America and Political Islam

P9-ELS-180

This book chronicles the policy debates on Islamism in the United States over the course of time, providing a comprehensive account of the origins of policy, followed by a balanced critique and recommendations for change. It delves deeply into the U.S. political scene to analyze the historical, political, cultural, and security issues that might help explain America's preoccupation with Islam and Muslims. Furthermore, the author sheds much light on the multiplicity of regional and international factors, such as the political decay of Middle Eastern regimes and the end of the Cold War, that shape the thinking of U.S. officials about the contemporary Islamist phenomenon. In addition to examining the domestic, regional, and international context of U.S. Islam policy, the book applies and tests the pronouncements of U.S. officials in four representative case studies – Iran, Algeria, Egypt, and Turkey – allowing decision makers and the shapers of foreign-policy opinion to speak with their own words. Finally, the author addresses the clash-of-civilizations debate and assesses the relative weight that culture and values have on the words and deeds of U.S. officials concerning political Islam.

One of the central and critical questions raised by Gerges is the extent to which culture and religion have replaced ideology and national interests as the independent variables in American foreign policy. This study indirectly considers whether the fault lines of national interests have dramatically changed in world politics; by doing so, it illuminates some of the conceptual and empirical implications for the study and practice of international affairs.

Fawaz A. Gerges holds the Christian A. Johnson Chair in International Affairs and Middle East Studies at Sarah Lawrence College. He was educated at Oxford University and the London School of Economics and has previously been a research fellow at Harvard and Princeton universities. He is the author of *The Superpowers and the Middle East: Regional and International Politics*, and his articles have appeared in several of the most prestigious journals in the United States, Europe, and the Middle East. Gerges is researching a follow-up book tentatively entitled *The Islamists and the West: Ideology versus Pragmatism?*

America and Political Islam

CLASH OF CULTURES OR CLASH OF INTERESTS?

FAWAZ A. GERGES
Sarah Lawrence College

CAMBRIDGE
UNIVERSITY PRESS

PUBLISHED BY THE PRESS SYNDICATE OF THE UNIVERSITY OF CAMBRIDGE
The Pitt Building, Trumpington Street, Cambridge, United Kingdom

CAMBRIDGE UNIVERSITY PRESS
The Edinburgh Building, Cambridge CB2 2RU, UK   http://www.cup.cam.ac.uk
40 West 20th Street, New York, NY 10011-4211, USA   http://www.cup.org
10 Stamford Road, Oakleigh, Melbourne 3166, Australia

First published 1999

Printed in the United States of America

Typeface Janson Text 10.25/13 pt.   *System* DeskTopPro$_{/UX}$® [BV]

*A catalog record for this book is available from
the British Library.*

Library of Congress Cataloging-in-Publication Data

Gerges, Fawaz A., 1959–
America and political Islam : clash of cultures or clash of
interests? / Fawaz A. Gerges.
p.   cm.
Includes bibliographical references
ISBN 0–521–63042–8 (hc.). – ISBN 0–521–63957–3 (pbk.)
1. Middle East – Foreign relations – United States.   2. United
States – Foreign relations – Middle East.   3. Islam and world
politics.   4. Islam – 20th century.   I. Title.

DS63.74.G46   1999
327.73017'671 – dc21   98–38600
                                                                                CIP

ISBN 0 521 63042 8 hardback
ISBN 0 521 63957 3 paperback

For Nora Ann

Contents

Acknowledgments

I owe a special thanks to Oxford Professor James Piscatori who initially commissioned me to write a monograph on the Clinton administration's approach toward political Islam for the Council on Foreign Relations, New York. That project planted the seed for this book. The more I reflected on Clinton's Islam policy, the more I recognized the need to contextualize this policy by examining how the previous administrations perceived and responded to Islamic activism. The result is a comprehensive and, one would hope, original book on an important subject that has not been sufficiently and completely analyzed and that will continue to be of global significance in the twenty-first century.

The book does several things. First, it chronicles the policy debates on Islamism in the United States over time, and it provides a comprehensive account of the origins of that policy, followed by a balanced critique and recommendations for change. Second, the study lets decision makers and the shapers of foreign-policy opinion speak with their own words. In this context, the book provides critical historical perspective. From that perspective, one can clearly see a recurring pattern in the U.S. foreign-policy process, in which officials strongly perceive the need for stability and dimly grasp the need for change. This tension in American policy may be explained by the oscillation between realpolitik and an idealism – often presented in pragmatic garb – that has often been played out in other areas of U.S. foreign policy and at other times as well.

Third, this book aims at something more than just providing a comprehensive presentation of the origins of U.S. policy on Islamism. It delves deeply into the U.S. political scene to analyze the historical, political, cultural, and security issues that might help explain America's fixation with Islam and Muslims. Furthermore, this study sheds much light on the multiplicity of regional and international factors, such as the political decay of Middle Eastern regimes and the end of the Cold War, that shape U.S. officials' thinking about the contemporary Islamist phenomenon. Analysis focuses in particular on the systematic efforts made by pro-Western Middle Eastern governments to influence the formulation of U.S. policy by portraying Islamic activists as mortal enemies of the West. In other words, special attention will be paid to both internal and external influences and the multiple forms of advocacy to which U.S. policy makers are exposed.

Fourth, in addition to examining the domestic, regional, and international context of U.S. policy toward political Islam, the book applies and tests U.S. officials' pronouncements in four representative case studies – Iran, Algeria, Egypt, and Turkey. The purpose of the case studies is not to render a full overview of every country in which political Islam plays a factor of consideration for U.S. interests. Rather, the goal is to select cases that represent a broad spectrum of Islamism, ranging from radical populist Islam to Islamically oriented political parties that are willing to play by the rules of the electoral game. This comparative methodology reveals the nuanced differences and similarities in the U.S. approach toward Islamic activism, including its mainstream and revolutionary facets.

Fifth, the book addresses the clash-of-civilizations debate and assesses the relative weight that culture and values have on the words and deeds of U.S. officials concerning Islamism. One of the central and critical questions raised is the extent to which culture and religion have replaced ideology and national interests as the independent variables in American foreign policy. This study indirectly considers whether the fault lines of national interests have dramatically changed in world politics; by doing so, it illuminates some of the conceptual and empirical implications for the study and practice of international relations.

The study is based on dozens of interviews with U.S. officials in the State Department, members of the National Security Council, and other policy participants. I also made extensive use of government and official documents, balanced by analytical studies that challenged Washington thinking. Official speeches, policy papers, congressional testimony, and other primary and secondary sources are all assembled to provide a full account of the debate as to whether political Islam has come to replace Communism as the post–Cold War equivalent of the "evil empire."

In writing this book, I have incurred many debts to colleagues who read more than one draft of the manuscript, and who shared their critical insights with me. These include Avi Shlaim, John Entelis, John Esposito, Michael Hudson, Mike Suleiman, Daniel Bell, William Quandt, Yvonne Haddad, Yezid Sayigh, Bill Mesmer, Douglas Simon, Peter Gellman, and Etel Solingen. I am grateful to the readers' comments at Cambridge University Press that helped improve the manuscript considerably. My editor at Cambridge, Alex Holzman, deserves credit and gratitude for his patience and professionalism.

I also owe an intellectual debt to my colleagues and students at Sarah Lawrence College whose critical feedback forced me to rethink some of my original ideas. Two of my research assistants – Benjamin Banayan and Louis Somma – were particularly helpful in collecting sources and organizing the bibliography. I could not have completed this book without the substantial assistance I received from the librarians at Sarah Lawrence. Sha Fagan, Judy Kicinski, and Janet Alexander always promptly accommodated my requests for more books and research materials.

Writing books is not easy; it requires discipline and a certain degree of selfishness and indulgence as an author spends many precious hours away from family and friends. In this sense, I dedicate this essay to Nora for her unconditional love and support. This project would not have been possible without her selfless generosity of spirit. Although I attempted hard to hide away in my study from my beloved children, Annie-Marie and Bassam, fortunately I did not succeed. Bassam's and Annie-Marie's presence saved me from exhausting work habits. This book is as much theirs as it is mine.

Fawaz A. Gerges
New York

1

Framing American Foreign Policy

This book examines the making of U.S. foreign policy toward Islamists from Carter to Clinton.[1] It focuses on the U.S. foreign-policy elite's thinking toward Islamist states and movements. This elite includes the executive branch – the presidents and their closest advisers – and the national security bureaucracies of the executive office, as well as domestic politics, particularly opinion makers and pressure groups. The multiplicity of domestic influences has the capability of simultaneously pulling U.S. policy in opposing directions. These influences include public opinion, media, private interest groups, policy-oriented academic programs and think tanks, Congress, and other institutional sources. American foreign policy is a product of the whole spectrum of domestic political realities.[2]

This book seeks to map the public pronouncements and some private musings of the U.S foreign-policy elite on Islamic revivalism

1. This study utilizes several terms – political Islam, Islamists, Islamic revivalism, Islamism, and Islamic activism – to delineate the contemporary Islamist phenomenon. Islamist activists contend that Islam possesses a theory of politics and the state and includes prescriptive notions for political and social activism. The various terms are always used interchangeably throughout this book. The term "Islamic fundamentalism," which is employed frequently and imprecisely by the media, the public, and some academics, fails to capture the complexity and eclectic nature of the Islamic revival. See Nazih N. Ayubi, *Political Islam: Religion and Politics in the Arab World* (London: Routledge, 1991), especially chapter 1, for an excellent definitional and conceptual explication of contemporary political Islam.
2. William B. Quandt, *Camp David: Peacemaking and Politics* (Washington, DC.: The Brookings Institution, 1986), pp. 6–29.

in order to illuminate the various administrations' positions and reveal the continuities and variations in American policy. Careful comparisons of public rhetoric with private statements reveal recurrent themes, values, and resonant notions that are critical to any understanding of the formulation and practical conduct of U.S. Islam policy.[3]

This study further analyzes actual U.S. policies. The analytical challenge is to assess the complex relationship between ideas and action, to see if the rhetoric or stance of various U.S. administrations serves as a reliable guide to comprehending their policies and if tensions persist between policy makers' words and deeds. Such a research strategy takes the level-of-analysis problem seriously by clearly distinguishing the level of rhetoric (discourse) from the level of policy (action).

This book raises a systematic set of questions, which serve as an analytical device to structure analysis and organize data. Do U.S. officials and their respective government bureaus perceive political Islam as posing a monolithic threat to Western interests, or do they also appreciate its often ambiguous and eclectic character? To what extent is official U.S rhetoric consistent with the policies actually implemented by the various administrations?

Even more to the point, is there any consensus within the U.S. foreign-policy elite regarding the compatibility between Islam and democracy? Do cultural differences influence U.S. officials' diagnosis of Islamic revivalism? To what extent does the bitter and troubled historic relationship between the two civilizations condition their peoples' thoughts and views of each other? Or is it more accurate to explain the anti-Islamic sentiments prevalent in the United States by reference to current political problems, rather than to cultural and historical encounters?

What kind of role do the mainstream media and scholarship coverage of Islam play in either legitimizing the U.S. approach toward Islamists or shaping U.S. politicians' attitudes? What is the input of the Congress, Israel, and pro-Western Middle Eastern states in mediating American views toward Islamists? Do popular perceptions and misperceptions of Islam influence American foreign-policy

3. Michael H. Hunt, *Ideology and U.S. Foreign Policy* (New Haven, CT: Yale University Press, 1987), pp. 15–16.

making? A major goal of this study is to determine the extent to which U.S. policy is driven by opinion makers, steered by popular emotions, daily headlines, and purely domestic political considerations.

It is clear from the evidence that the sum of U.S. public pronouncements on political Islam points to a conscious attempt to accommodate and reach out to moderate Islamists. Far from depicting Islam as a threat to the West, the Bush and Clinton administrations, in particular, lavishly praised Islamic religion and culture, recognizing the legitimacy of the renewed emphasis on traditional values in the Islamic world. Both administrations rejected the clash-of-civilizations hypothesis, viewing the present struggle as one that transcends civilization. Instead, the two administrations stressed America's role as a "bridge" between differing spiritual systems.

A closer and more critical reading of the various administrations' pronouncements, however, reveals some inconsistencies and strains. The U.S. approach toward Islamists is beset with ambiguities and tensions. American decision makers seem reluctant to take a strong, and decisive position on Islamic revivalism. This reluctance stems from Washington's inability to predict and assess the foreign-policy implications of Islamists if they gain power.

Three concerns underlie the U.S. stance on political Islam. First, the United States does not want to appear explicitly hostile toward Islamists so as not to add fuel to their flame. American officials do not want to repeat mistakes committed in dealing with the Islamic revolution in Iran. Second, the United States hesitates to support openly any Islamist group lest its regional interests and those of its allies be compromised. U.S. officials evince deep suspicions about the foreign-policy orientation and agenda of Islamist activists. Finally, a strain of skepticism exists within U.S. foreign policy-making circles regarding the compatibility between political Islam and democracy. U.S. discourse, replete with implicit references to Islamists' political behavior, views revolutionary Islam as antidemocratic and autocratic. Hence, far from providing concrete policy guidelines, U.S. official statements are couched in ambiguous language and open to multiple interpretations.

In addition, there is ample proof that the U.S. administrations' public statements are often inconsistent with their conduct toward Islamist movements and states. A gap exists between American officials' rhetoric and action. U.S. decision makers appear to be reluctant to apply their liberal pronouncements when formulating policy toward Islamists, standing solidly on the side of the Middle Eastern secular regimes. Although U.S. leaders reject the clash-of-civilizations hypothesis, American post–Cold War policy appears to be affected by the fear of an "Islamist threat." In U.S. eyes, some of Islamists' militant rhetoric and political program sound revisionist and threatening, making it unlikely that Washington would support them and abandon its loyal ruling allies.

Indeed, some Islamist movements have been deliberately provocative and confrontational, unwilling to recognize the limits of power and the categories of national identification and differentiation. For example, Ayatollah Khomeini of Iran dismissed the concept of ethnic and national distinctions as alien: "In Islam there are no frontiers."[4] Some Islamists regularly denounce the spiritual corruption of the West and proudly affirm the vitality and unchanging nature of Islam. This reality reinforces U.S. officials' perception that Islamists are intrinsically anti-Western and antidemocratic. On balance, the American foreign-policy elite views the good Islamists as the ones who are apolitical; moderate Islam is also equated with the pro-Western governments of Saudi Arabia, Egypt, Tunisia, Turkey, Pakistan, Malaysia, and Indonesia.

American Foreign Policy: Ideology versus Realpolitik

American foreign policy is frequently discussed in terms of a dialectical tension between two opposing patterns: realism–pragmatism and idealism–legalism. Or to put it differently, American foreign policy has oscillated between realpolitik and moralism. In the eyes of its advocates and practitioners, realism signifies a more orderly, clear-headed, and ruthless understanding of the formulation of policy based on well-defined national interests. These national interests are closely identified with national security is the essence of this realism.[5]

In contrast, moralism–legalism reflects a deeper cultural ethos and

4. Cited by Fred Halliday, *Islam and the Myth of Confrontation: Religion and Politics in the Middle East* (London: I. B. Tauris, 1995), p. 110.
5. Glenn P. Hastedt, ed., *American Foreign Policy: Past, Present, Future* (Englewood Cliffs, NJ: Prentice-Hall, 1997), pp. 28–34; Hunt, *Ideology and U.S. Foreign Policy*, pp. 1–18.

its values. These values are embedded in the core idea of national greatness, closely coupled with the promotion of individual liberty and democratic capitalism at home and abroad. Much of America considers itself a morally and politically superior society, a shining city on a hill, with a universal mission informed by a sense of exceptionalism. Dissenters argue that an active foreign policy devoted to international greatness will endanger the republican heritage of liberty.[6]

For the most part, however, the dominant views among influential policy makers have fluctuated across a wide range, falling considerably short of these two extremes – realpolitik and moral purpose. This debate between realists and moralists has its roots in the American national style, which is based on its geographic position, historic experience, economic system, and political culture and values. This American national style has led the country to a pendulum-like swing from isolationism in peacetime to moral activism in wartime.[7]

Nevertheless, over the past century one of the constants in U.S. foreign policy has been "to foster democracy abroad as a way of ensuring national security."[8] Although Americans associate democracy with peace and authoritarianism with aggression, this simple dichotomy fails to account for Washington's foreign policy. Historian John Gaddis notes that the United States has traditionally associated its security with the balancing of power in the world. At times, the U.S. foreign-policy elite has cloaked the balancing of power behind an idealistic facade and has used the democratic rhetoric as

6. Louis Hartz, *The Liberal Tradition in America* (New York: Harcourt Brace & World, 1955); Kenneth M. Dolbeare and Patricia Dolbeare, *American Ideologies* (Chicago: Markham, 1971); Dexter Perkins, *The American Approach to Foreign Policy* (Cambridge, MA: Harvard University Press, 1962), pp. 72–97; John Spanier and Steven W. Hook, *American Foreign Policy Since World War II* (Washington, DC.: Congressional Quarterly, 13th ed., 1995), pp. 15–18; Hunt, *Ideology and U.S. Foreign Policy*, pp. 19–45.

7. Seyom Brown, *The Faces of Power: United States Foreign Policy from Truman to Clinton* (New York: Columbia University Press, 1994), p. 7; John Spanier and Steven W. Hook, *American Foreign Policy Since World War II*, p. xii; Ronald Steel, *Temptations of a Superpower* (Cambridge: Harvard University Press, 1995), pp. 18–19.

8. Cited by Tony Smith, *America's Mission: The United States and the Worldwide Struggle for Democracy in the 20th Century* (Princeton, NJ: Princeton University Press, 1994), p. 348.

mere window dressing; democratic ideals were sacrificed at the altar of realpolitik calculations of self-interest. Interventionist policies have also been justified in terms of making the world "safe for democracy."[9] The U.S. stance on political Islam is pregnant with the same tensions and strains that have marked Washington's conduct toward other ideological movements and states.

Explications: (A) The Role of Culture and History

This book advances two key cultural, historical, and political explanations that account for U.S. ambivalence and suspicion of the Islamists. To begin with, although culture is not always the dominant factor in accounting for U.S. Islam policy, the underlying cultural values of Americans play a major role in shaping most policy makers' perceptions of Islamists. Culture, as defined by Clifford Geertz and others, is a historically transmitted pattern of meanings and symbols and a set of shared values, beliefs, attitudes, modes of living, and customs. Given American leaders' dependence and hypersensitivity to popular approval in public opinion polls, the society's cultural values have a direct impact on many of the country's international activities, including U.S policy toward Islamists. Most policy makers tend to be influenced by the dominant culture.[10]

Although the military threat to the West from the world of Islam had ceased to exist by the end of the seventeenth century, the religious and intellectual challenge of Islam continues to seize the imagination of many people in the West. Most Americans' cultural perceptions of Arabs/Muslims is that they are dangerous, untrustworthy,

9. John Lewis Gaddis, *The United States and the End of the Cold War: Implications, Reconsiderations, Provocations* (New York: Oxford University Press, 1992), pp. 9–11; Charles W. Kegley, Jr. and Eugene R. Wittkoff, *American Foreign Policy: Pattern and Process* (London: Macmillan Education, 1987), p. 259; Robert J. Art, "America's Foreign Policy," in Roy C. Macridis, ed., *Foreign Policy in World Politics* (Englewood Cliffs, NJ: Prentice-Hall, 1985), pp. 122–3.
10. Clifford Geertz, *The Interpretation of Cultures* (New York: Basic Books, 1973), p. 89; Richard J. Payne, *The Clash with Distant Cultures: Values, Interests, and Force in American Foreign Policy* (New York: State University of New York Press, 1995), pp. xiv, xvi, xvii, 5–9; William A. Haviland, *Cultural Anthropology* (Forth Worth, TX: Holt, Rinehart & Winston, 1990), p. 38.

undemocratic, barbaric, and primitive. Since the early 1980s, events in the Muslim world have become traumatic news in the United States. A *New York Times* editor noted that "thanks to current international politics, one form of ethnic bigotry retains an aura of respectability in the United States: prejudice against Arabs [Muslims]."[11]

Immediately after the Iranian revolution, a poll of representatives of mainstream America showed that a plurality of Americans taken immediately after the Iranian revolution think of "Islam" as a hostile culture and as synonymous with the specter of the Islamic Republic of Iran's revolutionary behavior. According to the poll, the American perception of Arabs/Muslims/Iranians – the poll showed an extremely close association of Muslim and Arab with Iran – is that of threatening people, with "all" or "most" Muslims being described as "barbaric" and "cruel" by 44 percent, "treacherous and cunning" by 49 percent, and "warlike and bloodthirsty" by 50 percent.[12]

Several polls and studies conducted since 1981 have confirmed the persistence of negative stereotypes of Arabs/Muslims among the majority of Americans. Michael Suleiman, who has written extensively on this topic, concluded that many Americans tend to see Arabs/Muslims as either extremely wealthy and immoral or as Bedouins who are indistinguishable from the deserts they inhabit.[13] During the 1991 Gulf War, many Americans evinced widespread hostility toward Arab Americans, including those who came from countries allied with the United States against Iraq. Hate crimes against Arabs/Muslims reached an "all time high" during the crisis, intensifying after the commencement of Operation Desert Storm.[14] This fact

11. "It's Racist, But Hey, It's Disney," *New York Times*, 14 July 1993; Michael W. Suleiman, *The Arabs in the Mind of America* (Brattleboro, VT.: Amana Books, 1988), p. 147; Payne, *The Clash with Distant Cultures*, pp. 96–7.
12. Shelley Slade, "The Image of the Arab in America: Analysis of a Poll on American Attitudes," *Middle East Journal* 35, no. 2 (Spring 1981), pp. 144–5, 147, 157.
13. Suleiman, *The Arabs in the Mind of America*, p. 147.
14. *1990 ADC Annual Report on Political and Hate Violence* (Washington, DC: American-Arab Anti-Discrimination Committee, February 1991), and "Hate Crimes Chronology, Update," 6 February 1991, in the ADC report; Nabeel Abraham, "The Gulf Crisis and Anti-Arab Racism in America," in Cynthia Peters, ed., *Collateral Damage: The 'New World*

prompted President Bush to deplore hate violence against Arab/
Muslim Americans and to appeal to the nation to be tolerant and
respectful of diversity.[15] Five national polls conducted in the 1990s
found that a plurality of Americans believed that "Muslims tend to
be religious fanatics," and that Islam is "basically an anti-democratic
religion."[16]

A 1994 Gallup poll compared and contrasted the views of the U.S.
public with that of American "leaders" – those in senior posts with
some international component in government, business, media, and
academe. This poll found that a goodly segment of the U.S. public
surveyed, 36 percent, thought that the "possible expansion of Islamic
fundamentalism" represented a "critical" threat to U.S. vital interests. In contrast, this poll found that 52 percent of American "leaders" were more inclined than the general U.S. public to consider the
expansion of Islamic fundamentalism an important threat. In fact,
this foreign-policy elite ranks the Islamist threat third among eight
possible critical threats mentioned in the survey.[17]

In other words, Islam is seen by many Americans as a hostile
culture and a threat to their interests and cultural values. Americans'
views of Muslims may to some extent be rooted in the country's
religious origins, and they may also be traced to the historical conflict
between Christians and Muslims, a confrontation that has been
transmitted and popularized through generations by history, litera-
ture, folklore, media, and academic discourse.[18]

Order' at Home and Abroad (Boston, MA: South End Press, 1992), pp.
255–72.
15. Abraham, "The Gulf Crisis and Anti-Arab Racism in America," pp.
268–9; *CBS Poll*, 9 January 1991. "U.S. Views Threat by Iraq as Strategy
to Split Critics," *New York Times*, 25 September 1990.
16. The five polls included a Roper survey of July 1993; a *Los Angeles Times*
survey of 1993; a joint survey by the American Muslim Council and the
Zogby Group in 1993; a Gallup poll of October 1994; and an American
Arab Institute survey of 1995. See David Pollock and Elaine El Assal,
eds., *In the Eye of the Beholder: Muslim and Non-Muslim Views of Islam,
Islamic Politics, and Each Other* (Washington: Office of Research and Media Reaction, United States Information Agency, August 1995), pp. 52–3;
"Muslims Don't Fare Well in Poll," *The Pantagraph*, 13 May 1993.
17. Pollock and El Assal, eds., *In the Eye of the Beholder*, pp. 53–4.
18. Robert J. Allison, *The Crescent Obscured: The United States and the Muslim
World, 1776–1815* (New York: Oxford University Press, 1995); Fuad

It is true that the United States neither exercised direct imperial control over Arab/Muslim societies nor developed the imperial structure of its European counterparts. Still, as Robert Allison shows in *The Crescent Obscured*, Americans inherited from Christian Europe the image of the specter of Islam as a religion born of tyranny, one that fosters religious and political oppression and economic stagnation. According to his thesis, Americans have not been concerned whether this description of Islam is accurate, but subscribe to it uncritically and for the sake of political convenience. Time and again, argues Allison, Americans have used the Muslim world as a reference point to highlight their exceptionalism – liberty, power, and human progress.[19]

Allison's critical book lays bare the historical and cultural roots of how Americans view Islam and Muslims. He also shows how Americans have readily reclaimed and reinvented those views, particularly during periods of crises. As a result, Americans have a rich, full reservoir of negative stereotypes about the Muslim world that are perpetuated and reinforced by the mass media. These stereotypes have a large role in the making of U.S. policy toward Arab and Muslim states.[20]

At the heart of this U.S. reservoir of images and ideas on Islam lie not only fear and bewilderment but also deep misgivings about mixing religion and politics. The blending of the two seems to challenge fundamental aspects of the U.S. liberal tradition – the separation of church and state and the reduced role that religious faith plays in the construction of identity in a secular society. This separation does not mean that America is not a religious nation. Unlike other industrial-

Sha'ban, *Islam and Arabs in Early American Thought: The Roots of Orientalism in America* (Durham, North Carolina: The Acorn Press, 1991); Maxime Rodinson, *Europe and the Mystique of Islam*, trans. Roger Veinus (London: I. B. Tauris, 1987), pp. 72–3.

19. Allison, *The Crescent Obscured*, pp. 35–59; Michael W. Suleiman, "Palestine and the Palestinians in the Mind of America," in Suleiman, ed., *U.S. Policy on Palestine: From Wilson to Clinton* (Normal, IL: Association of Arab-American University Graduates, 1995), pp. 9–14.

20. Allison, pp. 3–225; Michael W. Suleiman, "The Effects of American Perceptions of Arabs on Middle East Issues," in Edmund Ghareeb, ed., *Split Vision: The Portrayal of Arabs in the American Media* (Washington, DC: American-Arab Affairs Council, 1983), p. 338; Payne, *The Clash with Distant Cultures*, p. 139.

ized countries, religion plays a central role in American culture. However, the secularized U.S. ruling elite – and their Western counterparts – subscribe to the post-Enlightenment, modern notion of religion as a system of personal belief rather than as a total way of life. They view the Islamist phenomenon that seeks to re-establish a traditional form of rule "comprehensive in scope" as one that is abnormal insofar as it departs from an accepted modern norm. Thus Islam becomes "incomprehensible, extremist, and threatening."[21]

Graham E. Fuller, a former vice chairman of the National Intelligence Council at the CIA, concurs: "As a nation we are culturally ill-equipped to understand the passions of religious policy." Likewise, in his analysis of the U.S.–Iranian crisis of the late 1970s and early 1980s, Gary Sick, who was National Security Council staff member for Iran, notes that U.S. officials' profound cultural bias interfered fundamentally with how they assessed the balance of political forces in Iran, leading them to underestimate the strength and power of the mullahs.[22]

The fear of Islamism in power also stems from the unfortunate association in the minds of Americans of the form with the behavior of those governments; the tendency to deduce intentions from organization. The U.S. proclivity to confuse forms of governments with the behavior of those governments has caused repeated misunderstandings, and often gross exaggerations, of the dangers the nation actually faced.[23] Because Islamists are seen to be anti-democratic, there can be no interests in common with them, according to this view. It is also assumed that an Islamist government would likely threaten the regional balance of power and be internally repressive. At the heart of this perception lie two hypotheses: (1) Islam is incompatible with democracy, and (2) Islamists are inherently irredentists. Even if these two assertions are true, which is

21. John L. Esposito, *The Islamic Threat: Myth or Reality?* (New York: Oxford University Press, 1992), pp. 198–201; Payne, *The Clash with Distant Cultures*, pp. 26–31.
22. Fuller, "The Appeal of Iran," *The National Interest* (Fall 1994), p. 92; Sick, *All Fall Down: America's Fateful Encounter with Iran* (London: I. B. Tauris, 1985), pp. 164–8, 219–20.
23. Gaddis, *The United States and the End of the Cold War*, pp. 11–4.

disputable, it does not follow that form governs behavior, that an Islamist government would ignore political realities and act ideologically.[24]

(B) The Role of Politics and Security

It would be misleading to try to explain U.S. attitudes on Islamic resurgence by solely referring to cultural and historical factors. Contemporary security and political concerns are of great, if not greater, significance because they have a direct bearing on American officials' perceptions of their primary interests. These include U.S. strategic calculations in the Arab-Israeli theater, the vulnerability of access to Persian Gulf oil, and the vulnerability of pro–U.S. Middle Eastern regimes to an Islamist assault, the collapse of Soviet Communism, the prorogation of terrorism, and the potential proliferation of nuclear weapons.

Historically alarmed by the radical potential of all revolutions and the inherent challenge they pose to the principles of order and property, the U.S. foreign-policy elite has displayed hostility toward revolutions that have diverged from the American constitutional, liberal, and capitalist norm. The goal of American foreign policy remains wedded to the achievement of stability, understood partly as a process of orderly change.[25] Here lies the rationale for America's clash with revolutionary nationalism during the Cold War era and now with its successor and inheritor – revolutionary Islam.

In particular, U.S. decision makers fear the foreign-policy implications of revolutionary Islam, once it gains power. What the Amer-

24. Historian John Gaddis convincingly argues that a balance of power does not depend upon the ideological homogeneity of the states that make it up. States or political movements possessing radically different forms of governments can and often do share common interests, as the United States would discover in its relationship with both the former Soviet Union and China. Ibid., p. 15.
25. Stanley Hoffmann, *Dead Ends: American Foreign Policy in the New Cold War* (Cambridge: Ballinger, 1983), pp. 11–12, 275; William B. Quandt, *Decade of Decisions: American Policy Toward the Arab-Israeli Conflict, 1967–1976* (Berkeley and Los Angeles: University of California Press, 1977), p. 16; Spanier and Hook, *American Foreign Policy Since World War II*, pp. 11–12; Hunt, *Ideology and U.S. Foreign Policy*, pp. 92–124, 171–5.

ican foreign-policy elite dreads most is the destabilizing effects of Islamic militancy on the stability and security of the oil-producing states in the Gulf and the Arab-Israeli peace process – the two major pillars of American foreign policy in the region.[26] In U.S. eyes, these two pillars of traditional American diplomacy appear to be threatened less by external forces and more by internal Islamist opposition. U.S. officials' reference point is the 1979 Islamic revolution in Iran that attempted to export political radicalism to its Muslim neighbors. The Iranian experience has affected Washington's thinking on populist, revolutionary Islam, which is seen to be violent, antidemocratic, and anti-American.[27]

Furthermore, in the minds of many Americans, the menace of "extremist Islam" is multiplied by its equation with domestic and international terrorism and the specter of an Islamic nuclear bomb, particularly an Iranian bomb. As President Reagan put it: "I don't think that you can overstate the importance that the rise of Islamic fundamentalism will have to the rest of the world in the century ahead – especially if, as seems possible, its most fanatical elements get their hands on nuclear and chemical weapons and the means to deliver them against their enemies."[28]

The equation of Islam with "terrorism" has done considerable damage to the image of Muslims in the United States, thus constraining U.S. policy makers from pursuing an accommodationist policy toward Islamists. Several polls conducted in the 1990s clearly show that Americans' images of Islam and Muslims can be dramatically affected by the latest headlines, particularly with respect to suspicions about terrorism. For instance, a poll conducted by coincidence on the very day of the 1995 Oklahoma City bombing revealed a sharp increase in negative attitudes toward Muslims. Afterward it became clear that this bombing was not related to Islamist terrorism, and subsequent polls showed a steady, statistically significant

26. Edward P. Djerejian, "War and Peace: The Problems and Prospects of American Diplomacy in the Middle East," address before the Los Angeles World Affairs Council, 30 November 1993, *U.S. Department of State Dispatch*, 20 December 1993, p. 874.
27. Interview with a State Department official, Princeton, NJ, 27 May 1995.
28. Ronald Reagan, *An American Life: The Autobiography* (New York: Pocket Books, 1990), p. 409.

increase in "favorable" attitudes toward Muslims on a number of key issues.[29]

Washington's ambivalence and fear may also be explained by the changing nature of the global threat to U.S. interests in the post–Cold War era. The way in which the foreign-policy establishment began to view political Islam stemmed from Americans' changing attitudes toward the former Soviet Union. The end of the 1980s witnessed not only the political decay of the Soviet Union but also the intensification of Islamic activism in the Middle East and North Africa. The receding of the Soviet threat prompted American officials to reassess the new dangers confronting U.S. interests and allies. Given the U.S. tendency for crusades – the U.S.–Soviet rivalry as a struggle between good and evil – it is tempting to identify another global ideological menace to fill the "threat vacuum" created by the demise of Communism.[30]

Of all the new potential enemies, the idea of a unitary, timeless, and monolithic Islam on the march has recently gained currency in the West.[31] As a *New York Times* correspondent argued, "one threat

29. This intriguing new point was one of several findings revealed in the five polls mentioned above. See Pollock and El Assal, eds., *In the Eye of the Beholder*, p. 52.
30. Spanier and Hook, *American Foreign Policy Since World War II*, p. 16; Leon Hadar, "The Media and Islam," in Richard W. Bulliet, ed., *Under Siege: Islam and Democracy*, Occasional Papers 1 (New York: The Middle East Institute of Columbia University, 1994), pp. 64, 66; Esposito, *The Islamic Threat*, p. 4.
31. U.S. officials clearly recognize that the United States is confronting a new set of potential risks. These include tumultuous economic transitions, the proliferation of weapons of mass destruction, the intensification of ethnic conflicts, and a host of transnational issues, such as over-population, narcotics, refugees, terrorism, and the threat embodied by "extremist Islam." See Bill Clinton, "A Strategy for Foreign Policy," speech delivered to the Foreign Policy Association, New York, April 1992, in *Vital Speeches* 58, no. 14, May 1992, pp. 422–5; Warren Christopher, "America's Leadership, America's Opportunity," *Foreign Policy*, no. 98 (Spring 1995), pp. 8, 20–2, 25–7; Anthony Lake, "From Containment to Enlargement: Current Foreign Policy Debates in Perspectives," speech delivered at John Hopkins University, School of Advanced International Studies, Washington, DC, September 1993, pp. 15, 17–18.

has resonated in the public mind: Islamic holy war."[32] American strategists have identified "rogue states," such as Iraq, Iran, Sudan, and a variety of Islamist groups, as representing a grave threat to regional stability. In U.S. eyes, these "backlash," "outlaw," and "rogue" states sponsor terrorism and traffic in weapons of mass destruction; they also use and abuse the discourse of Islamist ideology by providing material and moral assistance to "extremist Muslims" who are bent on sabotaging the Middle East peace process and overthrowing the pro-Western Arab political order.[33]

For example, in its 19 March 1990 report, the U.S. House of Representatives Task Force on Terrorism and Unconventional Warfare warned that "the Mosque" is at the forefront of a Jihad of radical militancy against the contemporary Western world: "The combination of the rise of radical revivalist Islam and the crucial significance of oil for the economy of the West makes the struggle for the Near East the first crucial confrontation between revivalist Islam and the Judeo-Christian world."[34] The "myth" of confrontation is paradoxically propagated by a strange combination of rival political camps: Middle Eastern regimes, which are under assault by a vigorous Islamist opposition; those critics in the West, who seek to turn the Muslim world into another enemy; and some Islamic militants, who resent the West's growing influence and advocate confrontation.[35]

To begin with, important groups in the United States draw a parallel between the threat of Soviet Communism and that of political Islam and call on American officials to "contain" rather than "appease" the new enemy. However, these advocates of preemptive containment do not have a monopoly on public debate in the United States. A small but important intellectual segment is questioning the

32. Elaine Sciolino, "The Red Menace Is Gone. But Here's Islam," *New York Times*, Sunday, 21 January 1996, Week in Review section.
33. Anthony Lake, "Building a New Middle East: Challenges for US Policy," address by the National Security Adviser to the Washington Institute for Near East Policy, Washington, DC, 17 May 1994, in *U.S. Department of State Dispatch*, August 1994, pp. 36–9; Robert H. Pelletreau in "Symposium: Resurgent Islam in the Middle East," transcript in *Middle East Policy* 3, no. 2. (1994), pp. 1–5, 16–7.
34. "The Times of the Crusades Are Back," in *The House Republican Task Force on Terrorism and Unconventional Warfare*, Washington, DC, July 1989–May 1991), pp. 1–2, 11.
35. Halliday, *Islam and the Myth of Confrontation*, pp. 2, 6.

accuracy and applicability of the dominant discourse on political Islam in the United States.[36] Members of this segment view Islamic activism not as an absolutist threat but rather as the challenge of a variegated, splintered, and ambiguous phenomenon. Some American observers assert further that the new Islamists might even play the same constructive political role in reforming and liberalizing their societies that the Protestant reformers played in Europe five hundred years ago.[37]

It is essential to highlight this accommodationist view of political Islam to show the diversity and ambivalence within the U.S. intellectual milieu. Accommodationist voices are as numerous and vocal as confrontationalist ones. Explanations anchored in cultural determinism and reductionism fail to capture the complexity and fluidity of the American intellectual scene. Although considerable cultural antipathy colors U.S. public perceptions of Islam, it does less so in the case of the intelligentsia.[38]

Today, the pro-Western Middle Eastern regimes are in a state of crisis. They have failed to build stable and legitimate constitutional

36. Rashid al-Ghannoushi, the exiled leader of the Renaissance Party of Tunisia, recognizes the efforts of some Western scholars and certain sectors of the media, who have contributed immensely to bridging the ideological gap between the worlds of Islam and the Christian West, signaling a reversal of the ancient egocentrism and orientalism. See Ghannoushi, "Islamic Civilization Need Not Clash with Western Civilization," in *Islam: Opposing Viewpoints* (USA: Greenhaven Press, 1995), p. 51.
37. Leon Hadar, "Political Islam Is Not a Threat to the West," in ibid., p. 203; David Ignatius, "Islam in the West's Sights: The Wrong Crusade?" *Washington Post*, 8 March 1992; Robin Wright, "Islam, Democracy and the West," *Foreign Affairs* (Summer 1992), pp. 131, 133.
38. Edward Said, a perceptive critic of the Western discourse on Islam, contends that "there is a consensus on 'Islam' as a kind of scapegoat for everything we do not happen to like about the world's new political, social, and economic patterns. For the right, Islam represents barbarism; for the left, medieval theocracy; for the center, a kind of distasteful exoticism." See Said, *Covering Islam: How the Media and the Experts Determine How We See the Rest of the World* (New York: Pantheon Books, 1981), pp. x, xv. Although Islam is still negatively stereotyped in the United States today, the intellectual and political scene is much more diverse than it used to be in the 1980s, when Said wrote his critique.

institutions and to deliver the "goods" to their own people. As a result of internal discontent, these regimes have become increasingly vulnerable to existing ideological currents – one of the most powerful of which employs Islamic symbols to discredit and replace the secular ruling elite with an Islamist order. To augment their power base and stifle dissent, beleaguered Middle Eastern governments introduced some economic and political reforms. As with many political actions, liberalization produced the opposite effects: Islamists have been proven adept and effective at popular mobilization and very shrewd at playing the electoral game. They scored impressive political victories throughout the Arab Middle East and North Africa, thus exposing the weakness and unpopularity of the existing governments.

To justify their crackdown against Islamists, the U.S.–supported regimes, along with Israel, argued that Islamists could not be trusted because once in power, they would dispense with constitutional checks and balances and establish totalitarian theocracies. The pro-Western governments also warned the United States against the transhistorical nature of the Islamic threat to regional stability, as well as to Western interests and values.[39]

One cannot understand U.S. policy toward political Islam without considering the situation in Israel, Turkey, Egypt, and Saudi Arabia, America's four important regional friends. As long as Islamists continue to oppose the Arab-Israeli peace process and attack the pro-Western regimes, U.S. global interests will remain engaged. Yet the closer the United States identifies its interests with those of its regional allies, the more it finds itself locked in a bloody clash with

39. For example, President Hosni Mubarak of Egypt lashed out against the U.S. government for having contacts with the "terrorists from the Muslim Brotherhood," warning American officials that these groups "will never be on good terms with the United States." See Mary Anne Weaver, "The Battle for Cairo," *The New Yorker*, 30 January 1995, p. 69. Likewise, Tunisian President Zeine Abedin Ben Ali cautioned the West that the final aim of the Islamists is "the construction of a totalitarian, theocratic state," as quoted in *Le Figaro*, 2 August 1994. The Algerian Ambassador to Washington echoed this sentiment in the *Washington Post* of 1 April 1995: "It is misguided policy to distinguish between moderate and extremist fundamentalists. The goal of all is the same: to construct a pure Islamic state, which is bound to be a theocracy and totalitarian."

Islamist activists, since the latter remain potentially the most effective opposition force in the region today.

Paradoxically, some Islamists appear to confirm Western views by affirming that they would indeed replace Communism as the major challenge to the West, and would do so more effectively because their challenge is inspired by God.[40] Some of Islamists' rhetoric depicts the West as a unitary, imperial, and hostile civilization to Islam. These activists provide ammunition for those elements in the United States and the Muslim world who call for a war on Islamic revivalism. It seems that ideologues in the Islamist camp are their own worst enemies. At the risk of exaggeration, to reformulate a phrase of Regis Debray's, "Islam has Islamicized anti-Islam."[41]

As can be seen, U.S. official thinking is constructed within a polarized internal and external context. American policy makers, who must deal with these perplexing forms of advocacy, tend to be skeptical and ambivalent toward the Islamist phenomenon. On balance, however, U.S. officials' statements on political Islam are nuanced, steering away from blanket hostility and simplistic reductionism. American officials recognize the diversity among various Islamist movements, detecting no monolithic or organized international effort behind their political activities. With few exceptions, the U.S. foreign-policy elites do not appear to subscribe to the claim that Islam represents a threat to the West. Although widespread speculation about the new clash of civilizations is propagated by some opinion makers in the media and academe, it has not found a receptive audience in official Washington. An impressive measure of enlightened realism-skepticism colors U.S. officials' statements and attitudes on Islamism.

In sum, it seems clear that politics and contemporary security concerns, more than culture, propaganda, and history, account for America's preoccupation with Islamism. This point is an important one, given the tendency in both the Muslim and Western camps to

40. *Khomeini's Message to Gorbachev*, BBC Summary of World Broadcasts, ME/0354/A/4–6, 10 January 1989; Halliday, *Islam and the Myth of Confrontation*, pp. 111, 163.
41. Halliday, p. 193. This statement is not meant to justify or rationalize anti-Muslim sentiments but to show the strange convergence of stereotypes between the proponents and opponents of Islamic activism.

depict their complex relationship as a clash of cultures and civilizations. The wedding of the West's historical conceptions of Islam to current explosive problems has made Islamic activism traumatic news in the entire Western world.

The Division of the Volume

This book consists of nine main chapters and a conclusion. Chapter 1 has introduced the reader to the forces at play in the framing of American foreign policy. Chapters 2 and 3 focus on the domestic context of American policy making and the close links between ideas and policy directives. Chapter 2 surveys and assesses the debates on Islamic politics within the relevant U.S. intellectual constituencies. Responding to political Islam, American opinion makers and academics have tended to define the issues in black and white, polarizing them along confrontationalist/accommodationist lines. Chapter 3 examines the ways in which the U.S. public perceives and relates to Islam and Muslims, and analyzes the salient historical, cultural, and contemporary political developments that shape U.S. attitudes toward political Islam. One of the arguments maintains that the strongly held views of Congress and the public constrain the ability of U.S. officials to pursue an accommodationist policy toward Islamists.

Chapters 4 and 5 analyze the public speeches and pronouncements of Carter, Reagan, Bush, and Clinton administration officials on political Islam. These two chapters compare and contrast the positions of the various administrations in order to decipher the evolution of U.S. policy. Both Carter and Reagan failed to think out fully the problems of Islamic politics. Although the Islamic revolution in Iran made Carter and Reagan aware of the force and power of populist Islam, their response remained anecdotal and fragmentary. The Bush administration enunciated the first thorough policy statement on the Islamic revival in the Meridian House speech (June 1997) that established the intellectual context in which President Clinton subsequently addressed the Islamist question.

To compare and contrast U.S. official views with actual policies, Chapters 6 through 9 examine American foreign policy toward Iran, Algeria, Egypt, and Turkey, respectively. These four case studies represent a wide spectrum of Islamists currently in power or struggling to gain power. Islamic politics in the four countries also range from populist Islam to Islamically oriented political parties that are willing to play by the rules of the electoral process. By employing a comparative approach, this book will highlight the similarities and differences in U.S. policies toward the spectrum of Islamic activism, including its mainstream and revolutionary facets. Moreover, this blending of historical analysis with policy-relevant case studies should contribute to a better understanding of the theory and practice of American foreign policy in general.

Chapter 10, the conclusion, summarizes the major findings. It also offers lessons and recommendations about the implications of U.S. policy with respect to the relations between Islam and the West, the nature and structure of governance in Muslim societies, and the prospects for democratization there.

2

The Intellectual Context of American Foreign Policy

As is often the case, a vital policy debate occurs at the periphery of the policy process, amid an academic and intellectual milieu. Although some opinion makers and academics, owing allegiances to various benefactors and institutions, may be constrained by their positions in the institutional hierarchy, they do not voluntarily forgo the liberty to speak their own minds. There is ample room for divergent views, since academics and commentators are less inhibited than policy makers. Thus, to grasp and appreciate fully the complex dynamics and dialectics informing U.S. policy, one needs to situate it within the following underlying academic and intellectual moorings.

This chapter examines the differing views of opinion makers and academics toward Islamic politics. On no issue is the U.S. intellectual scene more polarized than on political Islam. Most opinion makers subscribe either to the confrontationalist or accommodationist camp.[1] The goal here is to illuminate the assertions of both camps and their conflicting policy recommendations inasmuch as the direct target of both is to influence the making of American foreign policy. The views of confrontationalists and accommodationists are well represented within the American foreign-policy–making elite. By comparing and contrasting the various positions of both camps, one hopes to shed light on the weight of domestic politics in affecting policy formulation and its intellectual foundation.

1. One should expect, however, a certain lack of tidiness and resistance to neat pigeonholing when examining the U.S. intellectual divide on Islamic activism.

Two themes set accommodationists and confrontationalists apart. The first concerns optimism versus skepticism regarding the prospects for democracy in Muslim societies as well as Islamists' democratic pretensions. At the heart of this "great debate" lies the belief that democracy, preferably America's version, is the model to which all less advantaged peoples aspire. What defines and unifies accommodationists and confrontationalists is a genuine conviction that democracy breeds moderation and eschews conflict and war. The second theme speculates about Islamists' political agenda once they assume power: Will they act in an irredentist manner and actively pursue anti-Western policies? Or will political realities dilute Islamists' ideological fervor and moderate their behavior?

The beauty of this great debate is that the two camps give radically differing answers as they make use of analogies and references from the Cold War lexicon. It is ironic how the accommodationist/confrontationalist debate resembles that of the Cold War. Both sides appear to be refighting it, but with Islamism replacing Communism as either the "new enemy" or "challenge" to U.S. vital interests.

The Confrontationalist Interpretation of Islam: The "New Enemy"

Many confrontationalists, who often lump all activist Islamists under the monolith rubric of "Islamic fundamentalists," argue that, in practice, Islam and democracy are antithetical.[2] Confrontationalists assert that like the Communist totalitarians, "Islamic fundamentalists" are intrinsically antidemocratic and deeply anti-Western, and invariably target the West. Bernard Lewis, for example, summarizes Islamic fundamentalists' attitude to the electoral process as "one man, one vote, once."[3] Gilles Kepel and Lewis contend further that liberal

2. Bernard Lewis, "Islam and Liberal Democracy," *Atlantic Monthly* (February 1993), p. 91; Daniel Pipes, "Same Difference: The Islamic Threat – Part I," *National Review* (7 November 1994), p. 63; Judith Miller, "The Challenge of Radical Islam," *Foreign Affairs* (Spring 1993), pp. 45, 51.

3. Lewis, "Islam and Liberal Democracy," p. 91. See also Peter W. Rodman, "Policy Brief: Co-opt or Confront Fundamentalist Islam?" *Middle East Quarterly* (December 1994), p. 64; Pipes, "Same Difference," p. 63; Miller, "The Challenge of Radical Islam," pp. 45, 47.

democracy is compatible with neither Islamic fundamentalism nor Islam itself.[4]

Samuel Huntington of Harvard University concurs: Deeply ingrained cultural traditions inhibit democratic development. Huntington implies that Islam is intrinsically nondemocratic: The only Arab country to sustain a form of democracy for a significant period was Christian Lebanon. "Once Muslims became a majority," asserts Huntington, "Lebanese democracy collapsed."[5] For Huntington and Martin Indyk – then at the Washington Institute for Near East Policy, a highly effective pro-Israel platform – in the Arab world Western-style democratic government strengthens anti-Western political forces.[6] In the same vein, Bernard Lewis reflects that Islamist influence on government has resulted in something not noticeably better but rather worse.[7]

According to Amos Perlmutter, the true nature of Islam is not merely resistant to democracy but wholly contemptuous of and hostile to the entire democratic political culture; it is "an aggressive revolutionary movement as militant and violent as the Bolshevik, Fascist, and Nazi movements of the past"; it cannot be reconciled with the Christian, secular West and, as such, the United States should make sure the movement is "stifled at birth."[8]

4. Kepel asserts further that "the rejection of even a chimerical notion of democracy is actually inherent in Islamic religious doctrine." See his *The Revenge of God: The Resurgence of Islam, Christianity and Judaism in the Modern World*, trans. Alan Braley (University Park: Pennsylvania State University Press, 1994), p. 194; Lewis, "Islam and Liberal Democracy," p. 93.
5. Samuel Huntington, "Religion and the Third Wave," *The National Interest* (Summer 1991), p. 41. See also Huntington, "Will More Countries Become Democratic?" *Political Science Quarterly* 99, no. 2 (Summer 1984), p. 214.
6. Huntington, "The Clash of Civilizations?" *Foreign Affairs* (Summer 1993), p. 32; Huntington, "Religion and the Third Wave," p. 41; Martin Indyk, "Concluding Remarks: The Implications for U.S. Policy," at "Islam and the U.S.: Challenges for the Nineties" Soref Symposium, Washington, DC, The Washington Institute for Near East Policy, 27 April 1992, p. 51; Jonathan S. Paris, "When to Worry in the Middle East," *Orbis* (Fall 1993), pp. 553, 557.
7. Lewis, "Islam and Liberal Democracy," p. 93.
8. Amos Perlmutter, "Wishful Thinking About Islamic Fundamentalism," *Washington Post*, 19 January 1992.

Confrontationalists contend further that the struggle between Islam and the West is not just about material and political interests; it is a clash of cultures and civilizations. In a widely noted article, Huntington affirms the primacy of culture in international politics: "[T]he fundamental source of conflict in this new world will not be primarily ideological or primarily economic. The great divisions among humankind and the dominating source of conflict will be cultural. The clash of civilizations will dominate global politics."[9]

The most important conflicts, contends Huntington, will occur along the cultural lines separating the West from non-Western civilizations: "On both sides the interaction between Islam and the West is seen as a clash of civilizations." He predicts that the next world war will be a war between civilizations.[10] Long before Huntington propounded his hypothesis, Bernard Lewis had sounded the alarm: the current struggle "is no less than a clash of civilizations – the perhaps irrational but surely historic reaction of an ancient rival against our Judeo-Christian heritage, our secular present, and the worldwide expansion of both."[11]

To support his assertion, Huntington cites the engagement of American forces in various military encounters with Iranian, Arab, and Islamic "terrorists," supported by at least three Middle Eastern governments.[12] According to Huntington, this warfare between Arabs/Muslims and the West culminated in the 1991 Gulf War, during which Islamic fundamentalist movements universally supported Iraq rather than the Western-backed governments of Kuwait and Saudi Arabia.[13] In the war's aftermath, he asserts, NATO planners increasingly targeted potential threats and instability along its southern tier: "This century-old military interaction between the West and Islam is unlikely to decline. It could become more virulent."[14]

In this context, confrontationalists draw a parallel between the Communist threat and Islam's: like Communism, Islamic resurgence is not only a proselytizing ideology but also revisionist. It is, accord-

9. Huntington, "The Clash of Civilizations?" p. 22.
10. Ibid., pp. 25, 31–2, 39.
11. Bernard Lewis, "The Roots of Muslim Rage," *Atlantic Monthly* (September 1990), p. 60.
12. Huntington, "The Clash of Civilizations?" p. 31.
13. Ibid., p. 35.
14. Ibid., pp. 31–2, 35.

ing to Daniel Pipes, "a militant, atavistic force driven by hatred of Western political thought, harking back to age-old grievances against Christendom."[15] In the words of Mortimer Zuckerman, "We are in the front line of a struggle that goes back hundreds of years, the principal obstacle to the extremists' desire to drive nefarious Western values into the sea, just as they once did with the Crusaders."[16]

For these advocates, Islam has replaced Communism as the principal strategic threat of the post–Cold War era: "The new threat is as evil as the old Evil Empire."[17] Daniel Pipes boldly asserts that Islamic "fundamentalists challenge the West more profoundly than Communists did and do. The latter disagree with our policies but not with our whole view of the world, including the way we dress, mate, and pray."[18] In some of his writings, Pipes does not make a very clear distinction between Islam as a religion and political Islam as an ideology, though he adamantly states he does. For him, Islam as such seems to be inherently opposed to the West: "Americans know an opponent when they see him," and "like communism during the cold war, Islam is a threat to the West."[19]

This line of thinking led a former assistant to Richard Nixon, Walter McDougall, to call for an alliance with Russia to hold the frontier of Christendom against its common enemy – the Muslim world.[20] Peter Rodman, a former White House and State Department official, echoes Pipes's sentiment: "Like leftist radicalism, Islamic rage is directed not only at the West but against the moderate, pro-Western elite in its own societies."[21]

15. "Political Islam Is a Threat to the West," in *Islam: Opposing Viewpoints*, (USA: Greenhaven Press, 1995), p. 192. See also Pipes, "Same Difference," p. 63; Rodman, "Policy Brief: Co-opt or Confront Fundamentalist Islam?" p. 64.
16. "Beware of Religious Stalinists," *U.S. News and World Report*, 22 March 1993, p. 80.
17. Charles Krauthammer, "Iran: Orchestrator of Disorder," *Washington Post*, 1 January 1993. See also Huntington, "The Clash of Civilizations?" p. 45.
18. "Same Difference," p. 64.
19. "Political Islam Is a Threat to the West," in *Islam: Opposing Viewpoints*, p. 190.
20. Cited by Pipes, "Same Difference," p. 64.
21. Rodman, "Policy Brief: Co-opt or Confront Fundamentalist Islam?" p. 61.

Confrontationalists claim that a political linkup exists among the various Islamic movements.[22] They contend that Islamic fundamentalists form a surging international network: "Iran is the center of the world's new Comintern. It is similarly messianic and ideological, ruthless and disciplined, implacably hostile to Western liberalism."[23] A domino-theory effect is thus postulated; "a success or two," assert some confrontationalists, "could transform Islamic fundamentalism into a revolutionary snowball that might reach across borders toward a greater 'umma,' or unity through Jihad," according to Jonathan Paris. All that is needed is a charismatic Sunni Arab fundamentalist, a Nasser with a beard to unite Muslims into a pan-Islamic political force.[24]

Such an eventuality, theorizes Paris, would usher in a unified "conquering army" of Muslims ready and willing to do battle with the West.[25] It is not surprising that confrontationalists call for smothering the Islamist awakening before it spreads into a deadly virus: "The four-fifths of the world that is not Islamic," asserts Paris, "cannot tolerate the violent pursuit of Jihad against them by the one-fifth that is Islamic."[26] In this argument, Islam is posited not only as the new enemy of the West but also of the rest of humanity.

Confrontationalist Policy Recommendations

The analogy with the Cold war is striking. Interventionists invoke familiar Cold War concepts to sharpen public concern and fear about a new Islamic threat. They sound the alarm in order to jolt U.S. policy makers from their sleep and push them to contain the marching Islamist hordes. To their way of thinking, the proliferation of state-sponsored terrorist groups and weapons of mass destruction in

22. Ibid., p. 63. Martin Kramer, "Islam vs. Democracy," *Commentary* (January 1993), p. 39; Paris, "When To Worry in the Middle East," p. 558.
23. Krauthammer, "Iran: Orchestra of Disorder." See also Pipes, "Same Difference," p. 63, and in "Symposium: Resurgent Islam," p. 7; Kramer, "Islam vs. Democracy," p. 39.
24. Paris, "When to Worry in the Middle East," p. 558.
25. Ibid. p. 558.
26. Ibid. p. 559.

the Middle East threatens the United Sates and its regional allies.[27] Confrontationalists argue further that Islamic extremism is bound to reach the shores of America through Muslim immigrants and visitors.[28] Accordingly, confrontationalists call on the U.S. government to prevent the entry of more Islamic fundamentalists and regard "those already in the West as potentially violent."[29] They also urge the United States to take active steps – just as the West did against the Soviet Union – to contain this new messianic creed.[30]

Pipes goes further by advocating not just containment of Islamists but also rollback and liberation. He puts the argument in blunt terms: Islamists must be battled and defeated.[31] He laments the fact that the "Left's soft approach" to fundamentalist Islam has become the hegemonic discourse in the United States.[32] Other confrontationalists warn the West not to be complacent about the recent failure of Islam, since the Islamic era may just be dawning: the West must realize that Islamic absolutism has replaced other secular, radical ideologies as the principal threat.[33] Again, the idea that the United States has to halt Islamists' advance everywhere echoes the Cold War's domino theory.[34]

Given their belief that democracy is incompatible with Islam, confrontationalists call on the U.S. not to press its Middle Eastern allies to make concessions on human rights and democratic reforms: Pressure for premature democratization can fatally weaken pro–U.S. regimes and lead to their replacement by a more ferocious, theocratic dictatorship. In this view, democracy in the Middle East is a luxury

27. Miller, "The Challenge of Radical Islam," p. 55.
28. Ibid., p. 56; Martin Kramer, "The Jihad Against the Jews," *Commentary* (October 1994), p. 41; *Jihad in America*, a PBS documentary produced by journalist Steven Emerson and aired 21 November 1994 (SAE Productions, 1994).
29. Kramer, "The Jihad Against the Jews," p. 42.
30. Krauthammer, "Iran: Orchestra of Disorder"; Huntington, "The Clash of Civilizations?" p. 49.
31. "Same Difference," p. 63.
32. Ibid., p. 65.
33. Judith Miller, "Faces of Fundamentalism," *Foreign Affairs* 73, no. 6 (November/December 1994), p. 142.
34. David Ignatius, "Islam in the West's Sights: The Wrong Crusade?" *Washington Post*, 8 March 1992; Leon T. Hadar, "Political Islam Is Not a Threat to the West," in *Islam: Opposing Viewpoints*, p. 200.

that friendly Middle Eastern regimes cannot afford because it enables antidemocratic forces to seize power.[35]

For example, before joining Clinton's National Security Council, Martin Indyk noted that the efforts of pro-Western regimes to bolster their legitimacy through the ballot box seem only to provide opportunities for Islamists to capture power through legitimate means.[36] Similarly, Jeane Kirkpatrick said she had no faith in the Arabs' and Muslims' capacity to make rational political choices through the ballot box: "The Arab world is the only part of the world where I've been shaken in my conviction that if you let people decide, they will make fundamentally rational choices."[37] Judith Miller's view echoes Kirkpatrick's: "Free elections seem more likely than any other route to produce militant Islamic regimes that are, in fact, inherently antidemocratic."[38]

In the views of Indyk, Kirkpatrick, and Miller, the unwillingness of Arabs and Muslims to imitate the democratic West is a sign of irrationality and backwardness. Thus, their solution lies in maintaining the authoritarian status quo and refraining from experimentation with electoral politics. Indyk, Kirkpatrick, and Miller take certain assumptions for granted. (1) Arabs/Muslims have been given many opportunities to elect liberal governments but they have opted for autocratic representatives; (2) Islamic politics is naturally antidemocratic and anti-Western; (3) unlike other peoples, Muslims are not ready yet for democracy; and (4) established authoritarian regimes are the least of the two evils, and thus the United States should continue to support them.

Although many confrontationalists feel that Middle Eastern governments treat their populations badly, they believe these regimes help the United States neutralize a radical ideology – political Islam – and preserve its interests.[39] Miller, therefore, counsels U.S. officials who are responsible for formulating new policies toward Islam to be

35. Lewis, "Islam and Liberal Democracy," p. 98; Rodman, "Policy Brief: Co-opt or Confront Fundamentalist Islam?" p. 64; Miller, "The Challenge of Radical Islam," pp. 52–3; Paris, "When to Worry in the Middle East," p. 560.
36. Indyk, "Concluding Remarks," p. 51.
37. Cited by Kramer, "Islam vs. Democracy," p. 37.
38. Miller, "The Challenge of Radical Islam," p. 52.
39. Ibid., p. 55; Pipes, "Same Difference," p. 64.

skeptical of those who seek to liberate Arabs through Islam, for in her view, Islamists have well learned the art of deceiving others by manipulating the words of democracy. She also advises Washington to oppose publicly the establishment of avowedly "Islamic states" because of their incompatibility with Western values and truths.[40]

Robert Satloff of the Washington Institute for Near East Policy calls on the United States to take active measures to join the battle that is being waged by Middle Eastern governments against Islamists. The United States should go on the offensive even if "this will find us acquiescing in some dirty deeds by some pretty odious fellows." After all, adds Satloff, it "is our battle too."[41]

Confrontationalists do not appear to be perturbed by concerns for human-rights violations and the political costs of intervention. They view the current struggle in the Muslim world as part of a broader confrontation between the democratic West and its secular friends on the one hand and "oriental despotism" on the other. Far from bringing about a peaceful world, the demise of the Soviet Union inaugurated a new, deadlier cultural war between Islam and the West. In this clash of civilizations, the United States can ill afford to be passive. Containment and rollback are the answer, not unilateral disarmament and appeasement.[42]

The Accommodationist Interpretation of Islam: The New "Challenge"

Accommodationists reject confrontationalists' portrayal of the Islamists as inherently anti-Western or antidemocratic. They distinguish between the actions of legitimate Islamist political opposition groups

40. "The Challenge of Radical Islam," pp. 51, 54. Miller criticized the Bush administration for not being harsh enough on the Islamists.
41. "An American Strategy to Respond to Political Islam," Soref Symposium, in Y. Mirsky, Matt Ahrens, and J. Sultan, eds., *Challenges to U.S. Interests in the Middle East: Obstacles and Opportunities* (Washington, DC: The Washington Institute for Near East Policy, May 1993), p. 38.
42. Krauthammer, "Iran: Orchestra of Disorder"; Rodman, "Policy Brief: Co-opt or Confront Fundamentalist Islam?" p. 64; Huntington, "The Clash of Civilizations?" p. 49; Pipes, "Same Difference," p. 64; Pipes in "Symposium: Resurgent Islam," p. 5; Miller, "The Challenge of Radical Islam," p. 45.

and the tiny extremist minority. John Esposito and Leon T. Hadar, two leading accommodationists, argue that too often academia, government, and the media emphasize the deeds of the small violent fringe and downplay those of the moderate political and nonpolitical movements. The construction of an imagined monolithic Islam, contends Esposito, leads to a religious reductionism that views political conflicts in the Islamic world in primarily religious terms – as Islamic-Christian disputes.[43]

Accommodationists contend that both in the past and today, the threat of a monolithic Islam has been a recurrent Western myth divorced from the reality of Muslim history. They see the world of Islam as much more fractured and fragmented than it is usually assumed to be; diversity and not timeless unity remains the major determinant in the formulation of foreign policy in the Arab/Islamic world.[44] Far from being inherently antidemocratic, Islam, accommodationists assert, lends itself to multiple and conflicting political interpretations, including democracy and dictatorship, republicanism, and monarchy; flexibility, even fluidity, rather than rigidity, is the norm within the Islamic tradition.[45]

Furthermore, accommodationists question the commitment of Western and Muslim governments to democratization. Robin Wright of the *Los Angeles Times* and others accused the Bush administration of preferring a "police state" to an Islamic democracy in

43. John L. Esposito, *The Islamic Threat: Myth or Reality?*, pp. ix, 180–1, 202, 208–9, 215. See also Leon T. Hadar, "Political Islam Is Not a Threat to the West," in *Islam: Opposing Viewpoints*, p. 198.
44. Richard W. Bulliet, "Rhetoric, Discourse, and the Future of Hope," in Bulliet, ed., *Under Siege: Islam and Democracy*, pp. 8–9, 11; R. Scott Appleby, "Democratization in the Middle East Does Not Threaten the West," in *Islam: Opposing Viewpoints*, p. 223; Mehdi Noorbaksh, "The Middle East, Islam and the United States: The Special Case of Iran," *Middle East Policy* 2, no. 3 (1993), pp. 79, 82; Jahangir Amuzegar, "The Truth and Illusion of Islamic Fundamentalism," *SAIS Review* 13 (Summer/Fall 1993), p. 129; Esposito, *The Islamic Threat*, pp. 182–3, 193, 213; Hadar, "Political Islam Is Not a Threat to the West," p. 204.
45. Robin Wright, "Islamist's Theory of Relativity," *Los Angeles Times*, 27 January 1995; John O. Voll and John L. Esposito, "Islam's Democratic Essence," *Middle East Quarterly* 1, no. 3 (September 1994), pp. 3–9; Gary Sick, "Islam and the Norms of Democracy," in Bulliet, ed., *Under Siege*, pp. 38–9; Hadar, "Political Islam Is Not a Threat to the West," p. 204.

Algeria; otherwise, they contended, how does one explain the admin-istration's silence about the suspension of the democratic process in Algeria but its active and outspoken advocacy of political pluralism elsewhere?[46]

Some accommodationists are also critical of the U.S. position on the proliferation of weapons of mass destruction in the Muslim Mid-dle East. Jochen Hippler claims that Western concern over nuclear proliferation in the region has less to do with actual military power than with control of the oil in the Persian Gulf. Hippler asserts further that the West's opposition to an "Islamic bomb" is based on a fear of the rebellion of the Third World out of its dominated power structure.[47]

Unlike confrontationalists, who consider political Islam as a radi-cal utopian ideology, accommodationists view Islamic resurgence as a product of socioeconomic and political woes; it is locally rooted. They argue that the various Islamic movements are basically moti-vated by the lack of economic opportunities and political freedom.[48]

46. Wright, "Islam, Democracy and the West," *Foreign Affairs* (Summer 1992), pp. 137–8. See also Yvonne Yazbeck Haddad, "The 'New En-emy'? Islam and Islamists after the Cold War," in Michel Moushabeck and Phyllis Bennice, eds., *Altered States: A Reader in the New World Order* (New York: Olive Branch Press, 1993), p. 91; Appleby, "Democratiza-tion in the Middle East Does Not Threaten the West," p. 229; Esposito, *The Islamic Threat*, pp. 186–7, 189, 204, 205, 214; Noorbaksh, "The Middle East, Islam and the United States," pp. 84, 86, 91; similarly, Ignatius is critical of the Bush administration for lending its ears to Saudi Arabia and of never uttering the word *democracy*. Ignatius ascribes too much weight to Saudi Arabia over U.S. policy: "When the Saudis have sneezed, the State Department has gotten a cold. Because the Saudis have been wary of Arab democracy, we have been wary. Because the Saudis have been a status-quo power, we have been a status-quo power. Because the Saudis have seemed comfortable with the political stalemate across the Arab world, we have been comfortable." See Igna-tius, "Islam in the West's Sights," in the *Washington Post*.

47. Hippler, "The Islamic Threat and Western Foreign Policy," in Jochen Hippler and Andrea Lueg, eds., *The Next Threat: Western Perceptions of Islam* (Boulder, CO: Pluto Press, 1995), pp. 118–19.

48. Bulliet, "Rhetoric, Discourse, and the Future of Hope," pp. 8–9; Espos-ito, *The Islamic Threat*, pp. 206, 210, 212; Hadar, "Political Islam Is Not a Threat to the West," p. 204; William Quandt, "The Middle East: What Is Our Long Term Vision?" (discussion held by the Middle East Policy Council), *Middle East Policy* 3, no. 3 (1994), p. 8.

Accommodationists also reject their counterparts' assertion regarding the inherently anti-Western attitudes of the Islamists:

> Few Muslims in their daily lives and in interaction with Western-ers nourish any kind of concept of implacable hostility or the need for confrontation. The West is a daily reality in the lives of nearly all Muslims; it is a culture many of whose features Muslims admire: education, technology, concepts of liberty, respect for human rights, rule of law, and improved standards of living.[49]

What Islamists oppose, contend accommodationists, are specific Western policies, which are seen to perpetuate the West's domi-nance and Muslim societies' dependence and subservience; these pol-icies include Washington's support for the corrupt and repressive Middle Eastern regimes, U.S. unconditional support for Israel, and the long history of American economic and military intervention in the region. In particular, the issue of Israel carries a great deal of historical and emotional baggage that extends across the Muslim world, becoming the center of the sense of grievance held by many Muslims against the United States.[50]

However justified some of these policies appear to U.S. politicians and observers, they help create deep suspicions of the United States and a sense that the peoples of the region are not masters of their own fate.[51] As a result of their perception of victimization by West-ern policies, Muslims often display "plot mentalities," blaming exter-nal forces for their political and economic ills. The implications of this conspiracy-theory tendency, argue accommodationists, lie in the rejection of universal values by many Muslims. The latter fear that the West's current promotion of human rights and democratization are among the new devices designed to impose its own values on the Muslim and Third World, again in the name of universal values.[52]

The question of democracy sets accommodationists and con-frontationalists apart. The latter claim that the lack of democracy in

---

49. Graham E. Fuller and Ian O. Lesser, *A Sense of Siege: The Geopolitics of Islam and the West* (Boulder, CO: Westview Press, 1995), pp. 102–3.
50. Accommodationists hope that the resolution of the Arab-Israeli conflict would help heal some of the wounds and repair bridges of coexistence within the Judeo-Christian-Islamic heritage.
51. Fuller and Lesser, *A Sense of Seige*, pp. 40, 42.
52. Ibid., pp. 38, 42.

Muslim states can be explained by reference to internal factors, mainly religion, culture, and history. In contrast, accommodationists assert that political considerations, including the West's recurrent meddling in the Muslims' internal affairs, account for the persistence of authoritarianism in Muslim societies. In their attempt to understand the dearth of democratic polities in the Middle East, accommodationists assign much more weight to external variables or externally inspired internal developments. Some of these include the impact of colonialism, the existing autocratic political order that is supported by the United States, the costs of the Arab-Israeli conflict, and recurrent external intervention. Accommodationists go further to challenge the very notion of democracy as defined by the West. Unlike their counterparts, accommodationists allow for a more encompassing form of democracy that takes into account Islamic practices and experiences.

Accommodationist Policy Recommendations

In contrast to confrontationalists, accommodationists advise the United States against opposing the implementation of Islamic law or the activities of Islamic movements, where such programs pose no threat to U.S. vital interests. The dominant Islamist current, they assert, represents a challenge rather than a threat to the United States and its Middle Eastern allies. Furthermore, John Entelis contends, the rise of fundamentalism presents not only challenges but also opportunities, including the potential for reformist and more representative governments. Accommodationists also call on the American government to recognize, accept, or at least tolerate the ideological differences between the Christian West and Islam: "Co-option is far more effective than confrontation in undermining a rival, in this case one perceived rather than real."[53]

Some accommodationists acknowledge that the democratic process is generally unfamiliar to many Muslims in the Middle East. Nevertheless, they call on the U.S. government to support the au-

53. Wright, "Islam, Democracy and the West," p. 143; See also John P. Entelis, "Islam and Democracy: A Dilemma for U.S. Policy – A Panel Discussion," at "Islam and the U.S.," Soref Symposium, p. 43.

thentic roots of Islamic democracy even if that means the coming to power of populist elements. They further assert that Islamists will have to deal with the harsh reality of their societies and the fact that they live in a globally interdependent world. Although Islamists might include some absolutists who reject the established political structure, the majority, predict accommodationists, will function within the political system.[54]

Far from being idealistic, some accommodationists impress on U.S. officials the need to adopt nuanced policies by making a distinction between pragmatic elements within Islamic movements and the more uncompromising and militant activists. While such accommodationists advocate the gradual inclusion of the former into the political process, they recommend the marginalization of the latter in ways that do not increase the use of violence on both sides, since, in their view, force has been ineffective in resolving the crisis of governance and legitimacy in the region.[55]

It would be misleading to think of accommodationists as being radical ideologues. Their critique of the dominant discourse on political Islam is informed more by pragmatic concerns and calculations than by any romantic fascination or deference to Muslims. Given the slow but steady decaying of the existing political order, they call for an inclusive, not exclusive, approach that preserves U.S. interests in the long term. In this context, accommodationists' policy prescriptions are anchored in political realities rather than in sentiments. According to Richard Bulliet of Columbia University, far from neglecting realpolitik, accommodationists are concerned with preserving U.S. national interests and avoiding a clash with Muslims.[56]

In the same vein, Esposito and Wright argue that Western interests would be far better served by pursuing policies of cooperation with friendly Muslim governments. They also call on Washington to pursue a clear, consistent public policy in support of real democratic

---

54. Hadar, "Political Islam Is Not a Threat to the West," p. 203; Wright, "Islam, Democracy and the West," pp. 143–5; Esposito in "Symposium: Resurgent Islam," p. 13.
55. Fuller and Lesser, *A Sense of Siege*, pp. 119–21.
56. Remarks at a seminar at the Middle East Institute, Columbia University, 29 February 1996.

openings that include Islamists, rather than toleration of authoritarian regimes that exclude them. The alternative, assert other accommodationists, is that U.S. support for repressive regimes will intensify anti-Americanism and encourage radicalization.[57]

Prevention of this alternative, assert Fuller and Lesser, requires a better grasp of Islamic history and Muslims' perceptions of the West. Two key themes most distinctly characterize Muslims' perceptions of their relationship with the other: "the reversal of Islamic civilization's long preeminence and a broad sense among Muslims that they are under siege from the West and are operating from a position of weakness and vulnerability."[58]

Fuller and Lesser also argue that once sensitized to the nature of Muslim grievances, American leaders can choose to ameliorate or eliminate those sources of grievance where possible. However, what U.S. policy makers cannot afford to do, add the authors, is continue to ignore Muslim hopes, aspirations, and fears: "The greater the scope and depth of grievances, the greater the likelihood of their consolidation into some broader brief against the West as a whole."[59]

To avoid such a polarized cultural trap, accommodationists call on Washington to appreciate Muslims' negative and hostile reaction to all external intervention in their internal affairs. Traditional Western support for strong but corrupt, ineffective Middle Eastern governments, as well as military moves against such rebellious Arab leaders as Qaddafi, are viewed as uncalled-for Western arrogation of privilege to discipline the Arab world.[60] According to Fuller and Lesser, another major source of grievance to which the United States should be sensitive is intra-Arab rivalries and the gap that exists between oil-rich Arab states and their poor neighbors. To prevent any catalytic event from setting the stage for a hostile Muslim coali-

57. Wright, "Islam, Democracy and the West," pp. 139, 143–5; Entelis, "Islam and Democracy," p. 43; Voll and Esposito, "Islam's Democratic Essence," p. 11; R. Scott Appleby, "Democratization in the Middle East Does Not Threaten the West," p. 229; Hadar, "Political Islam Is Not a Threat to the West," pp. 203–4; Esposito, *The Islamic Threat*, pp. 208–11, 213.
58. Fuller and Lesser, *A Sense of Siege*, p. 27.
59. Ibid., pp. 109–10.
60. Ibid., pp. 111–12.

tion, the authors urge the U.S. government to adopt moderate, constructive, and equitable policies toward Muslim societies.[61]

Fuller and Lesser agree that no single act of Western intervention will by itself lead to a confrontation in the Middle East. Nevertheless, they warn Western leaders that an accumulated sense of grievance by Muslims may build up into serious tensions, allowing the Islamists to rise to power on a wave of popular support.[62]

Conclusion

The previous analysis of accommodationist and confrontationalist positions and policy prescriptions shows clearly the diversity and fluidity of the U.S. intellectual scene. Political Islam is hotly debated in academic and policy circles. Far from advancing a monolithic interpretation of Islamic revivalism, American academics and policy specialists are split in their evaluation of Islamists and how to deal with them.

The importance of delineating the tensions within the American intellectual milieu lies in drawing the readers' attention to the plurality of views and lack of consensus on political Islam. Discord and contingency, not unity, mark Americans' perceptions of Islamists. This is a critical point to emphasize because America is often portrayed as a monolith, speaking with one voice. For example, throughout the Muslim world, the clash-of-civilizations hypothesis is read as representing the views of the U.S. government and the foreign-policy elite. The fact remains, however, that this thesis has not won many converts within the U.S. intellectual community or policy establishment. The subtle distinctions and tensions that mark America's intellectual and political landscape is hardly appreciated abroad.

In fact, accommodationists have competed effectively with the confrontationalists for the ear and attention of policy makers in Washington. At least on the level of rhetoric, U.S. diplomats use the symbols and terminology of accommodationists to delineate their stance on political Islam. Bush and Clinton administration officials soundly rejected the whole notion of cultural wars, as advocated by confrontationalists, and stressed their commitment to the common

61. Ibid., pp. 114, 117.
62. Ibid.

ties that bind civilizations together. Accommodationists' success lies in the heightening of U.S. officials' awareness of the fluid, ambiguous, and splintered nature of Islamic revivalism. They have influenced the manner by which American policy makers address this issue.

On the other hand, confrontationalists have left their imprint on individual U.S. policies toward Iran, Iraq, and other Islamist movements in the Arab-Israeli theater. If there is one characteristic that unifies confrontationalists, it is their explicit identification with Israel. Confrontationalists have been most effective in targeting policy areas related to the Arab-Israeli conflict on which a relative consensus exists in the United States. They have been less successful, however, in shaping the overall U.S. approach toward political Islam. Suffice it to say that the tensions and disagreements among academics and policy advocates parallel those within official government circles.

3

Islam and Muslims in the Mind of America

According to the eminent French scholar Maxime Rodinson, "Western Christendom perceived the Muslim world as a menace long before it began to be seen as a real problem."[1] This view is echoed by the late British historian Albert Hourani, who argued that Islam from the time it appeared was a problem for Christian Europe. Looking at Islam with a mixture of fear and bewilderment, Christians could not accept Muhammad as a genuine prophet or the authenticity of the revelation given to him. The most widely held belief among Christians, noted Hourani, was that "Islam is a false religion, Allah is not God, Muhammad was not a prophet; Islam was invented by men whose motives and character were to be deplored, and propagated by the sword."[2] As the thirteenth-century Crusader and polemicist Oliver of Paderborn claimed: "Islam began by the sword, was maintained by the sword, and by the sword would be ended."[3]

Centuries of interaction have left a bitter legacy between the world of Islam and the Christian West, deriving largely from the fact that both civilizations claim a universal message and mission and share much of the same Judeo-Christian and Greco-Roman heritage.[4] Separated by conflict and held together by common spiritual and material ties, Christians and Muslims presented a religious, in-

1. *Europe and the Mystique of Islam*, p. 3.
2. *Islam in European Thought* (New York: Cambridge University Press, 1991), pp. 7–8, 10.
3. Norman Daniel, *Islam and the West: The Making of an Image* (Edinburgh: Edinburgh University Press, 1960), p. 127.
4. Rodinson, *Europe and the Mystique of Islam*, chapter 1.

tellectual, and military challenge to each other.[5] The nineteenth-century German thinker Friedrich Schleiermacher argued that Christians and Muslims were "still contending for the mastery of the human race."[6] However, this portrait of unremitting Western–Muslim hostility is misleading. The pendulum of Western–Muslim relations has swung between rivalry/confrontation and collaboration/accommodation. Although conflict arising from cultural, religious, and ideological factors has been the norm, realpolitik and interstate interests have also shaped the relationship between the two civilizations.

Historically, Western powers felt no qualms about aligning themselves with Muslims against fellow Christian powers. Throughout the nineteenth century, the French, British, and Germans joined ranks with the Ottoman Muslims against their European opponents. Despite its inherent weakness, the Ottoman empire was an integral player in the inter-European balance-of-power system. The destruction of the empire in 1918 occurred as a result of its joining Germany in World War One against the Allied powers. The British and French also entered into alliances with Arab Muslims to counterbalance the Ottomans and Germans. Between 1919 and the 1950s, European interest in Muslim societies was more influenced by the requirements of colonial policy and decolonization than by religious sentiment.[7] British and French officials collaborated with whoever was willing to serve their interests, whether Islamist or nationalist. Political control and economic expediency, not religious or cultural variables, were the driving forces behind the Near East policy of Paris and London.

Unlike Europe, the United States did not engage in any prolonged, bloody encounters with Muslim states and societies. It never directly ruled over Arab and Muslim lands or developed Europe's complex imperial system. In the first part of the twentieth century, the United States, unrestrained by colonial and geographic require-

---

5. Hourani, *Islam in European Thought*, p. 8; John L. Esposito, *The Islamic Threat: Myth or Reality?*, p. 25; Bernard Lewis, "Islam and Liberal Democracy," p. 89.
6. *Der Christliche Glaube in Samtliche Werke*, 2d ed., vol. 3, pt. 1, (Berlin, 1842), p. 47; *The Christian Faith* English trans. (Edinburgh, 1928), p. 37.
7. Fuller and Lesser, *A Sense of Siege: The Geopolitics of Islam and the West*, pp. 19–20.

ments, established dynamic and cordial relations with Arabs and Muslims, who viewed America as a progressive island amid European reaction.

Even after it became a superpower, the United States was much less constrained by colonial, historical, and cultural factors than its European counterparts. Political and economic control have been the driving force behind Washington's Near East policy. Furthermore, in contrast to the Europeans, Americans do not appear to be concerned about the presence of a large immigrant Muslim community in their midst; in the United States, it is the Hispanics who are the focus of assimilationist fears concerning the "immigrant threat."[8] Although the religious and intellectual challenge of Islam continues to seize the imagination of many people in the United States, it is the security and strategic implications of the mass politics of Islam that resonates in the minds of Americans.

This chapter examines the ways in which the U.S. public, media, interest groups, and foreign-policy elites, including Congress, influence the making of American policy toward political Islam. Like the previous chapter, this chapter focuses on the domestic context of American politics, especially the linkages among society, politics, and government. Following an analysis of the historical, cultural, and current political developments that inform Americans' attitudes on Islamic resurgence, this chapter argues that contemporary security and strategic considerations, not merely culture and ideology, account for America's preoccupation with Islamism.

A Brief Historical Sketch

The emergence of a U.S. global role after World War Two dramatically changed the foreign-policy elite's attitudes toward rapid sociopolitical change in the third world. Although U.S. officials in the first part of the twentieth century supported the concept of self-determination and opposed the perpetuation of colonialism, in the second half of the century they looked with suspicion on populist third-world movements and ideologies. By the late 1940s, containing the perceived Soviet threat and ensuring the security of pro-Western

8. Fred Halliday, *Islam and the Myth of Confrontation: Religion and Politics in the Middle East*, pp. 182–4.

Middle Eastern regimes was higher on the U.S. foreign-policy agenda than coming to terms with third-world nationalisms. True, some officials in the Truman, Eisenhower, and Kennedy administrations advocated an alliance between the United States and local nationalist forces to contain Soviet expansionism, but they were a minority.[9]

The scale became weighted in favor of those U.S. policy advocates who mistrusted third world nationalists and suspected them of being allied with the Soviets in order to overthrow the existing regional order. On the whole, between 1955 and 1970, U.S. policy in the Arab world was framed in opposition to secular Arab nationalism led by President Gamal Abdel-Nasser of Egypt. In U.S. eyes, revolutionary nationalism, not political Islam, represented a security threat to the pro-Western, conservative monarchies. Symbolic representations, such as "extremist" and "satellite," were applied to radical nationalist elements throughout the Middle East.[10]

Ironically, in the 1950s and 1960s, the United States hoped to construct an alliance of Islamic states with sufficient prestige to counterbalance "godless communism" and the secular nationalist forces as represented by Nasser. In the mid-1960s, one of the reasons for the deterioration of U.S.–Egyptian relations was Nasser's belief that President Lyndon Johnson had encouraged King Faisal ibn 'Abd al-Aziz of Saudi Arabia to sponsor a holy Islamic alliance to isolate Egypt in the Arab world.[11] As importantly, in the 1950s and 1960s,

9. Dean Acheson, *Present at the Creation: My Years in the State Department* (New York: New American Library, 1969); Fawaz A. Gerges, "The Kennedy Administration and the Egyptian-Saudi Conflict in Yemen: Co-opting Arab Nationalism," *Middle East Journal* 49, no. 2 (Spring 1995), pp. 1–20.

10. Francis J. Russell, "U.S. Policies Toward Nasser," paper delivered by the Secretary of State's Special Assistant on 4 August 1956, in *Foreign Relations of the United States: Suez Crisis, 1956*, vol. 16 (Washington, DC: U.S. Government Printing Office, 1989), pp. 86, 142. See also Richard W. Cottam, "U.S. and Soviet Responses to Islamic Political Militancy," in Nikki R. Keddie and Mark J. Gasiorowski, eds., *Neither East Nor West: Iran, the Soviet Union and the United States* (New Haven, CT: Yale University Press, 1990), pp. 267–70.

11. *Foreign Relations of the United States, 1955–1957: Arab-Israeli Dispute, January 1–July 26, 1956*, vol. 15 (Washington, DC: U.S. Government

the United States exhibited an ambivalent and hostile attitude toward revolutionary Arab nationalism, whereas the politics of Islam was seen to serve Western interests. In the struggle between Islam and populist nationalism, the United Stated sided with the former. American policy was driven by Cold War considerations and strategic calculations, not by history, culture, or any intrinsic fear or hatred of Islam.

The U.S. perception of the Middle East situation and the nature of the threat, however, underwent a radical shift in the 1970s, largely because of the explosion of Islamic politics onto the scene. Regional events – the 1973 Arab-Israeli war, the consequent Arab oil embargo, and the 1978–79 Iranian revolution and ensuing hostage crisis – shocked many American officials into viewing Islam as a threat to Western interests.[12] Again, security calculations, along with related political and economic concerns, lie at the heart of the shift in U.S. perceptions.

Whereas Nasser had fought the 1967 Arab-Israeli war under the ideological banner of Arab nationalism, his successor, Anwar Sadat, could be argued to have fought the 1973 Ramadan War under the banner of Islam. The new Islamic assertiveness was accompanied by the OPEC oil boycott, which triggered escalating oil prices and inflation and, according to Zbigniew Brzezinski, Assistant for National Security Affairs for President Jimmy Carter, "had an acute effect on the daily life of virtually every American; never before had we felt such an impact in peacetime."[13] For the first time since the

Printing Office, 1989), pp. 325–6, 341, 343, 355, 362, 422–3. See U.S. Department of State, "Memorandum of Conversation. Subject: U.S.–UAR Relations, 17 September 1965," in *The Lyndon B. Johnson National Security Files, the Middle East: National Security Files, 1963–1969* (Frederick, MD: University Publications of America, 1989), reel 8 of 8. See also Ahmed Hamroush, *Qissa taura 23 Yulio: Karif Abdel-Nasser* [The story of 23 July revolution: The autumn of Abdel Nasser], vol. 5 (Cairo: Maktaba al-madbuli, 1984), pp. 82–3.

12. Esposito, *The Islamic Threat*, p. 17; Cottam, "U.S. and Soviet Responses to Islamic Political Militancy," p. 277; Edward Said, *Covering Islam: How the Media and the Experts Determine How We See the Rest of the World*, p. x.

13. Brzezinski, *Power and Principle: Memoirs of the National Security Adviser, 1977–1981* (New York: Farrar, Straus and Giroux, 1983), pp. 532–3.

dawn of colonialism, the U.S. government had to contend with a return of the power of Islam.[14]

Furthermore, in the early 1970s, Libyan President Mu'ammar al-Qaddafi employed Islamic symbols to legitimize his populist rule and to assist revolutionary movements throughout the Middle East and Africa. According to a U.S. official who served then as an ambassador to a Central African state, American diplomats, whether in Washington or Africa, became preoccupied with Qaddafi's proclamation of an Islamic state, his promotion of Islam as the religion of the "black man" in Africa, and his spreading of Islamic "radicalism" and "terrorism" worldwide. They feared that radical Islam was moving southward to engulf the whole desert. In fact, Qaddafi's Islamic campaign influenced U.S. official perceptions of Islamic revivalism long before the Iranian revolution.[15]

The Impact of the Islamic Revolution in Iran

Of all the regional developments in the 1970s, the Iranian revolution and the hostage crisis had the most formative effect on the U.S. foreign-policy establishment and the public's views of Islam. Accustomed to seeing their country as the most democratic and generous, Americans were shocked to hear Iran's Ayatollah Khomeini call it the "Great Satan." As one U.S. official noted in 1995, "the Iranian experience extremely conditioned U.S. thinking about the violent, anti-American nature of fundamentalist Islam."[16]

Never before had the U.S. government been subjected to this type of confrontation, which it deemed uncompromising and "irrational." President Carter described his negotiations with the Iranian mullahs thus: "We are dealing with a crazy group."[17] By holding 52 Ameri-

14. Esposito, *The Islamic Threat*, p. 17; Said, *Covering Islam*, pp. x, 33.
15. According to a State Department official, interviewed in Princeton, NJ, 27 May 1995.
16. Ibid. Other U.S. officials, with whom John Esposito had met, saw political Islam through the prism of Iran/Khomeini. See Esposito, ed., *Symposium: Voices of Resurgent Islam* (New York: Oxford University Press, 1983), p. 9.
17. Cited in Gary Sick, *All Fall Down: America's Fateful Encounter with Iran*, p. 277.

cans hostage for 444 days, Khomeini's Iran inflicted daily humiliation on the United States, eliciting an intense degree of hostility and a deep and unfamiliar sense of powerlessness. Eventually Iran became a national obsession.[18]

As with Arab nationalism in the 1950s and 1960s, such labels as "extremist," "terrorist," and "fanatical" were applied to the Islamic revolution in Iran.[19] In a poll of mainstream Americans conducted in 1981, 76 percent of the respondents indicated that they had a low opinion of Iran; 56 percent cited "hostage" as coming to mind when Iran was mentioned; after "Khomeini," "oil," and "the Shah," many also cited "anger," "hatred," "turmoil," and "troublesome country."[20] Iran's brand of revolutionary Islam appeared to be on a collision course with the United States. It was under the impact of the Iranian revolution, then, that Islamism replaced secular nationalism as a security threat to U.S. interests, and fear of a clash between Islam and the West crystallized in the minds of Americans. One of the major reasons given by former U.S. Secretary of State Cyrus Vance for his objection to a military mission to rescue American hostages in Iran was the specter of an Islamic-Western war: "Khomeini and his followers, with a Shi'ite affinity for martyrdom, actually might welcome American military action as a way of uniting the Moslem world against the West."[21]

On a practical level, the real damage to the U.S. presence in the

18. Ibid., p. 275.
19. Jimmy Carter, *Keeping Faith: Memoirs of a President* (New York: Bantam Books, 1982), pp. 12, 499, 506.
20. A corrective should be added here. This poll showed that the low opinion of Arabs/Muslims was largely due to Americans' perception that Arabs/Muslims are hostile to the United States and are anti-Christian. This finding indicated that Americans' low opinion of Muslims was a merely defensive reaction. For example, of those Americans who believed that Muslims have a respect for Christianity, 45.8 percent had a high opinion of Arabs. Conversely, of those respondents who believed that Muslims have contempt for Christianity, a mere 28.5 percent had a high opinion of Arabs. See Shelley Slade, "The Image of the Arab in America: Analysis of a Poll on American Attitudes," *Middle East Journal*, pp. 148–9, 158.
21. *Hard Choices: Critical Years in American Foreign Policy* (New York: Simon & Schuster, 1983), pp. 408, 410.

Middle East was the loss of the Shah of Iran, a staunch American ally whom President Richard Nixon and his Secretary of State, Henry Kissinger, once counted on to police the Persian Gulf.[22] Meanwhile, U.S. fears that the Iranian revolution would destabilize neighboring Gulf states were reinforced by Khomeini's vehement denunciation of Saudi Arabia and other Gulf monarchies as "un-Islamic" and his disdainful characterization of their ties with the United States as "American Islam." He further called on the Gulf countries to "follow the path of revolution, resort to violence and continue their struggle to regain their rights and resources."[23]

Events of the following years only sharpened U.S. fears of the power of resurgent Islam. At the end of 1979, Saudi Arabia, America's most valued client in the Middle East, was rocked by the two-week takeover of the Grand Mosque at Mecca by rebellious Islamists who denounced the Saudi royal family's monopoly on political and economic power. The 1981 assassination of President Sadat of Egypt and the bloody attacks against U.S. personnel and installations in Lebanon, Kuwait, and elsewhere, heightened U.S. officials' concern over the export of Iranian "fundamentalism."[24]

The Islamic revolution in Teheran colored U.S. attitudes toward political Islam. The result, note some observers, is that Iran's brand of revolutionary Islam overshadows much of the current U.S. debate about the rise of political Islam. The above-mentioned poll shows the extent to which Islam and Iran were linked for mainstream Americans. When asked what comes to mind when the words "Muslim" or "Islam" are mentioned, the two most common responses, which received an equal number of votes, were "Muhammad" and "Iran."[25] The politics of Islam were confused with the politics of

22. Kissinger said that "Iran under the Shah, in short, was one of America's best, most important, and most loyal friends in the world." See his *White House Years* (Boston: Little, Brown & Company, 1979), p. 1262.
23. Cottam, "U.S. and Soviet Responses to Islamic Political Militancy," p. 276. See also Jacob Goldberg, "The Shi'i Minority in Saudi Arabia," in Juan R.I. Cole and Nikki R. Keddie, eds., *Shi'ism and Social Protest* (New Haven, CT: Yale University Press, 1986), pp. 242–3.
24. Brzezinski, *Power and Principle*, pp. 484, 533; Esposito, *The Islamic Threat*, pp. 21–2.
25. Slade, "The Image of the Arab in America," pp. 148–9, 157. Iran's hostility toward the United States, coupled with its emphasis on the

Iran, with many Americans unable to imagine relations with an Islamist government in which the United States was not cast in the role of the Great Satan.[26] "U.S. perceptions of the Iranian experience," conceded one State Department official, "were projected to our experience of the Arab Middle East."[27]

The Fear of Terrorism and Its Effects on U.S. Policy

Terrorism has emerged as one of the most important political issues in the United States. Some U.S. officials and commentators have linked it to Islamic militancy, particularly to Iran. Secretary of State Warren Christopher said that "Iran is the foremost state sponsor of terrorism in the world," representing "one of the greatest if not the greatest threats to peace and stability in the region."[28]

Unlike its European partners, the United States virtually escaped the horror of terrorism during the Cold War era. This is no longer true. Terrorists now select targets in the United States itself. A series of explosions shattered America's peace of mind, raising fears about further attacks and calls for punitive action against the perpetrators and their alleged state sponsors. Perhaps the most memorable of these instances was the February 1993 World Trade Center bombing, as a result of which ten Muslims were convicted of waging "a war of urban terrorism" against America and of plotting to kill President Mubarak.[29] The subsequent trial – coupled with the revelations that the perpetrators had conspired to carry out a bloody campaign to destroy the United Nations and other New York landmarks and force the United States to abandon its support for Israel and Egypt – deepened Americans' fears about the security threats associated with Islamists.

According to Professor Richard Bulliet of Columbia University, Americans have quite readily accepted the notion that acts of vio-

conflict between Islam and the West, only furthers the perception of Arabs and Muslims as inherently anti-Christian and anti-Western.
26. Fuller and Lesser, *A Sense of Siege*, p. 22.
27. Continuation of interview, Princeton, NJ, 27 May 1995.
28. "Statement by Secretary of State Warren Christopher Regarding U.S. Sanctions Against Iran," State Department Briefing, in *Federal News Service*, 1 May 1995, p. 1.
29. *New York Times*, 2 October 1995.

lence committed by some Muslims "are representative of a fanatic and terroristic culture that cannot be tolerated or reasoned with." Bulliet expressed his fear that the United States might be witnessing the growth of a new kind of anti-Semitism, based not on theories of Semitic race but on Islam: "We at some point are going to reach a threshold where people no longer need evidence to believe in a generic terrorist threat from religious Muslim fanatics."[30] Some observers added fuel to the fire by warning of the existence of a coordinated international network of "Islamic terrorist" groups throughout the United States with its guns aimed against Western interests.[31]

Although no evidence emerged about the existence of an "Islamic Internationale," the World Trade Center bombing did considerable damage to the Muslim image and presence in the United States. As James Brooke commented in the *New York Times,*, by linking "Muslims and domestic terrorism in the minds of many Americans," the bombing made Muslims vulnerable targets for racism and political discrimination.[32] For example, in the first of two surveys on American attitudes toward Islam taken just after the bombing, more than 50 percent of the respondents said that "Muslims are anti-Western and anti-American."[33] In the second survey, the respondents were asked to rate various religious groups from favorable to unfavorable; Muslims topped the most unfavorable list.[34]

30. Preface, in Bulliet, ed., *Under Siege: Islam and Democracy*, Occasional Papers 1 (New York: The Middle East Institute of Columbia University, 1994), p. iii; see also pp. 4, 11. Ironically, Medieval Christians believed that Muslims were barbaric, irrational creatures, and Muhammad's actions were often invoked as examples of how Islam encouraged and praised the use of force. Jacques de Vitry wrote the "use of force in Islam derived from Muhammad's own practices." Cited in Daniel, *Islam and the West*, pp. 123–4.
31. See the PBS documentary *Jihad in America*, aired on 21 November 1994.
32. "Attacks on U.S. Muslims Surge Even as Their Faith Takes Hold," *New York Times*, 28 August 1995.
33. Survey sponsored by the National Conference on Inter-Group Relations, the Ford Foundation, and the Joyce Foundation. It was conducted between 6 and 8 August 1993 by L. H. Research. The number of the respondents was 2,755.
34. Survey sponsored by the American Muslim Council and conducted between 16 and 23 March 1993 by the John Zogby Group International. The number of the respondents was 905.

The explosion in New York City had broader implications for U.S. foreign policy. As a senior State Department official remarked, the World Trade Center bombing represented a setback to the Clinton administration's efforts to define a positive, accommodationist policy toward Islam and because of its link to the growth of Hamas on the West Bank and Gaza, of Hezbollah in Lebanon, and of other militant Islamists in Sudan and Algeria.[35] Some Middle Eastern regimes, particularly Israel and Egypt, sought to capitalize on the bombing by pressing the United States to support them further in the struggle against local Islamist opposition groups. In the United States, those subscribing to variations of the clash-of-civilizations hypothesis used it to advocate a tough policy toward Islamists.

Therefore, the World Trade Center blast provided confrontationalists in the United States and overseas with a golden opportunity to lobby the Clinton administration to formulate a forceful policy toward Islamists. Before the dust had settled in the April 1995 bombing of a federal building in Oklahoma City, some of the media's "terrorism experts" were linking Arabs, Muslims, and Middle Easterners to the explosion.[36] A *New York Times* commentator asserted that although the Oklahoma massacre was the work of American terrorists, most "other attacks against Americans came from the Middle East."[37] The evidence supplied to the FBI and the State Department shows otherwise, however.

According to FBI sources for the year 1993, radicals with Muslim backgrounds were responsible for the World Trade Center bombing; as reprehensible as it was, this was the only violent act committed domestically by people from Muslim background for that year. In contrast, the FBI reported the following terrorist attacks during the 1982–1992 period: Puerto Ricans, 72 attacks; left-wing groups, 23 attacks; Jewish groups, 16 attacks; anti-Castro Cubans, 12 attacks;

35. Continuation of Princeton interview, 27 May 1995.
36. *CBS Evening News*, 19 April 1995; *New York Times*, 20 April 1995; *Washington Post*, 20 April 1995; *International Herald Tribune*, 26 April 1995; See also Arthur L. Lowrie, "The Campaign Against Islam and American Foreign Policy," *Middle East Policy* 4, nos. 1 and 2 (September 1995), p. 213.
37. A. M. Rosenthal, "Things America Can Do to Curtail Terrorism, Domestic and Foreign," reprinted in the *International Herald Tribune*, 26 April 1995.

and right-wing groups, 6 attacks.[38] An analogous pattern can be seen with regard to anti-U.S. terrorist attacks abroad: In 1994, 44 took place in Latin America, 8 attacks in the Middle East, 5 in Asia, 5 in Western Europe, and 4 in Africa.[39]

It was within this charged atmosphere that Muslims in the United States became targets of harassment after the 1995 Oklahoma City bombing. In the following three days, more than 200 violent attacks against Muslim Americans were recorded.[40] The Oklahoma City bombing further exposed the latent negative imagery that character-izes and colors U.S. public views of Islam and Muslims. It also showed the media's willingness, when it comes to Arabs/Muslims, to abandon their principle of fair and accurate reporting. It should be stressed that the media's history of stereotyping Arabs/Muslims taps into a receptive political culture that feels skeptical and ambivalent about unfamiliar "others."

In moments of crisis, confrontationalists gain the upper hand and dominate the airways and media. It is at such a juncture that Ameri-cans' attitudes toward Arabs/Muslims harden. Several of the polls mentioned above confirm this reality. Instead of treating terrorist incidents as an aberration, some commentators exaggerate their im-portance and portray them as part of a systematic war against West-ern civilization. Instead of seeing terrorism for what it really is – a desperate and isolated act – these observers view it as part of a pattern of anti-Westernism and anti-Americanism. In this sense, ter-rorism has further poisoned Americans' perceptions of Islam and Muslims.

To his credit, President Bill Clinton was quick to caution against leaping to conclusions in the face of initial accusations that the Oklahoma City bombing bore the marks of Middle East–style terror-ism: "This is not a question of anybody's country of origin. This is not a question of anybody's religion. This was murder, this was evil, this was wrong. Human beings everywhere, all over the world, will

38. Federal Bureau of Investigation, Terrorist Research and Analytical Sec-tion, 1995.
39. U.S. Department of State, *Patterns of Global Terrorism* (Washington, DC: U.S. Government Printing Office, April 1995), p. 67.
40. Brooke, "Attacks on U.S. Muslims Surge," *New York Times*, 28 August 1995.

condemn this out of their own religious convictions, and we should not stereotype anybody."[41]

Nonetheless, a direct consequence of the Oklahoma City bombing was the new lease on life given to the 1995 Omnibus Counterterrorism Act, passed by the House of Representatives and the Senate and signed into law by President Clinton. One of the law's provisions allows the U.S. government to use evidence from secret sources in deportation proceedings against aliens suspected of terrorist involvement, without having to disclose the sources of the information. A second provision allows the government to deport aliens who have made charitable contributions to organizations branded as terrorist by the authorities.[42]

Despite the denials by Clinton administration officials, observers note that this counterterrorism legislation was partly aimed against "Mideast terrorism," a synonym for "Islamic terrorism."[43] At a Senate hearing in April 1993, Acting Coordinator for Counter-Terrorism Laurence Pope noted: "Twenty years ago in the Arab world, secular nationalism was the preferred ideology. And so it was the ideology that terrorists adopted as a cover for their actions. Increasingly, it's Islamic ideology, extremist Islamic ideology, which provides that cover."[44] An American official who works on terrorism at the National Security Council (NSC) corroborated this interpretation: In U.S. eyes, Islamists have replaced pan-Arab nationalists as the driving force behind terrorism in the Middle East; today terrorism is basically religiously inspired, lacking any nationalist inspiration.[45]

41. Quoted in the *New York Times*, 21 April 1995.
42. For background on the complex issues surrounding the counterterrorism legislation, see relevant articles in the *New York Times*, 21, 24, 27, 29, and 30 April; 8 and 9 June; and 3 October 1995.
43. Anthony Lewis, "This Is America," *New York Times*, 1 May 1995. Some Zionist groups said that they hoped the measure could be used to dry up potential contributions in the United States for terrorist groups like Hamas, as reported in the *New York Times*, 21 April 1995.
44. *Hearing of the Senate Judiciary Committee. Terrorism and America: A Comprehensive Review of the Threat, Policy, and Law, 21 April 1993.* Washington, DC: U.S. Government Printing Office, Serial No. J-103-9, 1994.
45. Interview, Washington, DC, 29 March 1995. A similar point was made by the State Department senior official interviewed 27 May 1995 in Princeton.

Although in agreement with the above assessment, two other NSC officials remarked that while individuals and states who practice terrorism do not represent Islam, they might succeed in doing so if the United States comes to be seen as anti-Islamic. Although the Clinton administration, according to these officials, does not accept the claims of the Israeli, Egyptian, and Algerian governments that the mainstream Islamist opposition fosters terror, the administration fails to distinguish effectively between Islamists who participate in the political field and those who carry out violence. The blurring of the lines between the two groups may explain the ambiguity in U.S. policy statements on political Islam.[46]

The Role of the Media

Although observers of the American scene agree that the mainstream media's negative news coverage of Islam and Muslims conditions public perceptions of and attitudes toward Muslim societies, they find it difficult to delineate the complex relationship between the mainstream media and U.S. policy. To some, the "dominant media are themselves members of the corporate-elite establishment," so fundamental tensions between the foreign-policy and media establishment seldom arise.[47] In this view, a number of factors contribute to the situation, including the media's overwhelming dependence on government sources for their news stories; the lack of public contestation of government propaganda campaigns; and the government's use of ideological weapons like anticommunism, a demonized enemy, or potential national-security threats. Only rarely do offbeat reporters dare to challenge the fundamentals of official policy.[48]

A slightly different perspective holds that the media subordinated their usual interests to Cold War requirements in the name of national security, resulting in a "journalism of deference to the national

46. Interview, Washington, DC, 29 and 30 March 1995.
47. Edward S. Herman, "The Media's Role in U.S. Foreign Policy," *Journal of International Affairs* 47, no. 1 (Summer 1993), p. 25. See also Leon V. Sigal, *Reporters and Officials: The Organization and Politics of Newsmaking* (Lexington, MA: D.C. Heath, 1973), pp. 42–9.
48. Sigal, Ibid., pp. 42–60; Herman, "The Media's Role in U.S. Foreign Policy," p. 26.

security state."[49] In the aftermath of the Cold War, Leon Hadar argues that the media, following either their own initiatives or the footsteps of the foreign-policy elite, speculated about the rise of new global enemies. This explains, in his view, the press's fascination with political Islam and Iran, or what he calls "the Green Peril."[50]

In this view, the press is not part of the foreign-policy establishment but has been a willing participant in foreign-policy making insofar as it helps "establish the boundaries within which policy can be made."[51] This is evident in the case of Islam and of Muslims, who are often portrayed in a negative light, thus placing them at a considerable disadvantage in U.S. public opinion. Although mass public opinion may not count much in the foreign-policy equation, elite opinion does; decision makers and members of the policy elite get much of their information from the press.[52] Both views – on the one hand, of the media as a supportive arm of the state, whose negative coverage of Islam reinforces and reflects U.S. policy makers' fears and prejudices, and on the other, of the press as an indirect participant in the process insofar as it contributes to the climate in which policy is made – have this in common: the notion that the media's coverage of Islam and Muslims sheds much light on the making of U.S. policy.

Many U.S. officials deny any connection between the negative portrayal of Islam in the press and American policy. Assistant Secretary of State Robert Pelletreau, for example, sharply criticizes the

49. William Dorman qualifies this assertion by noting that the U.S. media are not a monolith and that journalists do not take their orders from official Washington; rather, "the effects of ideology work their way more through cultural osmosis than directive." See his "Media, Public Discourse, and U.S. Policy Toward the Middle East," in H. Amirahmadi, ed., *The United States and the Middle East: A Search for New Perspectives* (Albany: State University of New York Press, 1993), pp. 289, 291–2, 304.
50. Leon Hadar, "The Media and Islam," in Bulliet, ed., *Under Siege*, p. 64.
51. Dorman, pp. 289, 291.
52. Ibid., p. 297. On another level, Andrea Lueg asserts that the Western media's portrayal of Islam is the primary source for Western conception of Islam and the region in which it predominates. See Lueg, "The Perception of Islam in Western Debate," in Hippler and Lueg, eds., *The Next Threat: Western Perceptions of Islam*, (Boulder, CO: Pluto Press, 1995), pp. 7, 15–16.

media for coverage that fosters the tendency, both in scholarship and public debate, to equate Islam with Islamic fundamentalism and extremism, but he does not consider the impact of the media's coverage on foreign-policy making, or vice versa.[53] Other U.S. policy makers, while agreeing that a flow of information exists on a multiplicity of levels between nongovernmental and policy-making agencies, assert that the desire of American decision makers to exchange ideas with the media and academia depends on the situation and the need for crisis management. A comment frequently heard is that U.S. officials base their decisions on their perception of national interests.[54]

Moreover, the way in which U.S. officials define national interests is related closely to their perception of reality, and policy is not formulated in a vacuum. The role of Congress, the media, and domestic considerations all drive policy and influence opinion within the foreign-policy community, especially on such issues as the Arab-Israeli conflict and political Islam.[55] Samuel Lewis, former director of the State Department's Policy Planning Staff, acknowledges that the media's hostile coverage of "extremist Islamist groups" reinforces American perceptions of Islam, thus complicating the task of U.S. policy makers.[56] In fact, the media's negative portrayal of Muslims, according to the poll mentioned above, has become an integral part of public consciousness.[57]

The Role of Israel and Its Friends

According to the Israeli writer Haim Baram, since the collapse of the Soviet Union and the fall of communism, Israeli leaders have attempted to enlist the United States and Europe in the battle against Islamic fundamentalism, portraying it as a larger-than-life enemy; their strategy is designed to convince U.S. public opinion and policy makers of Israel's continuing strategic value in a turbulent world.[58] A

53. Pelletreau in "Symposium: Resurgent Islam," p. 2.
54. Interview with NSC officials, Washington, DC, 30 March 1995.
55. Interview with a State Department official, Washington, DC, 30 March 1995.
56. Interview with Lewis, Chicago, IL, 23 February 1995.
57. Slade, "The Image of the Arab in America," pp. 144–5, 147, 150, 157.
58. Haim Baram, "The Demon of Islam," *Middle East International,* 2 December 1994, p. 8.

cursory review of Israeli politicians' pronouncements illustrates their strongly held views on political Islam. For example, as early as 1992, former President Herzog of Israel told the Polish Parliament that "the disease [of Islamic fundamentalism] is spreading rapidly and constitutes not only a danger to the Jewish people, but to humanity in general."[59]

In his frequent visits to the United States, the late Prime Minister Yitzhak Rabin often referred to the "Islamic peril" in order to convince Americans that "Iran is posing the same threat as Moscow in the good old days." Visiting the United States a few days after the World Trade Center bombing, Rabin told Clinton that "fundamentalism incited by Iran is infiltrating Muslim institutions in the West."[60] Shimon Peres, Israel's former Prime Minister, was more direct: "After the fall of Communism, fundamentalism has become the greatest danger of our time." In another speech, Peres recalled the evils of Nazism and Communism, warning against the current threat of Islamic fundamentalism, which, he said, "like Communism adopted the Machiavellian slogan that ends justify means, which is a license to lie, to subvert, to kill."[61]

According to Elaine Sciolino and to Arthur Lowrie, a former State Department official, the momentum of the anti-Islamist campaign in the United States suggests that "the purported views of Israeli leaders have been increasingly adopted by their supporters and others."[62] To what extent have Israeli views and lobbying efforts influenced the making of American policy on political Islam? Most U.S. officials at the State Department and NSC deny any Israeli connection in the formulation of American policy toward Islamists, contending that U.S. national interests are the sole consideration.[63]

59. Reported in the *Guardian*, 19 June 1992.
60. Reported in the *New York Times*, 23 February 1993. See also Baram, "The Demon of Islam," p. 8.
61. Quoted by Elaine Sciolino, "The Red Menace Is Gone," *New York Times* Sunday, 21 January 1996, Week in Review section. See also Todd Purdum, "Clinton to Order a Trade Embargo Against Tehran," *New York Times*, 1 May 1995.
62. Sciolino, ibid., and Lowrie, "The Campaign Against Islam and American Foreign Policy," p. 212.
63. Interview with a member of the State Department's Policy Planning Staff, Washington, DC, 27 March 1995. Interview with an NSC official, Washington, DC, 30 March 1995.

There were, however, a few dissenters. According to a senior State Department official, "we are very much influenced by the Israeli definition of Islamists. To a large extent, Israel's view of Islamic fundamentalism shapes U.S. officials' perception of this phenomenon."[64] Another member of the State Department noted that U.S. suspicions of Islamists is related partly to the latter's opposition to peace with Israel, a very important foreign-policy issue to the United States.[65]

President Clinton's vow before the Jordanian parliament in October 1994 to resist "the dark forces of terror and extremism" is a clear reference to militant Islamist groups, who oppose the Arab-Israeli peace process.[66] The impression conveyed by American officials is that the various U.S. administrations are well aware and responsive to Israel's definition of its security in the Middle East. Arthur Lowrie, a former State Department official, asserted that Clinton's dual-containment policy of Iran and Iraq and his subsequent 1995 announcement of a complete trade embargo on Iran were influenced by the lobbying efforts and political pressures of Israel's friends.[67] Similarly, the author of an article in the *Economist* suspected Clinton of relying partly on information supplied by Israel to appear personally tough on the issue of the day – terrorism.[68] The *Economist*'s point raises critical questions about the input of interest or pressure groups in shaping policy.

64. Princeton interview, 27 May 1995.
65. Interview with a member of the State Department's Policy Planning Staff, 27 March 1995.
66. "Remarks by President Clinton to the Jordanian Parliament," *The White House, Office of the Press Secretary*, Amman, Jordan, 26 October 1994, p. 1.
67. Lowrie, "The Campaign Against Islam and American Foreign Policy," pp. 215–16. More on Clinton's Iran policy below.
68. "Punishing Iran," 6 May 1995. In testimony before the House Foreign Affairs Committee in July 1993, Undersecretary for Global Affairs Timothy Wirth acknowledged that the U.S. government has "very, very good contacts with Israeli intelligence," especially on Iran. See U.S. House of Representatives, *The Future of U.S. Anti-Terrorism Policy*, "Hearing Before the Subcommittee on International Security, International Organizations, and Human Rights of the Committee on Foreign Affairs, 13 July 1993" (Washington, DC: U.S. Government Printing Office, 1993), p. 23.

Congressional Influence on U.S. Foreign Policy

More than anywhere else in the world, Congress plays a determining influence on U.S. policy toward the Middle East, having emerged as a decisive player in the last three decades. Although the President has much more leverage and leeway in that geopolitical sphere. Clinton administration officials whom I interviewed expressed their anxiety over the general atmosphere in the Congress. One NSC official remarked that Congress and the public hold "simplistic" and "prejudiced" views toward Islam and Muslims.[69] According to Elaine Sciolino of the *New York Times*: "In the absence of other compelling threats to the United States, Islamic radicalism has also seized the imagination of some in Congress."[70]

A cursory review of statements by some Congressmen reveals deep concern about security threats associated with the rise of political Islam. These include terrorism, acquisition of nuclear weapons, and the security of Israel and the Gulf states. Former House Speaker Newt Gingrich has called for "a coherent U.S. strategy for fighting Islamic totalitarianism."[71] Congressional hearings are rife with questions about the threat that Middle East and Islamic "terrorism" pose to the United States and Western security.[72] Representative Ileana Ros-Lehtinen accused the State Department of underestimating the uniform nature of "Islamic extremism" and of stressing instead its diffused and eclectic character; in her view, Islamic groups represent a monolithic movement "sworn to fight the Great Satan America for the global supremacy of Islam."[73]

The chairman of the House International Relations Committee, Benjamin Gilman, a New York Republican, attacked the Clinton administration's terrorism policy as ineffectual, using the security

69. Interview, Washington, DC, 29 March 1995.
70. "The Red Menace Is Gone," 21 January 1996.
71. Cited in Sciolino in Ibid.
72. According to Representative Ileana Ros-Lehtinen, chairperson of the Subcommittee on Africa, "Islamic militancy has emerged as one of the most serious threats to Western security." See "The Threat of Islamic Extremism in Africa," Prepared Testimony of the Honorable Ileana Ros-Lehtinen, Committee on International Relations, U.S. House of Representatives, *Federal News Service*, 6 April 1995, p. 1.
73. Ibid.

lapse in the World Trade Center bombing to demand radical changes in U.S. immigration laws: "We cannot continue to allow these people [Sheik Omar Abd al-Rahman and his followers] into our country. The laws are wrong. We've allowed our U.S. to become a dumping ground for hoodlums, terrorists, and people who are not interested in any good. They merely wish to destroy the U.S. I demand changes be made, and tomorrow will not be too soon."[74]

As to whether Congress has had an impact on the U.S. approach toward political Islam, some American officials have intimated that public and congressional perceptions of Islam do influence and set constraints on the policy-making process.[75] Demonizing Islamic movements, asserted a retired State Department official, complicates the United States' ability to adopt a constructive policy.[76] One striking example is the Clinton administration's approval in December 1995 of $20 million in covert aid to change the Iranian government or at least change its behavior.[77]

Speaker Gingrich, an ex-officio member of the House Intelligence Committee and the one who appoints its Republican members, used his great influence over government spending to force the President to fund the "secret mission," despite administration and CIA convictions that there is no viable alternative to the current Iranian leadership and that such a policy is likely to fuel paranoia and anti-

74. According to Gilman, this quote was taken from a letter sent to him by one of his New York constituents, as cited by Laurence Pope during the hearing of the Senate Judiciary Committee," *Terrorism and America*, p. 2. Gilman's point should be interpreted in a larger context. The World Trade Center and Oklahoma City bombings, noted sociologist Nathan Glazer of Harvard, focused attention in the United States on "Middle Eastern immigrants and their political activities, though the guilt [in the case of Oklahoma] turned out to lie elsewhere." See Nathan Glazer, "Debate on Aliens Flares Beyond the Melting Pot," *New York Times*, 23 April 1995.

75. Nevertheless, these diplomats have insisted that U.S. policy toward political Islam is ultimately determined by official statements, which are not "sensational and panic-stricken." Drawn from interview with a member of the State Department's Policy Planning Staff, Washington, DC, 27 March 1995 and interview with an NSC official, Washington, DC, 30 March 1995.

76. Lowrie, "The Campaign Against Islam," p. 215.

77. Tim Weiner, "U.S. Plan to Change Iran Leaders Is an Open Secret Before It Begins," *New York Times*, 26 January 1996.

Americanism in Teheran.[78] The result is that Congress tied the President's hands, forcing him to pursue a course of action that might have negative repercussions on U.S. interests. By agreeing to Gingrich's "secret" plan, however, Clinton bowed to Congress's wishes on an important foreign-policy issue. This is one way in which Congress indirectly participates in the making of U.S. foreign policy.

Another example was President Clinton's decision in April 1995, first announced before the World Jewish Congress, to impose a total trade embargo on Iran in an effort to change its behavior. Again, the President's decision, as Todd S. Purdum of the *New York Times* remarked, was suffused with domestic politics. Clinton administration officials were fully aware that anti-Iranian sentiment was building in the Senate and House, with some proposals aimed at punishing not only Iran but also foreign companies that continue to do business with it. By acting on its own, the White House hoped to seize the initiative and preempt the tougher anti-Iran Republican bills in the Congress.[79]

The President's actions, however, did not mollify influential Senate and House members. During a Capitol Hill hearing, Representative Gilman took credit for the additional sanctions against Iran by reminding Assistant Secretary of State Pelletreau that the administration would not have acted without sustained pressure from Congress. Gilman also stated that the Congress views the economic ban as "the beginning and not the end of the process," demanding a showdown with foreign companies that continue to trade with Iran.[80] Again, the President bowed to Congress's wishes when the latter passed legislation stipulating the punishment of any foreign company that invests $40 million or more in the Iranian oil and industrial sector. Despite warnings by Europe and Japan, Clinton signed this new legislation into law in summer 1996.

The effective pressure applied by Congress on the Clinton admin-

78. Ibid.
79. Purdum, "Cinton to Order a Trade Embargo Against Tehran," *New York Times*, 1 May 1995. See also "Punishing Iran," in the *Economist*, p. 14.
80. "Hearing with Defense Department Personnel; House International Relations Committee; International Economic and Trade Subcommittee – U.S. Sanctions on Iran," *Federal News Service*, 2 May 1995, p. 4.

istration shows the extent of the legislative influence in foreign-policy making. The case of Iran is just one example in which Congress keeps a watchful eye on foreign policy as well as participates in its formulation.

4

The Carter, Reagan, and Bush Administrations' Approach to Islamists

Lately we have seen the possibilities of, literally, a religious war – the Muslims returning to the idea that the way to heaven is to lose your life fighting the Christians or the Jews.[1]

President-elect Ronald Reagan

Understanding the chasm between accommodationists and confrontationalists is critical not only because it affects U.S. domestic politics but also because it provides the intellectual basis for American policy toward political Islam. Various U.S. administrations' perceptions of Islamists parallel those of the two opposing schools of thought. According to a member of the State Department's Policy Planning Staff, both confrontationalist and accommodationist views are well entrenched within the U.S. foreign-policy establishment: "[T]he hard-liners would like to draw a line in the sand against militant Islamists, whereas liberals prefer dialogue, diplomacy, and reconciliation with Islamists."[2]

Carter's Collision with Political Islam: The Iranian Revolution

Although presidents Carter and Reagan witnessed the rise to power of Islamic movements in the Middle East, as a result facing difficult policy choices in that sphere, neither one articulated publicly any

1. "An Interview with Ronald Reagan," *Time*, 17 November 1980, p. 37.
2. Interview, Washington, DC, 27 March 1995.

59

systematic set of ideas on political Islam. Both were preoccupied with the Cold War rivalry with the Soviet Union. Communism, not Islamic activism, was seen as the main enemy. Despite the intensification of Islamist sentiments in several Muslim societies, Carter and Reagan administration officials did not shift their strategic focus away from the Soviet Union, largely perceiving the new Islamists as a mere nuisance rather than a serious threat. Furthermore, the Carter and Reagan administrations showed a willingness to play down their differences with Islamists and align the United States with them in the common fight against the Soviets. American support for the mujaheden, the Afghan resistance movement in Afghanistan, was a case in point.

Nonetheless, Carter's and Reagan's first encounters with Islamists, and their inability to respond effectively to the new Islamist currents, negatively influenced Americans' view of Islam and of Muslims in general. Few events have had a more critical effect on U.S. thinking and policy toward political Islam than did the Iranian revolution of 1979. The Islamic revolution in Iran and the loss of an important client state shocked the Carter administration and may be seen as its greatest setback. For at least a decade, the United States had built its relations with Iran almost exclusively through the person of the Shah. In 1972, President Richard Nixon had told the Shah that he could purchase any U.S. conventional weapons he wanted, appointing him policeman of the Persian Gulf.[3] Therefore, "the fall of the Shah," stated former Assistant for National Security Affairs Brzezinski, "was disastrous strategically for the United States and politically for Carter himself."[4]

From the outset of the Iranian crisis, President Carter's task was complicated by conflicting advice from his aides. On the one hand, administration officials were divided over the most effective approach to adopt toward the new revolutionaries. On the other hand, "many

3. Gary Sick, *All Fall Down*, pp. 31–2, 157; Rouhollah K. Ramazani, ed., *Iran's Revolution* (Washington, DC: Middle East Institute, 1990), pp. 49–50. George Ball, former Undersecretary of State, said that by "anointing the Shah as the guardian of Western interests in the whole Gulf area, Nixon inadvertently encouraged the megalomania that ultimately contributed to the Shah's downfall." Quoted in William Shawcross, *The Shah's Last Ride* (London: Pan Books, 1989), p. 167.
4. Zbigniew Brzezinski, *Power and Principle*, pp. 354, 398.

of Carter's best intelligence sources," argues James Bill, "provided him with a deeply flawed and inaccurate picture of Iran."[5] Although initially the U.S. ambassador to Teheran, William Sullivan, called for quarantining Khomeini and working with the Shah, he subsequently changed his mind and advocated a dialogue between the military and Khomeini. Such a dialogue, stated Sullivan, might smooth the transition to a new political pact.[6]

With the exception of Sullivan and a few voices in the State Department, most U.S. officials strongly opposed any overture to Khomeini, fearing the adverse effects of Khomeini's seizure of power on Western interests: His Iran would become an easy target for radical leftist and religious forces. Brzezinski argued that Khomeini represented the forces of "Islamic fundamentalism that were now openly challenging the existing order."[7] Similarly, General Robert Huyser, who was sent to Teheran to "encourage the military to stage a coup," came to a similar conclusion: Khomeini's return to Iran would constitute the greatest potential for complete disaster.[8]

Of all Carter's advisers, Brzezinski and General Huyser lobbied hardest for a military solution in Iran – a military takeover if necessary. Contradicting Brzezinski and Huyser, Ambassador Sullivan reported that Iran's political structures were breaking apart, including the military.[9] Conflicting advice resulted in Carter's indecision and wavering posture, which in turn often led to the President following the advice of Brzezinski. After the Shah's departure from Teheran, some U.S. policy makers encouraged the Iranian armed forces to

5. James A. Bill, *The Eagle and the Lion* (New Haven, CT: Yale University Press, 1988), p. 258.
6. Barry Rubin, *Paved with Good Intentions: The American Experience and Iran* (New York: Oxford University Press, 1980), p. 237; Sick, *All Fall Down*, pp. 60, 150, 152.
7. Brzezinski, *Power and Principle*, pp. 377–8, 385, 394.
8. Sick, *All Fall Down*, pp. 60, 150, 152.
9. Brzezinski, *Power and Principle*, pp. 354–98; Rubin, *Paved with Good Intentions*, p. 247; Sick, *All Fall Down*, p. 170. In his memoirs, Brzezinski is very critical of Secretary of State Cyrus Vance and of Sullivan for their opposition to a military coup. U.S. failure in Iran discredited Brzezinski and his staff, who placed blame for the Shah's collapse on officials in the State Department. The latter were seen to be defeatist and perhaps disloyal to the Carter White House and to the Shah himself. See Bill, *The Eagle and the Lion*, p. 276; Rubin, *Paved with Good Intentions*, p. 247.

execute a coup in the event that Khomeini decided to return home from his exile in Paris. As Carter stated: "The threat of a military coup is the best way to prevent Khomeini from sliding to power."[10]

Nevertheless, when it came to formulating a consistent policy toward revolutionary Iran, the United States was at a loss. This difficulty arose not only because of conflicting advice within the Carter administration but also due to the fact that the administration, noted Iran desk officer Henry Precht, was ill-informed about the new religious men who controlled political life in Iran. Furthermore, argues Iranian specialist James Bill, powerful Pahlavi supporters in the United States sought to discredit the revolution by portraying the revolutionaries as uncivilized, barbaric, and fanatical and the revolution itself as a fleeting aberration that lacked the support of the Iranian people.[11] To this must be added the strong, anti-American behavior of the new revolutionaries who advocated the "export of revolution" into neighboring countries.[12]

Far from exploring the opportunities for reconciliation with the powerful clergy in Teheran once the Shah was overthrown, the Carter administration backed away from the unknown and untried Islamists, preferring to deal with the Western-educated moderates who were nominally in charge of the provisional government.[13] The advocates of change within the Carter administration usually lost on the Iran issue.[14] U.S. officials mistrusted the mullahs as well as underestimated their political strength and the captivating power of their message. President Carter had only contempt for the "street

10. Quoted in Brzezinski, *Power and Principle*, p. 387. See also Sick, *All Fall Down*, pp. 151, 153.
11. Bill, *The Eagle and the Lion*, pp. 276–7.
12. Fred Halliday, *Islam and the Myth of Confrontation*, pp. 64, 70.
13. Robin Wright, *Sacred Rage: The Wrath of Militant Islam* (New York: Simon and Schuster, 1985), p. 270; Sick, *All Fall Down*, p. 187. Warren Christopher, who as Deputy Secretary of State played a key role in the discussions within the U.S. government and in negotiations with Iran, acknowledged that it was only in late summer 1980 that U.S. officials shifted their focus from Western-educated Iranians to the right-wing fundamentalist group then in power. See Christopher, ed., "Introduction," in *American Hostages in Iran: The Conduct of a Crisis* (New Haven, CT: Yale University Press, 1985; a Council on Foreign Relations Book), p. 7.
14. Rubin, *Paved with Good Intentions*, p. 197.

mobs" who whipped up anti-American feelings to a fever pitch and for Khomeini's "irrational" statements and actions.[15] "We are dealing with crazy people in Iran," wrote Hamilton Jordan, Carter's Chief of Staff.[16]

Clash of Cultures or Clash of National Interests?

At the heart of this U.S. misreading of the Iranian scene, notes Gary Sick, NSC staff member for Iran and chief assistant to Brzezinski throughout the Iran crisis, lies a deep cultural bias: It is the contradiction between two value systems and world conceptions – Khomeini's Islamic-theocratic worldview versus Carter's essentially Western-secular one. According to Sick, although both Khomeini and Carter were deeply religious men, their faiths had almost nothing in common: "Khomeini was the archetype of the medieval prophet emerging from the desert with a fiery vision of absolute truth. His god was a harsh and vengeful deity – full of fury, demanding the eye and tooth of retribution for human transgressions of divine law. . . . He was a man riven with hate – hatred for the shah, hatred for Carter and America, hatred for those who dared oppose his vision."[17]

The tension between the religious and secular, adds Sick, was a major contributing factor to the failure of both Iranians and Westerners to understand and gauge properly each other's fears and aspirations. In his explanation of the U.S.–Iranian crisis, Sick puts a lot of weight on the unbridgeable chasm between two impossibly different cultures, as reflected in the very different personalities of Carter and Khomeini: "We are all prisoners of our own cultural assumptions."[18]

15. *Keeping Faith: Memoirs of a President*, pp. 451, 453.
16. *Crisis: The Last Year of the Carter Presidency* (New York: G. P. Putnam's Sons, 1982), p. 39.
17. *All Fall Down*, pp. 164, 219–20.
18. Ibid., pp. 164, 220. Christopher echoed Sick's point by remarking that in the negotiations leading to the release of American hostages, the Algerians played an indispensable role in interpreting two widely disparate cultures and reasoning processes to each other. See Christopher, "Introduction," *American Hostages in Iran*, p. 9. Likewise, Harold Saunders notes that the challenge facing members of the U.S. crisis team on Iran was how to bridge the wide gulf between the Iranian and American

Sick states that American officials found Khomeini's call for the establishment of an Islamic state to be "absurd"; it ran counter to the entire modern history of the Western tradition of secularizing revolutions. The U.S. foreign-policy elite was thus unprepared to deal with the unthinkable – the emergence of a cleric-dominated Islamic republic. U.S. officials failed to grasp the new revolutionary flame emanating from the mosques. According to Sick, Carter administration officials' profound cultural bias was "so persistent that it interfered fundamentally with the normal processes of observation and analysis on which all of us instinctively depend."[19]

Sick adds further that even after Khomeini constructed his Islamic state, the Carter administration's policy judgment continued to be impaired by an intrinsic cultural conviction that the "exotic extremes" of the Khomeini regime in Teheran – given its "wildly" "irrational" character, and its flouting of all the normal rules of accepted political behavior – was bound to destroy itself through its own excesses:

> Much of the deep emotion that permeated the policy-making process during the hostage crisis can, in my opinion, be traced to the underlying belief that we were dealing not only with a government that had flouted the law of nations but with a regime that was historically illegitimate, unfit, despicable. I suspect that all of us, reading the speeches and accounts coming out of Teheran, experienced a sense of physical revulsion at one time or another.[20]

The hostage crisis, which lasted for more than fourteen months, represented more than a test of wills between the United States and Iran; it was a clash of cultures. The crisis riveted and preoccupied the attention of Carter and the nation as few events ever have.[21] As the hostage drama dragged on, the Carter administration realized that the issue was becoming increasingly polarized along the lines of America versus Islam, sharpening anti-Muslim feelings in the United States. The outrage of the American people, according to Sick and Harold

worldviews. See Saunders, "The Crisis Begins," in *American Hostages in Iran*, pp. 47, 52.
19. Sick, *All Fall Down*, pp. 164–6.
20. Ibid., pp. 167–8.
21. Christopher, "Introduction," p. 1.

Saunders, was fully shared by U.S. policy makers at all levels, whose concern was to bring maximum pressure on Khomeini to free the hostages.[22] President Carter could not hide his anger after watching Iranian students demonstrate in front of the White House in support of the Iranian revolution. He took action to expel those students whose visas had expired: "I am not going to have those bastards humiliating our country in front of the White House! [I]f I wasn't president, I'd be out on the streets myself and would probably take a swing at any Khomeini demonstrator I could get my hands on."[23]

American diplomats suspected Khomeini of encouraging, if not orchestrating, militant Islamist students to take over the U.S. embassy and the hostages in order to consolidate his Islamic revolution at home and score political gains externally. In U.S. eyes, the moderate elements were being suddenly and unexpectedly undermined by the religious extremists.[24] As President Carter put it: "All our efforts were fruitless. The militants had become overnight heroes in Iran. Khomeini praised their action."[25] Secretary of State Vance also sounded the alarm: "We must be firm but cautious in dealing with this group of unknown and unpredictable Moslem fanatics."[26]

Brzezinski advised Carter to take some major steps not only to punish Iran but also "to unseat Khomeini." Carter concurred: "I want to punish them as soon as our people have been released; really

22. Sick criticizes U.S. officials for continually underestimating Khomeini's staying power and willingness to absorb punishment in the pursuit of his revolutionary objectives. See Sick, *All Fall Down*, pp. 206–7; Saunders, "The Crisis Begins," p. 47; Brzezinski, *Power and Principle*, p. 484.
23. Quoted in Jordan, *Crisis*, p. 40.
24. Christopher, "Introduction," p. 3; Sick, *All Fall Down*, pp. 197, 207. Harold Saunders, former Assistant Secretary of State for Near Eastern and South Asian Affairs, asserted that the hostage crisis was more of an internal struggle for power between "Islamic fundamentalists" and secular revolutionaries than an episode in Iran's international relations. In this context, a prominent Islamic statesman told Secretary Vance that "you will not get your hostages back until Khomeini has put all the institutions of the Islamic revolution in place." See Saunders, "The Crisis Begins," in *American Hostages in Iran*, pp. 45–7.
25. Carter, *Keeping Faith*, p. 458. The word *overnight* clearly shows how unaware U.S. policy makers were about the bloody struggle for power which accompanied the Iranian revolution from its inception.
26. Quoted in Jordan, *Crisis*, p. 38.

hit them. They must know they can't fool around with us."[27] The president, notes Sick, was persuaded that the diplomatic relationship with Khomeini's Iran was finished. Carter said he wanted to "get our people out of Iran and break relations. Fuck 'em."[28]

On a deeper level, Carter administration officials were particularly concerned about the security repercussions of the Islamic revolution and the potential effect of a spillover into neighboring Gulf states. They were mainly preoccupied with security and strategic calculations, not cultural variables. The latter indirectly impaired the policy judgment of some American diplomats. President Carter alluded to that when he intimated to his chief of staff, Hamilton Jordan, that they should stop "talking about cultural differences and Khomeini's irrationality," and spell out, instead, the serious strategic consequences inherent in Iran's actions.[29]

The security repercussions of the Islamic revolution were manifold. For example, in November 1979 the echoes of the Iranian revolution were felt in Saudi Arabia after Islamists temporarily seized the Grand Mosque in Mecca. The seizure of the holiest shrine for all Muslims, sent shock waves throughout the Muslim world and within the U.S. foreign-policy–making establishment. Subsequently, American diplomats and embassies were attacked and burned in Pakistan, Libya, Kuwait, and Afghanistan. Iran's defiance and challenge of the United States had a determining effect on succeeding U.S. policies toward Iran, Persian Gulf states, and other Islamic movements. The United States, argues Shireen T. Hunter, was not only bent on defeating Iran, thereby proving the bankruptcy of an Islamic revolution to other Muslims, but also on accomplishing this feat without driving Iran into Soviet arms or causing its disintegration.[30]

At this stage, the U.S.-Soviet rivalry took precedence over third-world problems, including revolutionary Islam. The latter was seen simply through the prism and lens of the Cold War, and Islamists were not viewed as posing a threat to U.S. security interests. The

27. Quoted in Brzezinski, *Power and Principle*, pp. 482–4. See also Sick, *All Fall Down*, p. 206.
28. Quoted in Sick, *All Fall Down*, p. 210.
29. Jordan, *Crisis*, p. 66.
30. *Iran and the World* (Bloomington: Indiana University Pres, 1990), pp. 59–60.

Islamic revolution in Iran marked Washington's first major encounter with political Islam.

Fearing that an anti-U.S. wave was sweeping the entire Muslim world, Secretary of State Vance ordered the evacuation of all nonessential American personnel from sensitive posts throughout the region. According to Saunders, Vance expressed his agony over the safety of U.S. citizens and diplomats in Muslim countries. Neither Vance nor Saunders could be confident that the attacks against U.S. targets would not be repeated in the Muslim world.[31] Brzezinski also felt alarmed: "The resurgence of fundamentalist Islam throughout the region, culminating in the fall of the Shah and the convulsions of Khomeini's Iran, created a continuing danger to our interests in a region on which the well-being of the West as a whole very much depends."[32] American officials felt the need to understand the tenets of Shi'i Islam and of the fundamentalist Islamic revival. They suddenly realized that the return of political Islam was there to stay.[33]

The December 1979 Soviet invasion of Afghanistan, however, reminded U.S. decision makers that the strategic clash with the Communist camp was of a higher order than a confrontation with the new Islamist challenge emanating from Teheran.[34] The latter paled in comparison with the Cold War rivalry that had preoccupied the United States since the late 1940s. Carter wrote in his diary that

31. Sick, *All Fall Down*, p. 233; Saunders, "Diplomacy and Pressure, November 1979–May 1980," in *American Hostages in Iran*, p. 91.

32. Brzezinski, *Power and Principle*, pp. 484, 533.

33. Saunders, "Diplomacy and Pressure," p. 124. The remark by Saunders about Shi'i Islam underscores one of the simplistic assumptions that were common in the early days of the Islamic revolution and have continued since, that the politics of Islamic revivalism is basically a Shi'i phenomenon. In the aftermath of the Iranian revolution, much ink was spent on analyzing the radical and revolutionary roots of Shi'i Islam, while ignoring the complex and universalist message of political Islam. Subsequent events in Saudi Arabia, Egypt, Sudan, and Algeria, with mostly Sunni populations, have shown the unviability of the Sunni-Shi'i divide. John L. Esposito and James P. Piscatori, "The Global Impact of the Iranian Revolution: A Policy Perspective," in Esposito, ed., *The Iranian Revolution: Its Global Impact* (Miami: Florida International University Press, 1990), pp. 318–19.

34. Gary Sick, "Military Options and Constraints," in *American hostages in Iran*, p. 151.

the Soviet invasion of Afghanistan was "the most serious international development that has occurred since I have been President."[35]
The implications of the Soviet move, added Carter, "could pose the
most serious threat to the peace since the Second World War."[36]

Moreover, the invasion of Afghanistan made it more important
for the Carter administration to mobilize Islamic resistance against
the Soviets by tapping into the anti-Communist sentiment of the
now dominant "fundamentalist clergy" in Iran. Containing Soviet
Communism, said Brzezinski, dictated an avoidance of anything that
might split Islamic opposition to the Soviets, especially a U.S.–Iranian military confrontation: "It now seemed to me more important
to forge an anti-Soviet Islamic coalition."[37] As in the 1950s and
1960s, the United States hoped to use Islam against radical, secular
forces and their atheist ally – the Soviet Union.

Carter administration advisers now recognized the new possibilities for cooperation with Islamic resurgence and hoped to harness its
ideological and material resources against Communist expansionism.
Uppermost in U.S. officials' minds were the lessons of the 1950s and
1960s, when Islam was employed as an ideological weapon in the
fight against secular, pan-Arab nationalism. Thus, despite the convulsions of the Islamic revolution in Iran and its global impact in
several Muslim states, the Carter administration did not enunciate a
clear policy statement, let alone a full-fledged policy, toward political
Islam. To U.S. officials, Islamic resurgence was a temporary distrac-
tion from the Cold War. American foreign policy still revolved
around the containment of Soviet Communism, not Islamism.

Nevertheless, the Islamic revolution in Iran and the hostage crisis
had a devastatingly negative impact on Americans' perceptions of
Islam and Muslims in general. In U.S. eyes, Islamic Iran threatened the security and stability of America's regional interests as well
as those of its Middle Eastern allies.[38] Indeed, Iran's impact was more

---

35. Carter, *Keeping Faith*, p. 473.
36. *Weekly Compilation of Presidential Documents*, U.S. Government Printing
    Office, vol. 16, no. 4, 28 January 1980, pp. 194–6.
37. *Power and Principle*, pp. 470, 478, 485, 489. See also Saunders, "Diplo-
    macy and Pressure," pp. 113–14; Sick, "Military Options and Con-
    straints," p. 151.
38. Esposito and Piscatori, "The Global Impact of the Iranian Revolution:
    A Policy Perpective," p. 317.

than academic. It has had a "profound effect" on the formulation and conduct of U.S. policy toward the larger Middle East ever since.[39] In the American mind, populist, revolutionary Islam came to be associated with terrorism and the promotion of subversive activities. Domestically, Carter's inability to respond effectively to the Islamic Republic of Iran – let alone free the U.S. hostages there – coupled with his failure to communicate his policy on Iran and on the hostages in particular to the American public, became one of the main rocks on which his presidential reelection bid crashed: "Iran, like a rock around the president's neck, helped pull him down."[40]

Reagan's Encounter with Islamic Resurgence: Rhetoric versus Action

Unlike Carter administration officials who wanted, at a minimum, not to "do or say things that would make us seem at odds with the whole Islamic world," Reagan aides often alluded to Islamic fundamentalism in highly antagonistic terms.[41] The Reagan administration's pronouncements on political Islam became hardened. For example, Secretary of State George Shultz equated Islamic fundamentalism with "radical extremism."[42] Defense Secretary Casper Weinberger referred to the Shi'ites as "the most fanatical and the most basically anti-Western Muslim sect. They do not place any great value on the preservation of human life."[43]

On several occasions, Reagan himself used hostile language to refer to Islam and Muslims. After his 1980 election, he gave an interview to *Time* magazine in which he claimed that Muslims were reverting to their belief that unless they killed a Christian or a Jew

39. Sick, *All Fall Down*, p. 221.
40. Ibid., p. 318; Brzezinski, *Power and Principle*, pp. 398, 509; Rubin, *Paved with Good Intentions*, p. 257; George Lenczowski, *American Presidents and the Middle East* (Durham, NC: Duke University Press, 1990), p. 201; Saunders, "The Crisis Begins," p. 48.
41. Saunders, "Diplomacy and Pressure," p. 124.
42. "The Future of American Foreign Policy: New Realities and New Ways of Thinking," testimony before the Senate Foreign Relations Committee on 31 January 1985, *U.S. Department of State Bulletin*, May 1985.
43. *Fighting for Peace: Seven Critical Years in the Pentagon* (New York: Warner Books, 1990), p. 137.

they would not go to heaven.[44] In the aftermath of the 1982 Israeli invasion of Lebanon, the President outlined a proposal to engage Arab moderates in the Arab-Israeli peace process before a rising wave of anti-peace fundamentalists put pro-Western governments on the defensive.[45] In his announcement of the 1986 U.S. bombing of Libya, President Reagan called Libyan President Mu'ammar al-Qaddafi a "barbarian," claiming that Libyan terrorism was part of a worldwide Muslim fundamentalist movement.[46] Similarly, in 1990 Vice President Dan Quayle drew a direct linkage between "the rise of Communism, the rise of Nazism, and the rise of radical Islamic fundamentalism."[47] Another senior U.S. official remarked in 1994 that with the death of Communism, "Islam is the global alternative."[48]

The Reagan administration's hostile attitude reflected the ideological style of the new President as well as the escalation of tensions between the United States and Islamists. However, the sharpening of rhetoric by Reagan administration officials did not herald a new focus or a shift in foreign-policy priorities. Like its immediate predecessor, the Reagan administration was far from preoccupied with the Islamist phenomenon. With the exception of Iran – along with its Shi'ite supporters in Lebanon whom Reagan tried to isolate – his administration did not encounter any large-scale Islamist challenges to the status quo in the Middle East.[49]

Reagan saw Soviet Communism and its local clients, not Islamism, as the real enemy. Under Reagan, U.S. policy remained wedded to supporting conservative religious elements against secular, socialist, and third world nationalist forces. Whereas the administration's pub-

44. "An Interview with Ronald Reagan," p. 37.
45. Leslie Gelb, "U.S. Sees Opportunities and Risks in Mideast After War in Lebanon," *New York Times*, 31 October 1982.
46. "Reagan Address on U.S. Air Strike against Libya, 14 April 1986," in *Historic Documents of 1986* (Washington, DC, Congressional Quarterly, 1987), pp. 347–54.
47. "Commencement Address at the U.S. Naval Academy for the Class of 1990, Annapolis, Maryland, 30 May 1990," in *U.S. Naval Academy Archives*, Nimitz Library, pp. 5–6.
48. John Esposito, quoted in the transcript of "Symposium: Resurgent Islam in the Middle East," *Middle East Policy* 3, no. 2 (1994), p. 9.
49. It was not until the late 1980s and early 1990s that Islamically oriented political movements won spectacular electoral victories in Egypt, Jordan, Tunisia, Algeria, and Lebanon.

lic statements were exceptionally hostile, no corresponding changes marked its actual behavior toward the new Islamists. For example, the Reagan administration strongly backed the mujaheden coalition in its fight against the occupying Soviet forces. Paradoxically, Reagan's action strengthened the most "militantly Islamic elements" within the mujaheden alliance, particularly the Party of Islam.[50] The Reagan administration was single-mindedly preoccupied with the containment of Soviet Communism. Reagan made it clear that he would assist any insurgency or revolt directed against the totalitarian Communist movement. He often reiterated his support for the Islamically oriented mujaheden "freedom fighters" because they resisted the Soviets.[51]

With hindsight, the U.S.-backed Islamic guerrillas in Afghanistan would come to haunt the United States and its allies. Having defeated the Soviet forces and the puppet Communist regime in Kabul, some of the Afghan veterans turned their guns on each other and on other targets in the United States and the Middle East, exploding their anger and frustration in the streets of New York, Cairo, Algiers, Benghazi, Islamabad, and Riyadh.[52] Some of Washington's allies blamed "the United States for creating the basis for an Islamic terrorist network by supporting so-called Islamic fighters against the Soviet occupiers in Afghanistan."[53]

Reagan's flirtation with the Islamist mujaheden factions in Afghanistan should be situated within the context of the second phase of the Cold War. Like his predecessors in the 1950s and 1960s, President Reagan allied the United States with Islamist groups and states – Afghanistan, Saudi Arabia, and Pakistan – to combat what he called the "evil empire" and its third world clients. The same logic explains the Reagan administration's swift reversal of its confrontationalist stand toward the Islamic Republic of Iran and a replacement with an accommodationist posture in the mid–1980s.

50. Richard W. Cottam, "U.S. and Soviet Responses to Islamic Political Militancy," in *Neither East nor West*, pp. 279–80. See also Lenczowski, *American Presidents and the Middle East*, pp. 226–7.
51. Reported in the *New York Times*, 26 January and 17 April 1988. See also Lenczowski, p. 227; Cottam, p. 280.
52. *New York Times*, 10 September and 20 November 1995; *Al Hayat*, 14 November 1995.
53. *New York Times*, 5 April 1993.

In this context, the Iran-gate episode, in which the United States traded arms with Iran in exchange for the freeing of U.S. hostages in Lebanon, signaled the Reagan administration's desire to associate with the "moderate forces of resurgent Islam as a natural ally in the objective of containing the aggressive intent of the Soviet Union."[54] By arming Iran, the Reagan administration hoped to arrest the deterioration in U.S.–Iranian relations and co-opt the rising Islamist forces on the side of the West. Furthermore, given the precariousness of the Islamic government in Teheran, some Reagan administration officials feared that Iran was a vulnerable target of Soviet expansionism. "The Khomeini regime," William Casey, director of the CIA, was reported to have said, "is faltering and may be moving toward a moment of truth; we will soon see a struggle for succession. The U.S. has almost no cards to play; the USSR has many."[55] Here lie some of the reasons for Iran-gate.

A partial corrective is in order here. Far from representing a strategic shift in the Reagan administration's view of the forces of Islamic resurgence, the Iran-gate episode was a tactical move, reflecting "inconsistency, uncertainty, and the absence of any serious strategic focus on Islamic political militancy." American foreign policy in the mid–1980s, asserts Richard Cottam, was torn between two diametrically opposed tendencies: Members of the National Security Council called for harnessing political Islam to the American anti-Soviet purpose, whereas the dominant view within the State Department advocated a policy that appeared to treat Islamic militancy and Iran as a preeminent negative target of the United States.[56]

Public exposure of the Iran-gate policy embarrassed Reagan, forcing him to accept the State Department preferences in favor of a much more vigorous tilt toward Baghdad in the Iran-Iraq war. As a result, U.S.–Iranian relations deteriorated further, culminating in the July 1988 shooting down of an Iranian civilian airliner by the *USS Vincennes* and Reagan's renewal of the economic embargo against Iran in November 1988. Like their predecessors, Reagan administra-

---

54. Cottam, "U.S. and Soviet Responses to Islamic Political Militancy," pp. 282–4.
55. Quoted in Bob Woodward, *Veil: The Secret Wars of the CIA, 1981–1987* (New York: Simon & Schuster, 1987), p. 407.
56. Cottam, "U.S. and Soviet Responses to Islamic Political Militancy," pp. 282–5.

tion officials developed an abiding suspicion that normal relations with Teheran were impossible. As Weinberger put it: "I feel that as long as the leadership in Iran remains as it is, it is futile to expect that any kind of agreements with such a government would be kept or would be of any value."[57]

This shift in the Reagan approach to Iran, argues Cottam, made Teheran a new surrogate enemy: Given the unwillingness and the inability of the Soviet Union to play the enemy role very convincingly by the second half of the 1980s, U.S. policy found Iran a convenient target. American foreign policy no longer revolved around containing Communism. Hence, the way in which Reagan administration officials began to view political Islam, asserts Cottam, was closely related to their changing attitude toward the Soviet Union.[58]

Despite the frequent negative utterances of Reagan administration officials on Islamic militancy, they did not articulate any policy statement on the subject. Islamists were not seen as representing a coherent, viable threat to the stability of the international order. However, U.S. officials' perception of Islamic politics would change by the end of the 1980s. President George Bush's assumption of office in 1989 coincided with a major Islamic revival in the Middle East and North Africa and the subsequent collapse of the Soviet Union. Unlike Carter and Reagan, Bush did not have the luxury to remain silent in the face of a political storm that was shaking the established Middle Eastern regimes to their foundations.

Bush and the Algerian Crisis

When President Bush assumed office in 1989, a major debate about policial Islam ensued within the U.S. foreign-policy establishment.

57. Weinberger, *Fighting for Peace*, p. 354. Secretary of State George P. Shultz echoed this sentiment: "Our guys got taken to the cleaners." See testimony before the Joint House–Senate Iran-Contra Investigation Hearings, 23 July 1987, as cited in *Report of the Congressional Committees Investigating the Iran-Contra Affairs*, 13 November 1987 (Washington, DC: Government Printing Office, 1987), p. 245. See also Esposito and Piscatori, "The Global Impact of the Iranian Revolution: A Policy Perspective," p. 326.
58. "U.S. and Soviet Responses to Islamic Political Militancy," pp. 284–6.

An American official who was involved in these discussions claimed that during the 1980s, the United States had felt no need to articulate a policy toward Islamists because Iran was the only theocracy in the region. By the late 1980s, however, Islamic movements were spreading throughout the Arab world and North Africa. This new development, coupled with the decline of Communism and the emerging global issue of democratization, brought the question of Islamic revivalism into the forefront of U.S. foreign-policy concerns; "we needed to know if Islam was compatible with democracy."[59]

Bush administration officials became particularly concerned about Islamists' impressive gains in parliamentary elections in Egypt, Tunisia, and Jordan. In Sudan, a 1989 military coup d'etat led by General Omar Hassan al-Bashir installed a precarious administration allied with the National Islamic Front. But the stunning victory of the Islamic Salvation Front (FIS: Front Islamique du Salut) in Algeria in the first round of elections held in December 1991 alarmed Washington. The FIS came within a step of acquiring control because the Algerian regime adopted an electoral system similar to the French two-cycle with a winner-take-all format.[60] In early January 1992, the hard-liners in the Algerian military annulled the elections, banned the FIS, and arrested hundreds of its rank and file, thus embroiling the country in a continuing, bloody civil war that as of the date of this publication has claimed 80,000 lives.

Here was the first, critical test to compel the Bush administration to articulate a response, if not a full-fledged policy, concerning Islamists in Algeria. The administration faced the challenge of proving that its rhetoric on political pluralism was genuine and applicable to the Arab/Muslim world. The Bush administration's response to the Algerian crisis was notable largely for its passivity, in contrast to its outspoken record in advocating political pluralism elsewhere. Bush deferred to the late French President François Mitterand, who backed the Algerian generals' cancellation of the election.

The extent of confusion in the Bush administration with regard to the Algerian military coup manifested itself in initial ambivalence

59. Interview with a member of the Policy Planning Staff, State Department, Washington, DC, 27 March 1995.
60. Andrew J. Pierre and William B. Quandt, "Algeria's War on Itself," *Foreign Policy*, no. 99 (Summer 1995), p. 135.

and subsequent vacillation. Initially, the State Department regretted the suspension of the electoral process and expressed hope that a way could be found to resume progress toward democracy. But far from criticizing the military's seizure of power in January 1992, the State Department said that the act was in accordance with the Algerian constitution. Concerned about being perceived as siding with the military generals, the State Department the following day revised its position to quell criticism that the United States had sacrificed democratic principles on the altar of realpolitik. Although Bush administration officials did not condemn the cancellation of the elections, they did decide that a wiser course would be to lower the U.S. profile by taking a neutral stand.[61]

Nonetheless, the Bush stance was widely seen as tacit approval of the military junta's action, thus reinforcing a view held by many Muslims that the United States was not serious about democratization in the Arab Middle East. Despite the Bush administration's subsequent assertion of neutrality, it continued to have little faith in the democratic credentials of the FIS. It is not surprising that a Senate study later found the Bush position to have been "something of a wink and a nod."[62] Some U.S. officials concurred with the above assessment. One State Department official remarked that "by not saying or doing anything, the Bush administration supported the Algerian government by default."[63] Other American diplomats privately agreed that a victory by Islamists in Algeria could have anti-

61. John M. Goshko, "U.S. Modifies Statement on Algerian Move," *Washington Post*, 15 January 1992. Editorials in the *New York Times* on 14 January and 24 July 1992 criticized the Bush administration for being "shamefully reluctant" to condemn the Algerian army's illegitimate and unwise move against the Islamist political opposition.

62. *The Battle Looms: Islam and Politics in the Middle East*, study commissioned by the Senate Committee on Foreign Relations (Washington: U.S. Government Printing Office, 1993), pp. 2, 6. This study criticized the Bush administration for being more concerned about the prospect of the FIS assuming power than about the complex reality of Algerian politics. Accordingly, the report recommended that the new Clinton administration take a more decisive and unambiguous stand in support of the restoration of the democratic process and human rights in Algeria. See p. 7.

63. Interview with a member of the Policy Planning Staff, State Department, Washington, DC, 27 March 1995.

Western effects and would spill across borders to cause upheavals in other countries.[64]

In particular, Bush administration officials were worried about "the march of Islamic fundamentalism" across Africa. The elections in Algeria reinforced their fears that Islamist governments, which are seen to be antipathetic to secular politics and Western culture, would pose a new challenge to Western policy makers after the collapse of Communism.[65] In this sense, U.S. perceptions of Islamists were related to the end of the Cold War and the strategic void created by the demise of the Soviet Union. Whereas the United States had concentrated its energy on combatting the "evil empire" in the Cold War era, it began to shift its attention to lesser evils in the early 1990s. Some U.S. leaders and opinion makers started speculating about the capacity of revolutionary, populist Islam to replace Soviet Communism as the new global enemy around which the United States could orient its new strategy.

It is within this light that the Bush administration's initial response to the Algerian crisis should be seen. Secretary of State James Baker made it clear that the U.S. government was unwilling to live with the results of the Algerian elections because it saw the FIS as an extension of radical Islamic fundamentalism, which is truly "antithetical to the West – to democratic values, free market principles, and to the principles and values we believe in."[66] It is not surprising then that the Bush administration turned a blind eye to the military's reversal of the democratic process in Algeria.

The following quotation by Baker exemplifies the reasoning behind the Bush administration's resulting policy toward Algeria:

When I was at the Department of State, we pursued a policy of excluding the radical fundamentalists in Algeria, even as we recognized that this was somewhat at odds with our support of democracy. Generally speaking, when you support democracy, you take what democracy gives you. If it gives you a radical Islamic fundamentalist, you're supposed to live with it. We didn't live with it in Algeria because we felt that the radical fundamentalists' views

64. *Washington Post*, 14 and 15 January 1992.
65. Barbara Crossette, "U.S. Aide Calls Muslim Militants Big Concern in World," *New York Times*, 1 January 1992.
66. "Interview with James A. Baker III," *Middle East Quarterly* 1, no. 3 (September 1994), p. 83.

were so adverse to what we believe in and what we support, and to the national interests of the United States.[67]

The Bush administration's reluctance to ride the Islamic current in Algeria, a country which occupied only a marginal place in U.S. foreign policy, exposed American policy makers' deep ambivalence about Islamists. According to an NSC official, the Bush administration feared that "Algeria would go the Iranian way."[68] Another U.S. official said that the Bush administration's reaction to the Algerian crisis was not only influenced by its fears of the Islamic revolution in Iran but also by the general political atmosphere in the 1980s: "Fundamentalist Iran was on the mind of American decision makers when the Algerian crisis erupted."[69] The United States was also worried about the potential negative impact of an Islamist government in Algeria on the Arab-Israeli peace process and the effect of any spillover into Egypt and North African states.[70]

This reality partially explains the Bush administration's decision after the Gulf War to allow the Iraqi regime to destroy the Shi'i uprising lest it augment the power of Islamic Iran. The U.S. administration also tried to establish new alliances to limit Iranian influence; it began building up pro-Western Turkey and Saudi Arabia as countervailing forces to Muslim regimes in Central Asia, which was the rationale for Secretary of State Baker's 1992 visit to that region. Baker urged the new Central Asian states to emulate secular Turkey rather than neighboring Iran. He stated publicly that the predominantly Muslim republics have "much more in common with American values, and much more of a future with the West, than they do with Iran and its fundamentalist brand of Islam."[71]

67. Ibid.
68. Interview, Washington, DC, 30 March 1995.
69. Interview, Washington, DC, 30 March 1995.
70. Interview with a member of the Policy Planning Staff, State Department, Washington, DC, 27 March 1995.
71. Quoted in Thomas L. Friedman, "Republics Promise to Protect Rights," *New York Times*, 13 February 1992. See also Friedman, "Baker's Trip to Nations Unready for Independence," *New York Times*, 16 February 1992; Robin Wright, "Islam, Democracy and the West," p. 143; Ignatius, "Islam in the West's Sights: The Wrong Crusade?" *Washington Post*, 8 March 1992; Leon T. Hadar, "Political Islam Is Not a Threat to the West," in *Islam: Opposing Viewpoints*, pp. 200–1.

Although U.S. officials, who were interviewed separately, acknowledged that supporting the generals was a "mistake," they cautioned against reading too much into Washington's initial position. They said that neither Bush nor Baker thought very deeply or clearly about the situation in Algeria; both were ambivalent about it, and this explains the tensions in the U.S. stance on Algeria.[72]

Security and strategic calculations lie behind Americans' suspicion of Islamists. U.S. officials appear to view political Islam as a populist movement with historical roots similar to those of revolutionary third world nationalism. Washington has not been disposed toward populist third world groups and states. Being a great power contented with the status quo, the United States does not tolerate revolutionary challenges, insignificant as they may be, to the international order; its prestige, interests, allies, and reputation are on the line. By sanctioning the military coup in Algeria, U.S. policy makers chose stability over experimentation with democracy. The Algerian generals were a much safer gamble than those untried, unknown Islamists. Once again, the United States underwrote the lesser of "two evils" to preserve its dominant position in the Middle East. Kantian principles were sacrificed on the altar of realpolitik.

The Meridian House Address: The Foundation of a New Policy on Islam

The Bush administration's ambivalence toward the FIS was made apparent in an address entitled "The U.S., Islam and the Middle East in a Changing World," delivered by Edward Djerejian, then Assistant Secretary of State for Near Eastern Affairs, at Meridian House International in Washington in June 1992.[73] Bush administration officials felt compelled to articulate a relatively clear, coherent policy statement on Islamic activism that would enable them to communicate and rationalize Bush's approach to the American public and the world. The result was the Meridian address, the first thorough statement given by any U.S. administration on the Islamist question.

72. Interview with a member of the Policy Planning Staff, State Department, Washington, DC, 27 March 1995. Interview with a State Department official, Washington, DC, 30 March 1995.
73. *U.S. Department of State Dispatch*, 2 June 1992, p. 3.

This speech represented a critical attempt by the Bush administration to resolve the tensions and ambiguity in the U.S. approach toward Islamic revivalism. It also inaugurated a subtle but important shift in the Bush administration's stance toward Algeria in particular and political Islam in general.

The Meridian address, along with other pronouncements by Bush administration officials, established the intellectual context in which the succeeding administration would address the Islamist phenomenon. This address represented the Bush administration's response to the collapse of the Soviet Union, the 1991 Gulf War, the Arab-Israeli peace process, and the new assertiveness and electoral successes of Islamic political movements.

In a veiled reference to the Algerian Islamists in the speech, Djerejian warned that "we are suspect of those who would use the democratic process to come to power, only to destroy the very process in order to retain power and political dominance. While we believe in the principle of one person, one vote, we do not support one person, one vote, one time."[74] On balance, however, the Meridian address struck a positive, flexible note with regard to U.S. perceptions of Islam.

The deterioration of the security situation in Algeria, coupled with the inability of the military to crush Islamists, forced the U.S. government to reevaluate and redefine its position. In this context, the Bush administration endorsed Algerian efforts toward economic and political reforms and liberalization. It also raised doubts about the viability of a military solution to the escalating conflict between Islamists and the regime, calling for a political settlement instead. Although American officials expressed understanding of the need to combat violence, they demanded that those arrested for security reasons be given due process of law.

Djerejian reaffirmed the continuity and significance of the two major pillars – resolution of the Arab-Israeli conflict and access to Persian Gulf oil – that have constituted basic U.S. foreign policy concerns in the Middle East for several decades. The end of the Cold War, stated the assistant secretary, necessitated the addition of a

---

74. In addition to the Meridian address, see Edward P. Djerejian, "One Man, One Vote, One Time," *New Perspectives Quarterly* 10, no. 3 (Summer 1993), p. 49.

third pillar to American policy: a core of fundamental values – such as support of human rights, pluralism, broad popular participation in government, and rejection of extremism, oppression, and terrorism. Yet Djerejian also emphatically rejected the confrontationalist interpretation of political Islam, treating it as the new enemy:

> the U.S. Government does not view Islam as the next "ism" confronting the West or threatening world peace. That is an overly simplistic response to a complex reality. . . .The Cold War is not being replaced with a new competition between Islam and the West. The Crusades have been over for a long time. Americans recognize Islam as a historic civilizing force among the many that have influenced and enriched our culture.[75]

Echoing the accommodationists, Djerejian said that there was considerable diversity, and indeed ambiguity, among the groups that were attempting to reform their societies along Islamic ideals: "We detect no monolithic international effort behind these movements." He then went further, expressing sympathy toward the renewed emphasis on Islamic principles throughout the Middle East and North Africa. Djerejian made a distinction, however, between moderate and extremist Islamist groups, accusing Iran and Sudan of sponsoring and exploiting the latter groups to spread terrorism throughout the region. Djerejian seemed to imply that extremist Islamist groups formed a concerted network, while the mainstream Islamists did not.

At the same time, Djerejian accepted accommodationists' premise that Islamic extremism could be explained in terms of the politics of frustration: It was the lack of socioeconomic and political opportunities that fueled Islamists and not, as confrontationalists asserted, any form of utopian ideology or intrinsic hatred of the West. Thus, in order to alleviate the threat of extremism, Djerejian recommended a strategy of privatization, liberalization, and the establishment of market economies.[76]

Djerejian was rather vague in referring to those Islamists whom he considered to be moderate and he failed to name any one group

75. All references to Djerejian here and below are taken from the Meridian House transcript, unless otherwise cited.
76. See "Hearing of the House Foreign Affairs Committee; Developments in the Middle East," *Federal News Service*, 17 March 1992, p. 33.

that fell within this classification.[77] He did stress, however, that U.S. opposition to extremist elements had nothing to do with their secular or religious orientation: "[R]eligion is not a determinant – positive or negative – in the nature or quality of our relations with other countries. Our quarrel is with extremism and the violence, denial, intolerance, intimidation, coercion, and terror which too often accompany it."[78]

The United States, Djerejian reminded his audience, had close relations with states whose political systems are firmly grounded in Islamic principles. He did not mention that such countries – Saudi Arabia and Pakistan – have been traditional U.S. clients. The challenge to American interests emanates from somewhere else, the myriad Islamically oriented political movements that are demanding change and calling for reformation of state and society.

Unfortunately, the Meridian address did not clarify the Bush administration's approach toward those very Islamist groups. In spite of Djerejian's assertion that religion was not a factor in U.S. foreign policy, his categories were loaded with implicit references to Islamist political behavior. His reluctance to be explicit about the phenomenon of Islamic resurgence reflected the Bush administration's sensitivity toward the issue and its fear to grapple with it.

The Bush administration's stance on elections seemed problematic as well. Djerejian said that the U.S. government would support those regimes that took specific steps toward holding free elections and expanding political freedom and would oppose those who used the democratic process to seize power indefinitely. Nonetheless, a thorny question remained: How could the administration determine if a particular group was bent on destroying the democratic process after attaining power legitimately? Neither the Meridian address nor subsequent statements by Bush administration officials specified any

77. This shortcoming was rectified by his successor, Robert Pelletreau, who would identify some Islamists whom the United States considered to be moderates. See the next chapter.
78. After Djerejian delivered his speech, it was reported that he was heard asking a retired U.S. ambassador, "Did that message about Islam come through?" This message was apparently the main point he wanted to get across. See Gene Bird, "Administration Official Assures Middle East the 'Crusades Are Over,'" *Washington Report on Middle East Affairs* 11, no. 2 (July 1992), p. 29.

Islamist group that had genuine democratic aspirations.[79] Or was Djerejian's qualification designed to justify U.S. acquiescence in the suspension of the Algerian election?

Chairing a hearing of the House Foreign Affairs Committee in March 1992, Representative Lee Hamilton quizzed Djerejian as to whether the Bush administration accepted the results of the election in Algeria. The assistant secretary declined to answer the question, hinting that the election might not have been fair. After repeated cross-examination by Hamilton, Djerejian's response in fact revealed the extent to which the Bush administration had accepted the Algerian regime's rationale for annulling the election: "What happened in Algeria is that the Algerian government made a decision and fundamentally that decision was that they felt that the people who had gained the votes in that election were the same people who did not have a commitment to democratic process and once in power would destroy the very process they came to power on."[80]

Again Djerejian failed to say whether he disagreed with the Algerian government's position. Little wonder that his subsequent statements in the Meridian address could easily be interpreted as justifying U.S. support for the suspension of the Algerian electoral process. Similarly, in a earlier hearing in February 1992, Secretary of State Baker had failed to condemn the Algerian army's coup and had expressed doubts about Islamists' intentions and democratic pretensions.[81]

Another ambiguous point contained in Djerejian's Meridian address was his emphasis on the importance of certain fundamental values that inspired U.S. foreign policy globally and regionally. These values – including respect and support of human rights, plu-

79. John L. Esposito, a vocal accommodationist, also raised a question mark about the administration's contention regarding some Islamist movements that allegedly sought to hijack democracy in the manner of one man, one vote, one time. Esposito queried: Does the Bush administration and its allies believe in risk-free democracy? In reality, risks exist, for there can be no risk-free democracy. See Esposito, *The Islamic Threat: Myth or Reality?* pp. 186–7, 189, 204, 205, 214, and "Symposium: Resurgent Islam in the Middle East," p. 11.
80. "Hearing of the House Foreign Affairs Committee; Developments in the Middle East," pp. 32–3.
81. "Hearing of the House Committee on Foreign Affairs; U.S. Foreign Policy," *Federal News Service*, 6 February 1992, pp. 38–9.

ralism, women, and minority rights – would also influence U.S. policy toward political Islam.[82] Although Djerejian denied having any ambitions to impose a "made in the USA" model on other societies, he made it clear that the U.S. government would establish enduring relations with those states and societies with which "we share fundamental values."[83] Of course, one cannot help but ask to what extent a number of Middle Eastern authoritarian regimes – traditionally Washington's staunch allies – share some of these ostensibly fundamental democratic values with the United States.

Furthermore, the danger of stressing the issue of values is that many political Islamists reject the U.S. list of fundamental values as being reflections of a struggle for cultural dominance and a sinister design to divest Muslims of the tenets of Islam. This collision of values has at times projected, by both sides, a civilizational war, since Islamists themselves lay claim to alternate universal values.[84]

Assessing the Meridian House Address

Far from clarifying U.S. policy toward Islamists, the Bush administration's major policy statement left many questions unanswered. Djerejian made several distinctions and qualifications, revealing tensions in U.S. thinking about the Islamist phenomenon. The Meridian address did not provide any specific guidelines for U.S. policy makers, being ambiguous and equivocal on the most pressing issues facing the American government. For example, one is still unable to discern from it whether the Bush administration was genuinely committed to the principle of free elections in a case in which political Islamists could win power. Would the United States be willing to accept an Islamist government in Egypt or Algeria? Djerejian's remarks were open to multiple interpretations, thus enabling the Bush administration to strike a delicate balance between its new liberal

82. Ibid.
83. Djerejian also reminded members of the House Foreign Affairs Committee that the promotion of American business and economic interests in the Middle East was a high priority on the Bush administration's agenda. Ibid., and Djerejian, "One Man, One Vote, One Time," p. 49.
84. For a sample of Islamists' views, see Yvonne Yazbeck Haddad, "The 'New Enemy'?: Islam and Islamists after the Cold War" in *Altered States: A Reader in the New World Order*, pp. 89, 92.

discourse on pluralism and the need to protect its Middle Eastern ruling allies.

Likewise, Djerejian's distinction between bad and good Islamists has little explanatory power. One thing is clear, however: Extremism, regardless of its secular or religious nature, is, by definition, the enemy of the United States. Moreover, although Djerejian recognized Islam as one of the world's great faiths and acknowledged its role as a historic civilizing force, he steered away from critically discussing the politics and agenda of the mainstream Islamists. One gets the feeling that while the Bush administration projected an enlightened interpretation of Islam, it still had lingering doubts about the new Islamists' agenda and politics. Despite the new accommodationist tone of the Meridian address, Bush's approach toward Islamists continued to be colored by historical fears. The mixing of Islam with politics made U.S. officials uneasy; they were obviously worried lest political Islamists, using the Islamic faith as a form of ideology, "cloak their message in another brand of authoritarianism" and threaten the stability of the U.S.-dominated regional order.

In spite of its inherent tensions and ambiguities, the Meridian speech represents a liberal declaration and conscious attempt by the Bush administration to build bridges to the world of Islam. Some Islamist leaders were impressed by Bush's new moderate and sensitive position toward Islam. For example, Rashid Ghannoushi, the exiled leader of the Renaissance Party in Tunisia, sang the praises of the unprecedented statements made by Djerejian and his clarification of the U.S. government's position. Ghannoushi commended Djerejian for recognizing Muslim contributions to world civilization and for not viewing Islam as a monolith. Such positive thinking, added Ghannoushi, may bring Islam and the Christian West to the "threshold of a new, mutually beneficial relationship."[85]

The fact remains, however, that the Meridian address was not matched by a corresponding policy shift. The liberal themes in Djerejian's speech were not translated into practical policy guidelines. American officials were reluctant to apply the new discourse while formulating American foreign policy. The Bush administration also did not exert any pressure on its traditional Muslim clients to open

85. Rashid Ghannoushi, "Islamic Civilization Need not Clash with Western Civilization," in *Islam: Opposing Viewpoints*, p. 51.

up the political process, accommodate the opposition, and expand popular participation in government. The United States took few, if any, concrete measures to try to convince the Egyptian, Algerian, Tunisian, or Saudi regimes of the need for a more inclusive vision of politics. Despite the collapse of the Soviet Union and the defeat of Iraq in 1991, U.S. Middle East policy remained preoccupied with traditional security issues at the expense of societal development and political liberalization.

In addition to Israel, Egypt, and Turkey, huge quantities of American arms continued to flow to the countries of the Gulf Cooperation Council (GCC).[86] Although the Bush administration recognized the role of the Islamic Republic of Iran in the release of American hostages in Beirut, it continued to berate Iran and Sudan for assisting and sponsoring acts of international terrorism and for opposing the Arab-Israeli peace process.[87]

The importance of the Meridian address lay in its symbolic and psychological, rather than practical or concrete, dimensions: It established broad parameters within which succeeding administrations could base their stance toward Islamists. Being the first major official U.S. statement on Islamism, the Meridian address set the intellectual framework that would influence American policy thinking for years. President Bill Clinton himself has approached the Islamist phenomenon within this context, having inherited Bush's legacy on political Islam with all of its constraints, opportunities, and ambiguities. A clear manifestation of the continuity of U.S. diplomacy in the Middle East was seen in Clinton's retaining of Djerejian, the main architect of Bush's Islam policy – along with other Bush administration officials – during his first term.

86. Edward P. Djerejian, "U.S. Policy Goals in the Near East," address before the National Association of Arab Americans, Washington, DC, 11 September 1992, *U.S. Department of State Dispatch*, 14 September 1992, p. 704.
87. Ibid. See also Djerejian, "Review of U.S. Efforts to Achieve Near East Policy Goals," statement before the Subcommittee on Europe and the Middle East of the House Foreign Affairs Committee, Washington, DC, 24 June 1992, *U.S. Department of State Dispatch*, 29 June 1992, p. 517.

5

The Clinton Administration:
Co-opting Political Islam

There are those who insist that between America and the Middle East there are impassable religious and other obstacles to harmony; that our beliefs and our cultures must somehow inevitably clash. But I believe they are wrong. America refuses to accept that our civilizations must collide. We respect Islam.[1]

President Bill Clinton

Although the Bush presidency witnessed international breakthroughs of historic importance – the collapse of the Soviet Union, the unification of Germany, and the 1991 Gulf War – it did not articulate a new vision or blueprint for U.S. foreign policy. Bush may have had a superb grasp of details, but he derided the "vision thing," opting instead for a pragmatic approach with common sense as an effective guide to action.[2] The Bush administration also did not reflect deeply on how it would cope with the strategic, ideological, and moral issues brought about by the end of the Cold War. Rather than initiate events, Bush and Secretary of State James Baker reacted to them as they unfolded in the international sphere instead.[3]

Nonetheless, Bush and Baker bequeathed Bill Clinton a Middle Eastern political landscape that had held considerable promise. The international coalition assembled by Bush had liberated Kuwait and

1. "Remarks by President Bill Clinton to the Jordanian Parliament," 26 October 1994.
2. James A. Baker III with Thomas M. DeFrank, *The Politics of Diplomacy: Revolution, War and Peace, 1989–1992* (New York: G. P. Putman's Sons, 1995).
3. Editorial in the *New York Times*, 6 October 1995.

86

soundly defeated Saddam Hussein. Responding to Arab and third world criticism of America's double standard toward Israel, Bush and Baker had successfully browbeaten the Likud government of Prime Minister Yitzhak Shamir into participating in the 1991 Madrid peace conference and to halting the building of new settlements in the occupied Palestinian territories. They also pursued a noninflammatory approach toward Iran that showed promise of reducing tensions. In short, with the elimination of the Soviet Union, the United States enjoyed unrivaled hegemony in the Middle East, with both its detractors and supporters looking to it for leadership.

Unlike his predecessor, President Clinton initially spent little time enmeshed in the details of foreign-policy making; he was more in his element with domestic politics – his real passion. Especially during his first term, the President essentially delegated foreign-policy formulation to a select team of aides – Secretary of State Warren Christopher, Deputy Secretary Strobe Talbott, Defense Secretary William J. Perry, National Security Adviser W. Anthony Lake, and Lake's deputy, Samuel R. Berger. After his reelection, Clinton assembled a new foreign-policy team: Secretary of State Madeleine Albright, Defense Secretary William Cohen, National Security Adviser Samuel Berger, and Strobe Talbott, who still serves as deputy secretary.[4]

Yet Clinton's personnel changes represent more of a change in style than substance. His reluctance to nominate assertive and strong-willed national-security advisers reflects his desire to downplay foreign policy and micromanage it personally. To be sure, the President has become more engaged in international affairs in the last three years, though focusing on issues related to world trade and the global economy. Clinton seems to have finally recognized the close links between political economy and international politics. His trips and tours abroad reflect a new awareness of the difficulty in separating internal and external politics.

In the first two years of the Clinton presidency, the lack of active presidential engagement in the formulation of foreign policy, coupled with the complexity and ambiguity of the post–Cold War era, raised critical questions about America's leadership and willingness to shoulder world responsibilities. Nonetheless, both of Clinton's

4. *New York Times*, 8 February 1993.

foreign-policy teams stressed the need for continued engagement in the outside world and for the strengthening of emerging market democracies.[5]

In the case of the Middle East, continued U.S. engagement implies a commitment to advancing the Arab-Israeli peace process and securing the flow of affordable oil from the Arabian peninsula. These two objectives are viewed as threatened by "extremist Islamist" groups, which receive support from the Islamic Republic of Iran and the Islamically based regime in Sudan. Iraq, and to a lesser extent Libya, are also considered a menace to Washington.

The current administration's global strategy – promotion and expansion of democracy and market economics – shows the accustomed contradictions in American policy toward the Middle East and North Africa. Like its Republican predecessor, the challenge facing the Democratic Clinton administration is how to strike a balance between the strongly perceived need for stability and the dimly grasped need for change. This is nowhere truer than in the Middle East, where the fault lines are rigidly drawn between authoritarian regimes, which are determined to maintain control, and opposition movements seeking to replace the old order with a new one. Most of these opposition groups use Islamic rhetoric and ideology as a legitimizing device in their struggle against the regimes already in power. Their revolutionary zeal has rekindled U.S. fears about the potential birth of a new radical third world force, which would be militantly hostile to the United States.

Complicating the situation, in U.S. eyes, is the appeal, durability, and rising potency of an Islamically inspired political message and

5. Anthony Lake, "From Containment to Enlargement: Current Foreign Policy Debates in Perspective," speech delivered at Johns Hopkins University, School of Advanced International Studies, in Washington, DC, September 1993. (In another address, "Foreign Policy in a New Age"– not referenced here – he reaffirmed the Clinton administration's commitment to continued engagement in world politics and the enlargement of market democracies, and its rejection of the new isolationism. In a more recent speech delivered at Freedom House, President Clinton denounced the so-called "isolationist backlash" in the country, warning that U.S. diplomacy "can only succeed if we continue to lead." He also rejected calls for unilateralism as a disguised form of the isolationism that is not a viable option in today's world. Quoted in the *New York Times*, 7 October 1995.

the concurrent decay of the existing political order. Far from declining, Islamists continue to challenge the status quo in Egypt, Algeria, the West Bank and Gaza, Jordan, Saudi Arabia, Tunisia, and other Middle Eastern states. From the onset of the Clinton presidency, the Islamist question has occupied a central place on its foreign-policy–making agenda.

For example, in February 1993 the administration held a weekend-long seminar on Islamic politics at the State Department attended by senior policy makers, including Christopher, then Secretary of State, and Albright, at the time ambassador to the United Nations. A White House official summarized the result of the meeting by saying, "We have a policy on Islam and Islamism." But all the administration did was to create a set of "talking points" to address the Islamist question.[6] The State Department set up a study group of midlevel officials to monitor and analyze Islamic revivalism. Later, a senior State Department diplomat praised the efforts of this study group for providing a nuanced and critical understanding of the Islamist phenomenon. (The workings of this study group are shrouded in secrecy. No mention of this group or its findings have been made public.) The State Department also organized a major conference in the region and invited many American officials from various agencies to participate in it. The purpose was to sensitize the U.S. foreign-policy establishment and husband its resources and talents in order to deal effectively with the new Islamists.[7]

Unlike the Bush administration, which had only one major statement – the Meridian address – on Islamic revivalism, Clinton administration officials, both at the senior and junior levels, have periodically given major speeches on the subject. Between 1993 and 1996, the President, Vice President, and even the first lady made important, symbolic gestures in order to dispel misconceptions about American views on Islam and Muslims. The administration's many statements constitute an impressive empirical record from which to examine official U.S. thinking on political Islam. Although this chapter utilizes the whole range of the administration's pronouncements

6. See "America and Islam: A Wobbly Hand of Friendship," *Economist*, 26 August 1995, p. 25.
7. The point about the State Department's activities was made by a former senior U.S. official at an off-the-record meeting of a group of policy makers and scholars in New York in September 1997.

on political Islam, it particularly examines in depth two major policy statements: Anthony Lake's May 1994 address to the Washington Institute for Near East Policy, and the May 1994 remarks of then Assistant Secretary of State for Near East Affairs Robert Pelletreau to the Middle East Council.[8]

Islam and the West: Coexistence and Harmony?

Lake remarked in his May 1994 address that the Middle East faced a stark choice between two roads: one leading to a future in which extremists, wielding weapons of mass destruction, dominate the Middle East and pose an existential threat to Israel and other U.S. friends in the region; the other leading to democratic progress, economic prosperity, and regional stability and security. To Lake, the fundamental divide in the Middle East was between violence, regression, and isolation, on the one hand, and peace, freedom, and dialogue on the other.

Like the commentator confrontationalists, Lake saw the struggle in the Middle East in moral terms as a clash between the forces of good and evil; the lines of demarcation were clearly defined without

8. Anthony Lake, "Building a New Middle East: Challenges for U.S. Policy," address by the National Security Adviser to the Soref Symposium of the Washington Institute for Near East Policy, Washington, DC, 17 May 1994, *U.S. Department of State Dispatch*, August 1994. See Pelletreau's remarks in "Symposium: Resurgent Islam." All references to Lake and Pelletreau below will be taken from these transcripts, unless otherwise cited. Long before Lake and Pelletreau delivered their addresses, several junior officials had made important critical comments about Islamic resurgence, thus laying the groundwork for Lake's and Pelletreau's policy statements. Refer to the various statements of Edward Djerejian, who continued to serve as Assistant Secretary for Near Eastern affairs for a while. See also Martin Indyk, "The Clinton Administration's Approach to the Middle East," address by the special assistant to the President to the Soref Symposium, 18–19 May 1993, in Mirsky, Ahrens, and Sultan, eds., *Challenges to U.S. Interests in the Middle East: Obstacles and Opportunities*; testimony of Laurence Pope, *Hearing of the Senate Judiciary Committee, Terrorism in America* and "House Foreign Affairs Committee Hearing," *Reuter Transcript Report*, 21 April 1993; Mark R. Parris, "Update on the Crisis in Algeria," statement before the Subcommittee on Africa of the House Foreign Affairs Committee, 22 March 1994, *U.S. Department of State Dispatch*, 4 April 1994.

ambiguities or uncertainties. At one end stood "reactionary backlash states" – Iran, Sudan, Iraq, and Libya – that need to be contained and isolated because they sponsor terrorism and traffic in non-conventional weapons.[9] At the other end stood the moderate, "like-minded Middle Eastern states which share our goals of free markets, democratic enlargement, and controls on proliferation of weapons of mass destruction."[10] Lake did not bother to name those Middle Eastern states that are democratic and are not bent on acquiring weapons of mass destruction. The reason is simple. The Middle East has few democracies and many weapons of mass destruction.

President Clinton also saw the conflict in the Middle East in terms of black and white. In his speech to the Jordanian parliament in October 1994, he said that the United States does see a contest in the Middle East and elsewhere – "a contest between tyranny and freedom, terror and security, bigotry and tolerance, isolation and openness. It is the age-old struggle between fear and hope."[11]

Echoing accommodationists, however, Lake and Clinton denounced the hard-liners' assertion that, in the post–Cold War world, a clash of civilizations pitted the West against Islam: Today, the real conflicts that confront the world, argued Lake, are manifestly not conflicts of civilizations:

> In the Middle East as throughout the world, there is, indeed, a fundamental divide. But the fault line runs not between civilizations or religions; no, it runs instead between oppression and responsive government, between isolation and openness, and between moderation and extremism. . . .
>
> Our foe is oppression and extremism, whether in religious or secular guise. We draw the line against those who seek to advance their agenda through terror, intolerance, or coercion.[12]

9. See also Lake, *From Containment to Enlargement*, p. 17.
10. "Building a New Middle East," p. 38. Lake's remarks echoed those of Martin Indyk, which he had given at the same forum a year earlier. It is likely that Indyk, being a senior director for Near East and South Asian Affairs at the NSC, had a hand in writing Lake's speech. See Indyk, "The Clinton Administration's Approach to the Middle East," p. 1.
11. "Remarks by President Bill Clinton to the Jordanian Parliament," 26 October 1994.
12. Lake, "Building a New Middle East," p. 37.

Likewise, despite his unambiguous moral tone, President Clinton rejected confrontationalists' "clash-of-civilizations" hypothesis, viewing the present struggle as one that transcended civilization.[13] The conflict that grips the Middle East today, stated Clinton, has nothing to do with Islam but is more about "the forces of terror and extremism, who cloak themselves in the rhetoric of religion and nationalism, but behave in ways that contradict the very teachings of their faith and mock their patriotism."[14]

In the same vein, Djerejian had argued earlier that the United States should be wary of magnifying Islamic threats to U.S. interests: "Otherwise, we may fall victim to misplaced fears or faulty perceptions."[15] Similarly, his successor, Pelletreau, cautioned against stereotyping an important regional development – Islamic resurgence – lamenting the fact that the U.S. media often depict Islam as an "undifferentiated movement hostile to the West, ready to use violence and terrorism to achieve its ends. Such an image is, of course, skewed, over-simplistic and inappropriate."[16] Djerejian's and Pelletreau's criticism should be considered a strong rebuff of confrontationalists' policy prescriptions.

Clinton administration officials proffered a much more liberal interpretation of political Islam than did Bush's aides. For example, Djerejian, Lake, and Pelletreau said that a renewed emphasis on traditional values in the Muslim world would not inevitably come into conflict with the West or with democratic ideals.[17] To the

13. "Remarks by President Bill Clinton to the Jordanian Parliament," p. 3. Clinton's statement was a jab at, among others, Samuel Huntington, who has predicted a clash between cultures, not least Islam and the West. See "America and Islam: A Wobbly Hand of Friendship," in the *Economist*, p. 25.
14. "Remarks by President Bill Clinton to the Jordanian Parliament," p. 3.
15. "U.S. Policy on Recent Developments and Other Issues in the Middle East, statement before the Subcommittee on Europe and the Middle East of the House Foreign Affairs Committee, Washington, DC, 27 July 1993," *U.S. Department of State Dispatch*, 9 August 1993, p. 572.
16. "Current Issues in the Middle East," address to the Harvard Law School: Islamic Legal Studies Program in Cambridge, 11 April 1994, p. 4.
17. Ibid; Djerejian, "U.S. Policy on Recent Developments and Other Issues in the Middle East," p. 572; Pelletreau in "Symposium: Resurgent Islam," p. 4.

contrary, these traditional values, declared President Clinton, were compatible with the West's: "[T]he traditional values of Islam – devotion to faith and good works, to family and society – are in harmony with the best of American ideals. Therefore, we know our people, our faiths, our cultures can live in harmony with each other."[18] Clinton often cited the message of tolerance that the Prophet Muhammad brought to his followers and peoples of other faiths.[19]

By rejecting a view held by many confrontationalists both in the Middle East and in the United States, the President's remarks were meant to dispel any lingering doubts in people's minds about an unavoidable clash between the world of Islam and the Christian West. In his speech to the Jordanian parliament, Clinton chose to highlight the theme that the United States should be able to act as a "bridge" between differing spiritual systems, not as a crusading nation: "Every day in our land, millions of our citizens answer the Moslem call to prayer"; their values "are in harmony with the best of America's ideals."[20]

18. "Remarks by President Bill Clinton to the Jordanian Parliament," p. 3. Visiting the Islamic Center of Washington, DC, Vice President Al Gore also praised Islam for having a great deal to teach all people about tolerance and coexistence. He compared Islamic teachings to those of his Christian faith: Islam urges citizens to submit to God's will and live their lives in conformity with that understanding. "Submission to God," concluded Gore, "is part of what I have been taught within my religious tradition all my life." See "Remarks of Vice President Gore as He Meets with Arab and Muslim Ambassadors," *Federal News Service*, 10 June 1994.

19. "Remarks by President Bill Clinton to the Jordanian Parliament," p. 4. See also "The President's remarks at White House welcoming ceremony for King Hussein of Jordan and Prime Minister Yitzhak Rabin of Israel, Washington, DC, 25 July 1994," in *U.S. Department of State Dispatch* 5, no. 7, August 1994, p. 3; "Statement by the President on the occasion of the Islamic holy month Ramadan," the White House: Office of the Press Secretary (Boston, MA), 31 January 1995. Welcoming King Hassan of Morocco to the White House, President Clinton praised the king for serving as a "force for tolerance and progress rooted in Islamic values." See "Remarks by President Clinton and King Hassan of Morocco upon Arrival at the White House," *U.S. Newswire*, 15 March 1995, p. 1.

20. "Remarks by President Bill Clinton to the Jordanian Parliament," p. 4.

It was reported at the time that Clinton decided to stress the idea of Muslim tolerance in part so as to further a basic strategy of offering support to moderates within the larger Muslim community. With his strong remarks, Clinton not only plunged himself into the center of a major intellectual debate in the Western and Muslim worlds but also reaffirmed his belief in coexistence and dialogue, rather than in confrontation.[21] According to a senior U.S. diplomat, who participated along with other officials in writing Clinton's speech for the Jordanian parliament, the President's aides wanted to put him on record as advancing the harmony thesis and as rejecting that of the clash of civilizations.[22]

Five months later, holding a joint press conference with King Hassan, President Clinton delivered the same message:

> Islam can be a powerful force for tolerance and moderation in the world, and its traditional values are in harmony with the best of Western ideals. As I said in my speeches to the parliaments of Jordan and Israel, the United States has great respect for Islam and wishes to work with its followers throughout the world to secure peace and a better future for all our children.[23]

The President returned to the same theme a month later during the ceremony welcoming Pakistani Prime Minister Benazir Bhutto. Clinton praised Pakistan for blending the ideals of a young democracy with the traditions and practices of Islam: "[S]he [Bhutto] was elected to lead a nation that aims to combine the best traditions of Islam with modern democratic ideals."[24] In addition to highlighting its assistance in fighting international terrorism, Clinton stressed the positive role that Pakistan, as a moderate democratic Islamic country of 130 million people, could play in the Muslim world.[25]

Clinton underlined Pakistan's moderate orientation in a politically

21. David Lauter, "Clinton Seeks to Build Bridge to Muslim World," *Los Angeles Times*, 27 October 1994.
22. This point was made by a former senior State Department official at an off-the-record meeting of a group of policy makers and scholars in New York in September 1997.
23. "Transcript of Remarks by President Clinton and King Hassan II of Morocco in Press Conference," *U.S. Newswire*, 15 March 1995, p. 2.
24. "Joint Press Conference with President Bill Clinton and Pakistani Prime Minister Benazir Bhutto," *Federal News Service*, 11 April 1995, pp. 1–2.
25. Ibid., p. 2.

volatile region: an Islamic country that might serve as a model for the newly emerging Muslim states in Central Asia. Whereas the Bush administration had tried to sell the Turkish model to the Muslim states of the former Soviet Union, the Clinton administration leaned more toward Pakistan's. Yet both administrations paid scant attention to Turkey's and Pakistan's dismal human rights records. U.S. policy makers appeared to be interested mainly in the two countries' foreign policy orientation – seen to be "moderate" and above all pro-Western. It is in this context that American officials deemed Turkey's and Pakistan's brand of Islam tolerant, progressive, and appealing.

During his visit to Indonesia in 1994, Clinton made a high-profile appearance at the main mosque in Jakarta, declaring that "even though we have had problems with terrorism coming out of the Middle East, it is not inherently related to Islam – not to the religion, not to the culture."[26] Clinton's pronouncements show a consistent pattern of political correctness toward Islam – certainly on the symbolic and rhetorical level. He has also reached out to Muslims, highlighted the commonalities (and not the differences) between the Christian West and Islam, and rejected reductionism and stereotypes of Islam and Muslims. The President's stand thus puts him squarely in the accommodationist camp. The critical question that needs to be addressed, however, revolves around the consistency between this administration's rhetoric and its actual policies (see below).

Other junior and senior officials had already laid the groundwork for Clinton's discourse on Islam. The revival of religion – read: of

26. Quoted in Arthur L. Lowrie, "The Campaign Against Islam and American Foreign Policy," *Middle East Policy*, p. 216. Clinton and Vice President Al Gore also met with Arab and Muslim Americans, fielding questions on domestic and foreign issues facing their community in the United States. Al Gore acknowledged the mistreatment Muslim Americans had faced following the Oklahoma City bombing, promising that the U.S. government would not sacrifice the rights of citizens in its fight against terrorism. See the *Washington Report on Middle East Affairs*, no. 6 (January 1996), p. 63. As another example of the Clinton administration's efforts to reach out to the American Muslim community, first lady Hillary Rodham Clinton hosted a group of Muslims at the White House in celebration of the completion of the month-long Ramadan fast. Announced in an American Muslim Council press release, 18 February 1996.

Islam – asserted Lake, is not specific or unique to Muslims; it is part of a universal quest by people everywhere for ways to achieve responsive government, receive basic human rights, and find a moral guide for their lives.[27] To be sure, in a separate speech, Pelletreau qualified Lake's positive message by noting that there are certain manifestations of the Islamic revival that are "intensely anti-Western aimed not only at eradicating Western influences in their societies, but at resisting any form of cooperation with the West or modernizing evolution at home. Such tendencies are clearly hostile to U.S. interests."[28]

What distinguishes Islamic extremism, contended both Lake and Pelletreau, is that it uses religion as a mask to hide its naked pursuit of political power: "Islam is not the issue." Lake and Pelletreau's point had been made more forcefully by State Department Counselor Timothy Wirth during a Capitol Hill hearing back in July 1993. Wirth drew a clear distinction between terrorism and Islamist political ideology:

> The misuse of Islamic political rhetoric by these groups should not cause us to confuse in our minds terrorism and Islam. Our problem is not, of course, with Islam or with the people who practice that religion. It is, instead, with the use of violence and terrorism by any person, regardless of religion, national origin or ethnicity.[29]

Wirth's distinction was important because he rejected the existence of any connection between the actions of certain Islamists and Islam both as a religion and ideology. He also rejected the notion of collective responsibility and guilt by association. Wirth's point was echoed by Djerejian two weeks later: "We must never permit the actions of a violent minority of any creed to form our attitudes toward entire groups."[30] Wirth's and Djerejian's differentiation laid

27. Lake, "Building a New Middle East," pp. 37–8.
28. Pelletreau, "Current Issues in the Middle East," p. 6.
29. *The Future of U.S. Anti-Terrorism Policy*, hearing before the Subcommittee on International Security, International Organizations, and Human Rights of the Committee on Foreign Affairs, House of Representatives, 13 July 1993, pp. 85–6.
30. Djerejian, "U.S. Policy on Recent Developments and other Issues in the Middle East," p. 573.

the basis for the subsequent assertion by Lake and Pelletreau that Islam was not a factor in U.S. foreign-policy considerations toward any state or group.[31]

Pelletreau asserted further that the United States did give serious consideration to the legitimate role Islam played in societies and governments of the region, notwithstanding some extremists' manipulation of the symbols and ideals of Islam.[32] Like Djerejian, Lake and Pelletreau praised Islam's many contributions to world civilization over the past fourteen hundred years, stressing the close historical bonds and core values between Islam and the Judeo-Christian beliefs of most Americans: "We have no quarrel with Islam. We respect it as one of the world's great religions and as a great civilizing movement."[33]

Moreover, Lake rejected confrontationalists' contention that Islamic fundamentalism had replaced international Communism as the West's designated threat. Lake and Djerejian expressed their skepticism of confrontationalists' recommendation that "the United States, as the sole remaining superpower in search of a new ideology to fight, should be bent on leading a new crusade against Islam."[34] Borrowing an identical phrase from the Meridian address, Pelletreau said that the United States did not view Islam as the next "ism" confronting and threatening Western security. He then added an important qualification: "We do, however, object strongly when we are labeled a 'Great Satan' [a reference to Khomeini's habitual depiction of the United States], or when our culture and values are derided, or our citizens taken hostage or violence and terrorism practiced either randomly or to advance political ambition."[35]

31. Former Secretary of Defense William J. Perry reiterated this point in an address to the Council on Foreign Relations in New York City, 18 May 1995, p. 2.
32. Pelletreau, "Current Issues in the Middle East," p. 5.
33. Pelletreau's remarks in "Symposium: Resurgent Islam," p. 2–3. See also Lake, "From Containment to Enlargement," p. 17; Djerejian, "U.S. Policy on Recent Developments and Other Issues in the Middle East," p. 572.
34. Lake, "Building a New Middle East," p. 37. See also Djerejian, "War and Peace: The Problems and Prospects of American Diplomacy in the Middle East," p. 875.
35. Pelletreau in "Symposium: Resurgent Islam," p. 4.

Islam and Democracy

Like that of its predecessors, the Clinton administration's rhetoric on political Islam combines carrots and sticks, alternating between accommodationist and confrontationalist language. It is unclear if this vacillation is part of the administration's conscious strategy or due to uncertainty and ambivalence regarding Islamists' real agenda. What is clear is that U.S policy, as will be argued below, is full of unresolved tensions.

Echoing Djerejian, Pelletreau noted that although the United States was seriously concerned about Iran's and Sudan's exploitation of Islamic extremist groups throughout the Middle East and North Africa, "we see no monolithic international control being exercised over the various Islamic movements active in the region."[36] Refuting confrontationalists' assertion about the existence of a coordinated Islamist network, Clinton administration officials have pointed out that a considerable diversity existed among various Islamist movements.

This said, a corrective is in order here. A minority view within the first Clinton administration claimed that a regional network of fundamentalist troublemakers provided religious extremists with material support and spiritual inspiration. For example, Indyk has argued that both the Islamic Republic of Iran and Sudan have demonstrated their "regional reach by fishing in troubled waters all the way from the Gulf, through Egypt and Lebanon to Algeria."[37] Hence, the challenge facing the United States, added Indyk – former executive director of the Washington Institute for Near East Policy – was to help Middle East friendly regimes confront this emerging threat by containing extremism. It was Indyk who coined the term "dual containment" of Iran and Iraq as a way, among other things, to isolate and defeat religious and nationalist extremists.[38]

36. Ibid., p. 3. See also Djerejian, "War and Peace," p. 876.
37. Indyk, "The Clinton Administration's Approach to the Middle East," pp. 2–3.
38. Ibid., pp. 1, 3–4. According to an NSC official in an interview, Washington, DC, 29 March 1995, although the dominant view within the Clinton administration does not believe that political Islam is monolithic, attitudes differ in the Congress and among the U.S. public. The

Martin Kramer, an Israeli academic who knows Indyk, acknowledges that the latter "believes that Islamists represent a threat to American interests."[39] William Quandt has also said that Indyk is one of few American officials who came close to viewing political Islam as a threat.[40] Will Indyk's replacement of Pelletreau as assistant secretary of state for Near Eastern affairs – inasmuch as they are advocates, respectively, of the confrontational and accommodationist points of view – bring about a marked change in the U.S. approach toward Islamic activism? Will Indyk's appointment change the current balance between accommodationists and confrontationalists within the Clinton administration? Or will Indyk adhere to the main tenets of U.S. policy? So far, Indyk's replacement of Pelletreau as assistant secretary of state has not brought any marked shift in the U.S. approach. Indyk seems to adhere to the main tenets of U.S. policy, despite his vocal view on Iran, Iraq, Sudan, and Libya.

Whereas Djerejian and Pelletreau said that certain manifestations of the Islamic revival are a cause for concern, Lake went further by arguing that "Islamic extremism" – particularly some Islamist movements, which use the cover of Islamic resurgence to suppress freedom and engage in terrorism – pose a threat to U.S. interests and allies.[41] Lake's distinction between Islam as a religion and "Islamic extremism" as a political-military movement is problematic: It obscures more than clarifies. The critical point is not to ask whether Islam is a great religion or not but rather to determine how U.S. policy makers view the role of Islam within the larger political process. By taking issue with the political-military manifestation of the Islamist phenomenon, Clinton administration officials have shown deep uneasiness and anxiety about mixing religion and politics. This position also appears to be true in the second Clinton term.

According to Lake, the U.S. government very carefully watched

latter, asserts this official, hold "simplistic" and prejudiced views about Islam and Muslims in general.

39. Interview, Washington, DC, 31 March 1995.
40. Interview, Washington, DC, 31 March 1995.
41. Lake, "From Containment to Enlargement," p. 17.

Islamic extremists in Algeria, Egypt, Sudan, Jordan, southern Lebanon, and the West Bank and Gaza, and he warned that it will resist those militant Islamists who seek to expand their influence by force.[42] Other Clinton administration officials have made it clear that they oppose the use of revolutionary means or "internal terrorism" by Islamists, even "in countries where they are repressed or prohibited by strong state action from participation." Violence is not a path to legitimate political participation, stated Pelletreau, and opposition movements that use or espouse violence and terrorism as the path to political power will pose a threat to regional stability and thus to U.S. interests.[43] Another American official said that Washington would oppose any Islamist extremist movement that uses violence to subvert the existing order.[44]

Pelletreau's attempt to rationalize this U.S. position "on the basis of morality" is questionable. The Clinton administration is on record as supporting and assisting the military activities of opposition elements in Iran, Iraq, and Libya to topple their regimes there. Conversely, Pelletreau's response shows that the U.S. government is opposed to violent acts by Islamists against its friends regardless of whether such acts were legitimate responses to the repression practiced by various Muslim states.

Furthermore, although "extremism" (or "Islamic extremism") was the operative term in Lake's text, it was not delineated or clearly defined. Lake's use of this label is thus open to multiple inferences and interpretations. In contrast, Djerejian and his successor, Pelletreau, offered a much broader definition of Islamic extremism: Islamists who operate outside the bounds of law – espousing violence to achieve their aims and opposing the democratic process – are extremists; whereas Islamist groups that function within the bounds of law are legitimate. Pelletreau went even further: "We will oppose those

42. Ibid. Lake reiterated the Clinton administration's stand on political Islam in an op-ed piece titled "The Middle East Moment; at the Heart of our Policy: Extremism Is the Enemy," *Washington Post*, 24 July 1994.
43. Pelletreau's remarks in "Symposium: Resurgent Islam," p. 21. See also Pelletreau's "Statement Before the Subcommittee on Europe and the Middle East of the House Foreign Affairs Committee, 4 October 1994," in *U.S. Department of State Dispatch*, 10 October 1994, pp. 683, 685.
44. Interview with an NSC official, Washington, DC, 30 March 1995.

who substitute religious and political confrontation for constructive engagement."[45]

In U.S. eyes, extremism is no longer just synonymous with the use of violence but also with the Islamists' political agenda. Thus, Djerejian redefined American foreign policy in the Middle East in ambitious terms – as preventive diplomacy and deterrence: It was an offensive strategy designed not "just [to] prevent the outbreak of conflict and promoting the peaceful resolution of disputes, but also in changing the behavior and limiting the means at the disposal of potential warmakers and in isolating extremists willing to pursue the options of destabilization and conflict."[46]

Djerejian's new definition of U.S. strategy echoed Indyk's ambitious call for the United States – being "the dominant power in the Middle East and the custodian of that region's balance of power" – to use its clout to (1) transform the Middle East, and (2) create a new regional order based on a deterrence of revolutionary secular (Arab) nationalism and religious (Islamist) extremism.[47] In spite of the statements of Djerejian and Indyk, the Clinton administration has not yet used either the actions of Islamists or their rhetoric and presumed intentions as a yardstick by which to formulate a policy toward them. Such a shift in American policy would increase the potential for further misunderstanding between the United States and Islamists.

The first Clinton administration appeared to have accepted its predecessor's view that elections should not be used as the only criterion to measure the democratic process. In his address at the Washington Institute, Lake introduced a new definition of democ-

45. Pelletreau's remarks in "Symposium: Resurgent Islam," pp. 2–3. See also Djerejian remarks at the House *Hearings Before the Subcommittee on Africa of the Committee on Foreign Affairs*, 12 May 1993 (Washington, DC: U.S. Government Printing Office, 1994), p. 91.
46. Djerejian, "War and Peace," pp. 874, 876.
47. See Daniel Pipes's "Interview with Martin Indyk on 13 November 1993 – Perspectives from the White House," *Middle East Quarterly* 1, no, 1 (March 1994), p. 61. Indyk also made similar remarks in his capacity as executive director of the Washington Institute in "Beyond the Balance of Power: America's Choice in the Middle East," *National Interest*, no. 26 (Winter 1991/92), pp. 33, 42–3. He was appointed special assistant to the president and senior director for Near East and South Asian Affairs at the NSC a year later. In 1997 President Clinton promoted Indyk to assistant secretary of state.

racy, supposedly to prevent Islamists from "hijacking" it through elections; this definition included not only elections but also an independent judiciary and the protection of human rights.[48] Pelletreau also stressed the importance of Western democratic values. "Our societal values," he argued, cause the United States to oppose those who oppress minorities, preach intolerance, practice terrorism, and violate human rights, adding: "We're suspicious of those who would use the democratic process to come to power only to destroy that process in order to retain power and political dominance."[49]

Although never explicitly articulated, a deep residue of skepticism colored U.S. officials' views regarding the compatibility of political Islam with democracy, and American decision makers remain ambivalent. A strong tendency exists in U.S. policy circles to view the Islamic Middle East as an exception to other regions undergoing liberalization.[50] American officials conceded that the issue of democracy in the Arab Middle East is low on the Clinton administration's list of priorities, notwithstanding assertions to the contrary.[51] A telling remark by one official summarizes the U.S. stand: The Clinton administration would not oppose Islamists if the latter kept their focus on domestic issues.[52] Another official was more blunt: "We are prepared to live with Islamic regimes as long as they do not endanger or be hostile to our vital national interests. We have no intrinsic interest in human rights in the Middle East."[53]

48. Lake, "From Containment to Enlargement," p. 17.
49. Pelletreau's remarks in "Symposium: Resurgent Islam," pp. 2–3. See also Pelletreau, "Current Issues in the Middle East," p. 5; Djerejian, "U.S. Policy on Recent Developments and Other Issues in the Middle East," p. 573.
50. Interview with an official of the State Department's Policy Planning Staff, Washington, DC, 27 March 1995.
51. For example, President Clinton said that the ideals of democracy are compatible with "the traditions of Islam." To demonstrate his point, he cited the words of Pakistan's first President, Muhammed Ali Jinnah: "Islam and its idealism have taught us democracy. It has taught us the equality of man, justice, and fair play to everybody." See "Joint Press Conference with President Bill Clinton and Pakistani Prime Minister Benazir Bhutto," p. 1.
52. Interview with a member of the State Department's Policy Planning Staff, Washington, DC, 27 March 1995.
53. Interview with a State Department official, Princeton, NJ, 27 May 1995.

Most Clinton administration officials interviewed by this author stressed their concern with the potential implications of Islamists' foreign-policy agenda, not with their internal politics. The end of the Cold War did not bring about a radical change in U.S. attitudes toward political governance in the Middle East. The American position toward democratization in the region contrasts sharply with its approach toward the rest of the world. As one U.S. official said, "The notion of enlargement never caught up in the Clinton administration. American decision makers are skeptical about the process of democratization because they do not know if the whole regional order would not crash."[54] This skepticism explains Washington's conditioned preference for stability over political experimentation in the Middle East.[55]

To American eyes, the Middle East, unlike other regions, remains outside the circle of democracies: the winds of change bypassed the authoritarian regimes there. One might wonder further if the United States does not prefer to deal with predictable and manageable autocratic Muslim leaders than with those maverick and untested democrats. Washington's ambivalence toward the results of the 1991 parliamentary elections in Algeria and the Islamist opposition in Egypt raises many questions about American commitment to democratization in the Muslim Middle East.

Here, then, was another striking similarity between U.S. and Soviet behavior toward the third world. In the heyday of Arab nationalism in the 1950s and 1960s, the United States tried very hard to convince Nasser and other Arab nationalist leaders to divert

54. Interview with a senior State Department official, Princeton, NJ, 27 May 1995.
55. Interview with William Quandt, Washington, DC, 31 March 1995. Quandt argues that a retreat has occurred in U.S. rhetoric regarding support for liberalization and democratization in the Arab world. In contrast, the United States has supported the process of liberalization and even democratization in Indonesia, Malaysia and Pakistan. American officials appear to have little faith in the Arabs' ability to construct and sustain constitutional experiments. When asked if he could see any light of democracy for Arab countries, a senior State Department official said he could see none. Asked if the United States had any inclination toward democratization of Arab states, again his answer was negative. See Aydin Nurhan, "Turkey and Middle Eastern Stability," *Vital Speeches of the Day* 63, no. 5 (15 December 1996), p. 131.

their attention from external to internal affairs. U.S. policy makers promised Nasser economic and technical assistance if he would turn his focus inward. The Eisenhower, Kennedy, and Johnson administrations were more concerned with Nasser's meddling in regional and world politics than about his authoritarian behavior at home. [56]

According to a senior State Department official, in the 1950s and 1960s the United States was much more willing to accept, at least theoretically, the compatibility between Islam and democracy than it is today. Middle Eastern states had relatively open social systems, did not engage in wholesale violence against their population, and were closely allied with the United States.[57] American decision makers had hoped that Muslim governments and individual groups would adopt colonial institutions and remain firmly linked to the West; to their dismay, the situation began to change with the further closing of the social systems in Muslim societies in the 1970s. Herein lay the origins of Washington's current ambivalence about the prospects for democracy in the Middle East.[58] Therefore, the Clinton administration accepted the gradualist argument, moving ever so slowly and cautiously with regard to advocating social and political change in the region. American officials fear for the survival of Egypt and Saudi Arabia – "the two most important states in the Arab Middle East" – were they to be pressured to accelerate the pace of change.[59]

Culture as a Factor in U.S. Perceptions of Islamists

Although American officials privately acknowledge the important role that culture plays in influencing their perceptions of political Islam, they tend to steer clear of any public discussion regarding this issue. For example, Lake noted that culture shapes politics and economics. He hastened to add, however, that just as the idea of freedom

56. Fawaz A. Gerges, *The Superpowers and the Middle East: Regional and International Politics, 1955–1967* (Boulder, CO: Westview Press, 1994), especially chapters 3, 5, 6, and 8.
57. Interview with a State Department official, Princeton, NJ, 27 May 1995.
58. Ibid.
59. Ibid.

has universal appeal, transcending cultural and civilizational frontiers, so does the democratization process. In this spirit, Lake gave
the impression that a global consensus exists on the subject, thus
universalizing the unique American experience.[60]

Lake's successor, S. Berger, appears to subscribe to a similar view.
After Clinton's 1998 visit to Africa, Berger stood before representatives of refugee and development organizations. Recounting that half
a million people greeted the President in Ghana, he said: "I wish
Americans could see us as others do. We are a beacon, an incandes-
cent light that gives power through our ideals, our culture, our way
of life."[61] Berger's Africa speech fit into the Clinton administration's
thesis that the United States must use its dominance to help create
new capitalist democracies in its own image.

Some U.S. officials have been more forthcoming than Lake, however. One admitted that the United States utilizes the Western
model when discussing democracy in the developing world because
certain ideas, such as democracy, have evolved in the West, becoming universal in the process.[62] Although American diplomats interviewed by this author made it clear that they did not subscribe to
Huntington's hypothesis regarding the clash of civilizations, they
stressed the existence of negative cultural perceptions which color
public and official views of Islam and of Muslims in general. They
also noted that Huntington puts his finger on this negative cultural
perception, writing that "the issues are mostly joined in the axis of
Islam and the West [and where] a potential for confrontation exists
between the two civilizations."[63]

A State Department analyst also said that American women feel
offended by the manner in which their counterparts are treated in
Muslim societies. Thus, continued the same analyst, one cannot ne-
glect the effects of cultural differences that divide the two civiliza-

60. Lake, "From Containment to Enlargement," p. 14.
61. Quoted in Elaine Sciolino, "The Point Man: Berger Manages a Welter
    of Crises in the Post–Cold War White House," *New York Times*, 18
    May 1998.
62. Interview with a member of the State Department's Policy Planning
    Staff, Washington, DC, 27 March 1995.
63. Ibid. Interview with a member of the NSC, Washington, DC, 29
    March 1995.

tions: "For ideas have an impact on policy. The end of the Cold War has not changed that. We are still hostages of history."[64] Another senior U.S. ambassador was more blunt: "Violent Islam is seen as wilfully blind – witness the case of Shaykh 'Umar 'Abd al-Rahman, who was convicted along with nine other Muslims of conspiring to carry out a day of terror in New York and who was bent on destroying American values. Islam is a conquering religion threatening the American way of life."[65]

Underlying this negative perception of Islam is a cultural divide between two competing value systems. Some U.S. officials are well aware of this, and of the forces that underpin the American public's generally hostile views of Islam and Muslims. The question then becomes, to what extent are American policy makers influenced by similar prejudices? And can they escape such a culture trap when formulating policies toward nations with cultures different from theirs? The record appears mixed on this score. For although Clinton administration officials generally take note of the role of culture, they, like their predecessors, have attributed the rise of Islamic extremism to socioeconomic and political alienation and exclusion, rather than cultural traits per se or any inherent anti-Western attitudes.[66] This stand remains true today.

As Edward Djerejian put it above during his May 1993 congressional testimony: "Experience suggests to us that political Islamic movements are to an important degree rooted in worsening socioeconomic conditions in individual countries."[67] A year and a half later, Clinton himself attributed the rise of extremist forces to disillusionment, poverty, and alienation: "[I]f poverty persists in breeding despair and killing hope," added Clinton, "then the purveyors of

64. Interview with a member of the State Department's Policy Planning Staff, Washington, DC, 27 March 1995.
65. Interview, Princeton, NJ, 27 May 1995. This ambassador stressed, however, that the majority of U.S. policy makers do not share this radical view of Islam.
66. Lake, "The Middle East Moment." Lake, "Building a New Middle East," p. 37. Interview with a member of the NSC, Washington, DC, 29 March 1995. Pelletreau, "Symposium: Resurgent Islam," pp. 3–4.
67. Djerejian, at House *Hearings Before the Subcommittee on Africa of the Committee on Foreign Affairs*, p. 97.

fear will find fertile ground [to] stoke the fires of violence."[68] This diagnosis, rooted in economics, led Pelletreau and other U.S. officials to suggest that the most viable, long-term means to defeat extremism is to address the conditions under which it thrives by supporting initiatives toward sustainable economic and social development. "Our goal must be to spread prosperity and security to all," concluded Clinton.[69] The United States, seconded Pelletreau, should also encourage governments in the region to open up the political field and advance the rule of law, decentralization, and liberalization.

The consensus within the Bush and Clinton administrations has been that the roots of political Islam lie in the lack of economic, educational, and political opportunities for the masses. If this is so, would it not be more conceptually useful to substitute other analytical concepts to that of Islam that might better explain the current social upheaval in Muslim societies? The analytical usefulness of the notion of Islam is indeed open to question. In fact, an argument can be made that this notion has often been more of a hindrance than a help in understanding what moves people or states in Muslim societies.

Some Clinton administration officials respond to this sort of criticism by contending that certain manifestations of the Islamic revival are intensely anti-Western and aim at eliminating Western influences while resisting any form of cooperation with the West, including modernization at home.[70] The layman is thus left wondering if Islamists are driven by the lack of economic, educational, and political opportunities at home or by innate, anti-Western biases, or by both factors. Lake's and Pelletreau's policy statements can in fact be interpreted in accommodationist as well as confrontationalist terms. Obviously, the Clinton administration's public statements on political Islam have had more than one audience in mind.

Having in any event ostensibly articulated U.S. thinking regarding

68. "Remarks by President Bill Clinton to the Jordanian Parliament," p. 3. During his press conference with King Hassan of Morocco, President Clinton said that the way to consolidate stability and defeat extremism is "to strengthen economically the forces of progress and tolerance." See "Transcript of Remarks by President Clinton and King Hassan II of Morocco in Press Conference," p. 3.
69. "Remarks by President Bill Clinton to the Jordanian Parliament."
70. Pelletreau in "Symposium: Resurgent Islam," p. 3.

political Islam, the national security adviser and the assistant secretary of state outlined two further strategies: peacemaking and containment.[71] First, Lake and Pelletreau identified the Arab-Israeli peace process as one of the administration's highest foreign-policy priorities. They reiterated Clinton's commitment to advancing the peace process energetically and to resisting acts of terrorism, extremism, and the politics of rejection aimed at halting the process. To be sure, the Clinton administration's stand on the Arab-Israeli peace process pits it against the majority of political Islamists, who vehemently oppose it. Not surprisingly, this is one of the issues that has poisoned U.S. perceptions of Islamists, and that carries the potential of escalating into a full-fledged confrontation.

Second, Lake stressed Clinton's determination to contain actively those "backlash," "rogue" states – particularly Iran, Iraq, and even Sudan – and any organizations that promote and support extremism. The two strategies of peacemaking and containment are meant to complement each other in order to preserve and protect American interests in the Middle East. To what extent have such containment policies succeeded in advancing the cause of the Arab-Israeli peace and in suppressing religious and nationalist extremism? As already mentioned, the analytical challenge is not just to assess the consistency of U.S. thinking on political Islam but also to appraise the efficacy of its application to concrete policy choices.

Analysis of the Clinton Administration's Rhetoric

As was the case with those of its predecessor, the many different pronouncements by Clinton administration officials reveal serious strains and tensions in U.S. thinking. For example, the administration's distinction between bad and good Islamists has little explanatory merit. The ambiguities in U.S. policy statements stem from the fact that the lines are blurred between those Islamists who adopt

71. In his May 1993 address to the Washington Institute, Indyk listed "dual containment" of Iran and Iraq and promotion of the Arab-Israeli peace process as being the core of the Clinton administration's regional strategy. Again, the influence of Indyk's views on Lake is undeniable. See Indyk, "The Clinton Administration's Approach to the Middle East," pp. 3–6; Pipes's interview with Indyk, "Perspectives from the White House," p. 62.

violence to overthrow the status quo and others who play by the rules of the political game to gain power.[72] While U.S. officials have condemned the former, they have also refrained from initiating, and sustaining, any kind of open and meaningful discussion with mainstream political Islamists.

Although Clinton and his aides have lavishly praised Islamic religion and civilization, they have hardly had anything useful to say about political Islamists and their bloody struggle against the established order. Like their predecessors, Clinton administration officials have vehemently criticized the use of violence and terrorism by certain Islamist groups. Yet they have not dared censure some of America's Middle Eastern allies, who habitually practice violence against their own population.[73] In U.S. eyes, the good Islamists appear to be the ones who are apolitical; moderate and liberal Islam are also equated with the pro-Western regimes of Saudi Arabia, Egypt, Turkey, Pakistan, and Malaysia. The administration's unwillingness to engage moderate Islamist elements seriously lies in the fact that the latter represent the most effective threat so far to the regional order.

The Bush and Clinton administrations resisted establishing and maintaining contacts with mainstream Islamists. Although initially the Clinton administration opened a discreet dialogue with the Algerian FIS and Egyptian Muslim Brothers, it promptly discontinued these contacts after the Algerian and Egyptian regimes vocally complained and pressured it to stop. U.S. officials feared that their dialogue with the Islamist opposition would undermine the stability of their Middle Eastern ruling allies.

Furthermore, Bush and Clinton administration officials feared that Islamists might use free elections to seize political power. At best, the Clinton administration's thinking on elections is ambigu-

72. Interview with a member of the Policy Planning Staff, State Department, Washington, DC, 27 March 1995, and interview with a member of the NSC, Washington, 29 March 1995.
73. Tunisia is a case in point. For example, Pelletreau blamed Islamists in Tunisia for precipitating a confrontation with the Tunisian authorities in the early 1990s. See Pelletreau in "Symposium: Resurgent Islam," p. 16. Although Islamists in Tunisia had refused initially to participate in the political process, they did not engage in any violent campaign against the regime. In fact, the weight of evidence suggests that it was the other way around.

ous, attempting to strike a delicate balance between the need, on the one hand, to highlight America's commitment to pluralism and liberal values and, on the other, to protect U.S. geostrategic and material interests in the region along with its traditional Middle East allies.

Clearly, to the United States, militant Islam has replaced radical Arab nationalism as the major threat to American national interests in North Africa, the Middle East, and the Persian Gulf. Islamist groups are challenging Washington's conception of a desirable Arab-Israeli peace settlement, as well as its continuing dominance in the internal affairs of the oil-producing Gulf states.[74] According to a State Department official, the Clinton administration's dual containment policy toward Iran and Iraq – and, one might add, of Sudan – should be seen within this context.[75] The adoption of the dual containment policy signaled the triumph of confrontationalists' view within the administration.[76]

The Clinton administration's stand on political Islam is more complex than that, however. The sum total of its pronouncements on Islam points to a conscious attempt to accommodate and reach out to moderate Islamists. As a State Department official put it, "our policy is to keep the lines of communications open to the moderate Islamic movements."[77]

At least in its public pronouncements, the Clinton administration has gone much further than its predecessor in trying to build bridges to Muslims and put to rest any lingering doubts about the potential of a new civilizational clash between the West and the Muslim world. The President and his closest aides have rejected confrontation-

74. Interview with a senior State Department official, Princeton, NJ, 27 May 1995.
75. Ibid.
76. Special Assistant to the President Martin Indyk, a hard-liner within the administration, was the coauthor, along with Lake, of the dual containment policy.
77. Interview with a State Department ambassador, Princeton, NJ, 27 May 1995. Djerejian, the architect of the Bush and Clinton policy approach toward political Islam, often echoed and confirmed this sentiment during his service and after his exit. See Djerejian, "War and Peace," p. 875, and "United States Policy Toward Islam and the Arc of Crisis," *Baker Institute Study*, no. 1 (1995), p. 2.

alists' call to arms and their warnings about a "green" menace replacing the old "red" one. Clinton officials have demonstrated considerable sensitivity in their statements, cautioning against tarring Islam and Muslims with the brush of extremism. In private, some officials have said that the administration does not share the widely held view in public and Congress that Islam is the new threat or bogeyman: "This administration is more sophisticated," argued one state department official.[78]

Although, on the whole, the Clinton administration has stressed the need for coexistence and accommodation with Islamists, its rhetoric is strewn with hostile references to "Islamic extremism" and "Islamic terrorism." And yet, conceded an NSC official, the administration perceives Islamic revolutionary fervor as a source of instability and a threat to U.S. interests.[79] Another American official agreed that some Clinton administration aides have called for an offensive strategy to dilute the Islamist ferment; however, the problem with such a course of action is that no one group or faction claims the mantle of revolutionary legitimacy within the Muslim world. The Islamist movement, added this State Department official, is fragmented, and that is good news for the United States because it implies that a rough balance of power exists between Islamists and established regimes.[80] In other words, both Islamists and Middle Eastern ruling elites remain unable to challenge U.S. dominance in the region.

Thus, the fear of revolutionary Islam has motivated the Clinton administration to follow the activities of Islamists closely, especially in the Persian Gulf, Egypt, and the Arab-Israeli theater – as well as Turkey and Algeria. According to an NSC official, given the huge size of U.S. investment in the Gulf, the United States is naturally worried about the rise of Islamic fundamentalism in Saudi Arabia, Bahrain, and Kuwait; for example, Bahrain serves as a major financial center for the Persian Gulf and as an American naval base that

78. A member of the Policy Planning Staff, State Department, Washington, DC, 27 March 1995. Also, interview with a member of the NSC, Washington, DC, 29 March 1995.
79. Interview, Washington, 29 March 1995.
80. Interview with a member of the State Department's Policy Planning Staff, Washington, DC, 27 March 1995.

Washington would find very costly and difficult to replace in the case of a crisis.[81] Although American policy makers do not see any immediate threat to the survival of the family-based regimes in the Gulf, they are less sanguine about their survival prospects in the longer term.[82]

The tensions inherent in U.S public discourse on Islam is reflected quite clearly in the unhappiness expressed by both accommodationist and confrontationalist critics of the Clinton administration's policy approach to Islamic activism.

Accommodationists, like John Esposito and Yvonne Haddad, both professors of religion at Georgetown University, have faulted the Clinton administration for not clearly and decisively specifying which of the various elements within the Islamist movements it considers to be moderate or extremist. Esposito asserted that the administration has not listed any of the Islamist groups that it regards nonextremist, thus failing to allay Islamists' fears.[83] Haddad further contended that Arabs/Muslims "continue to provide the convenient target for proving U.S. virility."[84] In particular, she focused on Indyk's May 1993 address to the Washington Institute for Near East Policy, accusing him of outlining a "Manichean vision" of the world should Islamists gain influence and power.[85]

For opposite reasons, confrontationalists are even more vehement in their criticism. Judith Miller, a *New York Times* correspondent, Martin Kramer, and Daniel Pipes, commentator, have accused the

81. Interview, Washington, 29 March 1995.
82. Ibid. In the last two years a series of defections, protests, sabotage activities, and bloody bombings in Saudi Arabia and Bahrain have shaken the deceptive calm of the two pro-Western states, setting off wide reverbations among their Persian Gulf neighbors, whose sheikdoms and emirates depend on the United States for protection against domestic and regional enemies. From articles and editorial opinions in the *Wall Street Journal*, 25 October 1994 and 12 June 1995; *New York Times*, 16 November 1995, and 24 and 28 January 1996; *Al-Hayat*, 19 January 1996.
83. John L. Esposito, in "Symposium: Resurgent Islam," p. 9.
84. Yvonne Yazbeck Haddad, "Islamist Perceptions of U.S. Policy in the Middle East," in David W. Lesch, ed., *The Middle East and the United States: A Historical and Political Reassessment* (Boulder, CO: Westview Press, 1996), p. 16.
85. Ibid.

Bush and Clinton administrations of "fudging" their response to the threat posed by radical Islam. They dismiss the distinction between good and bad Islamists: to confrontationalists, all militant Islamist movements "are likely to remain anti-Western, anti-American and anti-Israeli."[86]

The false distinction between moderates and extremists, asserted Miller, was simply politically useful to the Bush and Clinton administrations.[87] Similarly, Kramer at least indirectly accused American decision makers of hypocrisy for drawing a distinction between good and bad Islamists without concretely identifying any of the so-called moderates: The Clinton administration has not found a Muslim leader to "crown" as a moderate.[88]

Kramer claimed that "fundamentalists' apologists" in U.S. academia have succeeded in influencing American policy makers. Little wonder, he said, that the United States is ill-informed about Islamic fundamentalism, viewing it as a movement of reform, itself susceptible of reform. Such wishful thinking "promises to be the riskiest policy venture of the next decade in the Middle East and North Africa."[89] Washington's policy of appeasement, Kramer concluded, would inaugurate a new Islamist era.[90] Likewise, Patrick Clawson, an observer, criticized former National Security Advisor Lake for his defense of the renewed emphasis on traditional values in the Islamic world: Lake's statement smells of condescension toward Muslims.[91]

Richard Haass, a national security adviser in the Bush administration, and Mark Paris, commentator, questioned the Clinton administration's premise that the promotion of democracy everywhere is inevitably in the U.S. national interest.[92] An FIS takeover in Algeria,

86. Miller, "The Challenge of Radical Islam," *Foreign Affairs*, p. 45. See also Kramer, "Islam vs. Democracy," *Commentary*, p. 39; Daniel Pipes in "Symposium: Resurgent Islam," pp. 5–6.
87. Miller, "The Challenge of Radical Islam," pp. 46, 54–5.
88. Interview with Kramer, Washington, DC, 31 March 1995.
89. Ibid. See also "Islam vs. Democracy," p. 41.
90. Kramer, "Islam vs. Democracy," p. 42.
91. Patrick Clawson, "Liberty's the Thing, not Democracy: Ripostes," in *Middle East Quarterly* 1, no. 3 (September 1994), p. 13.
92. Jonathan S. Paris, "When to Worry in the Middle East," *Orbis*, p. 553; Richard Haass, "Paradigm Lost," *Foreign Affairs* (January/February 1995), p. 44.

predicted Paris, might "snowball into a pan-Islamic Jihad that under-mines all of North Africa."[93] He also contended that further democ-ratization in Egypt and Jordan might pose unacceptably high risks to American security interests: The solution lies in supporting the es-tablished regimes in Cairo and Amman because "authoritarian rulers can more easily make peace with Israel than can those incipient democracies that have expanded political participation, even if de-mocracy is not dominated by Islamist parties."[94]

The criticism leveled by both accommodationists and confronta-tionalists against the Clinton administration shows the ambiguity of its public statements and the rough balance that the administration has tried to maintain between the two sides. In spite of the appoint-ment of Indyk as assistant secretary, this rough balance, though a little tilted toward accommodationists, has basically remained the same during Clinton's second term. The U.S. approach toward Is-lamic activism was devised by the Bush administration, and it has been consistently adhered to by the Clinton presidency since 1993. This nuanced approach serves a multiplicity of interests, including domestic and foreign constituencies. Being politically correct – stressing the common bonds between Islam and the Christian West – the U.S. stance presents the United States in a good light without having to commit it to any concrete courses of action.

In the end, what one has to scrutinize is not just U.S. public pronouncements but actual U.S. policy initiatives toward Islamists; one has to link American officials' statements to tangible issues and particular countries. Indyk might succeed in keeping the pressure on the so-called "rogue" or "backlash" states – Iran, Iraq, Sudan, and other "religious extremists" that he has identified as representing a threat to the United States and its regional allies. It is thus well worth observing the Clinton administration's second-term policies – even if only selectively – to see if a shift has taken place in the U.S. approach. The following chapters do precisely this by analyzing ac-tual U.S. foreign policy toward Islamists in Iran, Algeria, Egypt, and Turkey. The purpose is to highlight the harmony or dichotomy that exists between the Clinton administration's discourse and policy and assess the weight and relationship between ideas and action.

93. "When to Worry in the Middle East," p. 560.
94. Ibid., p. 563.

6

The Islamic Republic of Iran

Few foreign-policy relationships evoke as much anger and emotion in the United States as does the U.S. relationship with Iran. Although U.S.–Iranian relations were poor in 1979, they have reached their nadir under the Clinton administration. Unlike some of its predecessors, this administration has decided to confront rather than co-opt postrevolutionary Iran. Since 1995, the Clinton administration has waged an undeclared economic, political, and covert war against Iran's cleric-dominated regime.

In contrast to its general statements on political Islam that are accommodationist, the Clinton administration's discourse on Iran is exceptionally hostile, as are its actions toward that country. In the Iranian context, U.S. rhetoric serves as a gauge to policy. Iran thus makes an ideal case study from which one can examine U.S. thinking and action toward revolutionary Islam, despite American policy makers' efforts to downplay the Islamic factor behind Iranian behavior.

Culture or Security?

From the outset of the Clinton presidency, administration officials have expressed deep objections to Iran's policies, branding it an "international outlaw," "terrorist," and "rogue" state. U.S. officials have made no secret of their plan to isolate and contain Teheran in order to force it to change its threatening behavior.[1] Iran's policies,

1. Elaine Sciolino, "Christopher Signals a Tougher U.S. Line Toward Iran," *New York Times*, 31 March 1993; "Remarks by President Clinton at a Dinner of the World Jewish Congress," *Federal News Service* (30 April 1995), p. 4; "Statement by Secretary of State Warren Christopher

stated Clinton, include its active opposition to the Arab-Israeli peace process, its support of local and international terrorism, and its quest to acquire nuclear weapons. The result is that Iran has become "a threat not only to its neighbors, but to the entire region and the world."[2]

Secretary of State Christopher echoed Clinton's sentiment: "We view Iran's action as a major threat to United States interests and international security, and we're determined to stop them."[3] To Christopher, Iran's "evil hand" is responsible for a "trail of carnage."[4] The chairman of the House International Relations Committee, Gilman, went further by comparing the potential threat of a nuclear-armed Iran to that of "Nazism and Hitlerism."[5]

On one level, the U.S.–Iranian crisis represents a cultural and ideological clash between two different systems of politics and government. On a deeper level, however, the demonization of Iran reflects a hardening of U.S. officials' perceptions and their fear that the clerically dominated regime is using and abusing Islam to attack

Regarding U.S. Sanctions Against Iran," pp. 1, 3; Robert H. Pelletreau at the House "Hearing with Defense Department Personnel," pp. 1–2.

2. Remarks by President Clinton at a Dinner of the World Jewish Congress," pp. 2–3. In his speech, Clinton did not stress Iran's dismal human-rights record. Although this administration, like its predecessors, is interested mainly in Iran's foreign policy, not its human-rights performance, a subtle difference distinguishes Clinton's behavior. When Salman Rushdie, the British author, visited the United States in March 1992, not only did Bush aides decline to meet with him but also intervened to prevent his meeting with congressional leaders. The White House spokesperson, Martin Fitzwater, subsequently justified this rebuff by stating: "There's no reason for any special relationship with Rushdie. I mean he's an author, he's here, he's doing interviews and book tours and things that authors do. But there's no reason for us to have any special interest in him." Quoted in the *Washington Post*, 26 March 1992. In contrast, Clinton invited Rushdie for a meeting in the Oval Office in 1993, though the President demoted the meeting by moving it to a lesser office (Lake's). See "America and Islam: A Wobbly Hand of Friendship," p. 26.
3. "Statement by Secretary of State Warren Christopher Regarding U.S. Sanctions Against Iran," p. 2.
4. Quoted in Thomas W. Lippman, "No More Mr. Nice Guy: On the Subject of Iran, Warren Christopher Is the Hardest of the Hard-Liners," *Washington Post*, 15–21 May 1995, National Weekly Edition, p. 18.
5. "Hearing with Defense Department Personnel; U.S. Sanctions on Iran," p. 4.

American vital interests and allies. In this view, the importance of Iran lies in its summoning of Islamic ideology in direct opposition to the secular West and its client Middle Eastern states.

Since 1979, Iran has contested the legitimacy of the regional order by using the powerful sword of Islamic politics. Islam has thus provided the Iranian leadership with a convertible currency to finance and buttress its regional ambitions. That leadership, as well as the outside world, view today's Iran through the prism of Islamic messianism. In the case of the U.S. foreign-policy elites, the Islamic revolutionary experience in Iran has to a large extent shaped their views of the whole Islamic revivalist phenomenon.

American officials have attempted to draw a distinction between the government of Iran with whom they disagree and its Islamic character. In April 1993, Laurence Pope, the acting coordinator for counter-terrorism at the State Department, said that the United States is concerned about Iranian actions, not the Iranian regime, per se, or the fact that it is an Islamic Republic.[6] Similarly, in his May 1993 address enunciating the policy of "dual containment" of Iran and Iraq, Martin Indyk, then senior Middle East specialist at the White House, said that Washington was not opposed to the Islamic government in Iran but to some specific aspects of the Iranian regime's behavior.[7] Some U.S. officials noted that the Clinton administration realizes that Iran's use and misuse of Islam is a smoke screen designed to mask its ambition to be the "traditional hegemon" in the Persian Gulf.[8]

Despite these disclaimers, noted a member of the Policy Planning Staff, the Islamic aspect of the Iranian revolution is relevant because the Iranian leadership articulates and defines its rhetoric and policies in Islamic terms. Another U.S. official concurred: "We are aware of the Islamic aspect of the Iranian revolution and that is how most U.S. policy makers view it."[9] A senior State Department official ascribes U.S. ambiguity on Iran to the fact that American decision

6. *Hearing of the Senate Judiciary Committee*, p. 48.
7. "The Clinton Administration's Approach to the Middle East," in *Challenges to U.S. Interests*, p. 5.
8. Interview with a member of the State Department's Policy Planning Staff, Washington, DC, 27 March 1995; interview with an NSC official, Washington, DC, 30 March 1995.
9. Interview with an NSC official, Washington, DC, 29 March 1995.

makers think in terms of nation–states, not in socioreligious terms, when formulating policy; hence they tend to identify Islam with a nation–state, the same way they identified Communism with the Soviet Union. The importance of the Iranian factor in the Clinton administration's stand on Islamists lies in the fact that political Islam has become synonymous with Iran.[10]

In a similar vein, Richard Cottam, a specialist on Iran, argued that by *Iran*, everyone understood that what was meant was the forces of Islamic political militancy.[11] Graham Fuller, a former intelligence official at the CIA, agreed. Much more is involved in U.S. policies toward Iran, contended Fuller, than simply a falling out with the dominant power in the strategic Gulf region: The true centrality of Iran for the United States lies most profoundly in Teheran's mobilization of "the resources of an entire culture – that of Islam – to marshal forces against the evil Americans and its "evocation of deeper Third World grievances against the West."[12] Iran's cultural and ideological challenges to the United States, asserted Fuller, are also accompanied by other threats, also global in nature, including nuclear proliferation, terrorism, and the quest for regional hegemony, especially in the oil-producing Gulf region, that conflict with U.S. strategic aims.

The debate over whether ideology or security influences the making of U.S. Iran policy is inconclusive. The difficulty lies in measuring the relative weight of each variable. While cultural and ideological factors indirectly affect American officials' views of the Iranian regime, current security and strategic concerns directly inform and fuel U.S. policy. The role of culture and religion are important inasmuch as they reinforce U.S. officials' fears of the Iranian threat. This includes Iran's support of international terrorism to sabotage the Arab-Israeli peace process and its attempt to undermine the stability of the oil-producing Gulf states. Compounding the situation is Teheran's alleged pursuit of a nuclear weapon program and unwillingness until recently to lift a death edict against author Salman

10. Interview with a State Department ambassador, Princeton, NJ, 27 May 1995.
11. "U.S. and Soviet Responses to Islamic Political Militancy," in *Neither East nor West*, pp, 281, 285.
12. "The Appeal of Iran," *National Interest*, p. 93.

Rushdie, who was accused of blaspheming Islam in his 1988 novel, *The Satanic Verses.*

Of all U.S. grievances against Iran, American officials are particularly annoyed at Teheran's financial and political support for Islamist elements in the Palestinian territories and Lebanon in order to undermine the Arab-Israeli peace process. The Clinton administration waxes indignant about Iran being of one of the few states in the world that has publicly condemned the peace process. In fact, Iranian leaders are on record as opposing the Arab-Israeli peace process. Former Iranian Foreign Minister Ali Akbar Velayati stated: "We consider the signing of this accord [Palestinian-Israeli agreement] as a conspiracy against Islam and Palestine and we disagree with it."[13] Likewise, after four Palestinian suicide bombers killed fifty-nine Israelis in March 1995, Hussein Sheikholeslam, an Iranian foreign ministry official whose duties include spreading revolutionary activities, took pleasure announcing the collapse of the peace process. After meeting with the leaders of Palestinian Hamas and Islamic Jihad (Holy War), Sheikholeslam stated that "the Islamic resistance movement is in for a glorious future. There is no peaceful solution. The Israelis must return to the countries they came from."[14]

Here lies the immediate, direct reason for the Clinton confrontational approach toward Iran. From the beginning, this approach was entwined with American policy on the Arab-Israeli peace process, the administration's most important foreign-policy initiative.[15] Clinton has committed his administration to providing long-term security for Israel by helping it normalize relations with its Arab neighbors. The President and his senior aides have often stressed the paramount role that the peace process plays in U.S. foreign policy. As Clinton put it: "Securing a lasting and comprehensive peace must be our urgent priority. . . . And we will not stop working until the

13. Text of statement by Velayati before the forty-eighth session of the UN General Assembly, 4 October 1993. See also James A. Bill, "The United States and Iran: Mutual Mythologies," *Middle East Policy* 2, no. 3 (1993), p. 99.
14. Quoted in John Kifner, "Alms and Arms: Tactics in a Holy War," *New York Times*, 15 March 1995.
15. Gary Sick, "The United States and Iran: Truths and Consequences," *Contention* 5, no. 2 (Winter 1996), p. 71.

circle of peace is complete."[16] Christopher, and later Secretary of State Madeleine Albright, rearticulated the President's main point: "From the outset, advancing the Arab-Israeli peace process and maintaining security in the Gulf have been among the highest foreign-policy priorities of our administration."[17]

Furthermore, American officials fear that if Iran's brand of revolutionary Islam is left unchecked, it might subvert the established, pro-Western Arab regimes, especially in the Gulf region. The Clinton administration is concerned about the cumulative effects of internal political decay in the Gulf states as well as the impact of Iran's increasing military power and assertiveness, on the stability of Saudi Arabia and Bahrain. The dual containment policy is designed to weaken the ruling mullahs' ability to threaten U.S. primary interests and allies in the Gulf by reforming the regime in Teheran.

The Evolution of American Policy toward Iran

When President Clinton assumed office in 1993, he inherited a wide array of executive and legislative constraints imposed by Presidents Jimmy Carter, Ronald Reagan, and George Bush on Iran to block most military and many economic transactions between the two states. Seventeen years after U.S. diplomats were taken hostage in Teheran, the United States has maintained a continuous state of national emergency with respect to Iran, having severed diplomatic relations with Teheran in 1980 and placed it on the State Department's list of state supporters of terrorism in 1984.[18]

These restrictive legal and diplomatic measures contrasted sharply, however, with large-scale trade between Iran and the United States. American exports, for example, increased steadily over the early 1990s, from zero in 1989 to $1 billion in 1993.[19] American oil

16. Remarks by President Clinton at a Dinner of the World Jewish Congress, p. 4.
17. "Statement by Secretary of State Warren Christopher Regarding U.S. Sanctions Against Iran," p. 1.
18. Bill, "The United States and Iran," p. 105; Geoffrey Kemp, *Forever Enemies: American Policy and the Islamic Republic of Iran* (Washington, DC: The Carnegie Endowment for International Peace, 1994), p. 6; Esposito and Piscatori, "The Global Impact of the Iranian Revolution: A Policy Perspective," in *The Iranian Revolution: Its Global Impact* p. 326.
19. Kemp, *Forever Enemies*, p. 326.

companies were the largest purchasers of Iranian oil, buying about 30 percent of Iran's oil exports, or more than $4 billion worth on the open market in the early 1990s. The Iran issue presented the Clinton administration with a difficult dilemma by highlighting two conflicting pillars of American policy: desire to promote U.S. economic interests around the world and a determination to exert pressure on Iran to change its behavior.[20]

Initially, President Clinton – like his predecessors – had difficulty formulating a consistent policy toward Iran. Although in its first few months in office the Clinton presidency intensified its rhetoric on Iran, it broadly retained the basic policy of past administrations. Trade flowed relatively unhindered between the two countries, making the United States the eighth largest exporter to Iran by mid–1993.[21]

Within a few months, however, it became clear that this two-pronged approach – ostensible diplomatic sanction but open and growing trade – was becoming untenable. Largely in response to Iran's opposition to the Arab-Israeli peace process and its apparent military buildup, domestic pressure to take more forceful initiatives to isolate Teheran began to grow, and Israel and some Arab governments attempted to convince Washington that Iranian-inspired Islamic extremism represented a major threat to the stability of the Middle East and the interests of the West.[22] The anti-Iranian cam-

20. Elaine Sciolino, "Christopher Proposes Tighter Curbs on Trade with Iran," *New York Times*, 31 March 1995.
21. Kemp, *Forever Enemies*, p. 9.
22. Clyde Haberman, "Israel Focuses on the Threat Beyond the Arabs – in Iran," *New York Times*, Sunday, 8 November 1992; David Hoffman, "Israel Seeking to Convince U.S. That West Is Threatened by Iran," *Washington Post*, 13 March 1993; Douglas Jehl, "Iran-Backed Terrorists Are Growing More Aggressive, U.S. Warns," *New York Times*, 18 March 1993; Steven A. Holmes, "U.S. Says Terrorist Attacks Dropped Sharply in 1992," *New York Times*, 1 May 1993; Rowland Evans and Robert Novak, "Ripe for Retaliation," *Washington Post*, 1 August 1996. After his return from his first Middle East trip, Secretary of State Christopher testified before the Appropriations Committee's international operations panel that many leaders in the Middle East had told him they greatly feared Iran because of its support for terrorist groups. Cited by Sciolino, "Christopher Signals a Tougher U.S. Line Toward Iran"; Israel Shahak, "With Iraq Neutralized, Israelis Seek Catalyst for War with Iran," *Washington Report on Middle East Affairs*, (April/May

paign was welcomed within U.S. official circles, whose response came in the form of the May 1993 "dual containment" policy of Iran and Iraq.[23]

Dual containment was designed to exert economic and political pressure on Iran, including the use of covert Central Intelligence Agency (CIA) operations to curb what the administration called Iran's expansionist ambitions. In 1994, President Clinton signed an intelligence order in which he defined the purpose of future covert action as enhanced containment through an aggressive anti-Iranian propaganda campaign.[24]

But even dual containment soon reached its limits. Since 1993 the administration has appealed to its European allies to join in a policy

1993), p. 15; Sick, "The United States and Iran," pp. 62–5; Bill, "The United States and Iran," p. 98.

23. See Indyk's Soref Symposium address in which he outlined the dual containment policy, "The Clinton Administration's Approach to the Middle East," pp. 5–6. As early as March 1993, U.S. officials expressed their concern over the expanding activities of Iranian-backed terrorist groups opposed to the Middle East peace process. As Christopher bluntly put it, "Iran is one of the principal sources of support for terrorist groups around the world." See Sciolino, "Christopher Signals a Tougher Line Toward Iran." The State Department also condemned Iran as the world's "most dangerous state sponsor of terrorism." See Jehl, "Iran-Backed Terrorists Are Growing More Aggressive, U.S. Warns."

24. Elaine Sciolino, "C.I.A. Asks Congress for $19 Million to Undermine Iraq's Rulers and Rein in Iran," New York Times, 12 April 1995. Edward Shirley, a former Iran specialist at the CIA, argued that the fear of Saddam Hussein was not the primary impetus behind the new policy; rather, dual containment called for collective economic action against the Islamic Republic of Iran to force it to change its unacceptable behavior. Shirley contended further that dual containment is America's most coherent attempt to establish a blueprint for coping with Iranian Islamic militancy: It may even "become the cornerstone of a new American doctrine for a radicalized Islamic Middle East." See "The Iran Policy Trap," Foreign Policy, no. 96 (Fall 1994), pp. 75–6. (Shirley is the pseudonym, not the real name, of the CIA specialist.) Echoing Shirley, senior Iranian officials accused the United Stated of punishing Iran because of its Islamic government. See Agis Salpukas, "Conoco Signs Contract with Iran to Develop Persian Gulf Oilfield," New York Times, 7 March 1995.

of firm containment and economic pressure on Iran. It has also tried to block the rescheduling of Iran's external debts and to restrict many categories of technology transfer to Iran.[25] American officials have failed, however, to persuade their European counterparts to curb their economic ties to Iran. European countries have preferred "critical dialogue" to isolation as a means of moderating Iran's behavior; they also have accused the United States of inconsistency, citing the American purchases of Iranian oil.[26]

When Russia signed a $1 billion contract in January 1995 to build two nuclear reactors in Iran, congressional leaders threatened to cut aid to Russia, underlying the Iranian issue's importance to Washington.[27] Clinton called the sale profoundly disturbing and warned that if it went ahead, "Russian national security can only be weakened in the long term."[28] Thus the United States was willing to risk a crisis with Russia by putting the Russian-Iranian reactor before its priorities for the May U.S.–Russia summit.[29]

Pressure for a more activist containment of Iran reached a peak in March 1995, when Teheran concluded a deal with an American company (Conoco) to help explore for oil. As the United States was being accused by Europeans of hypocrisy for trading with Iran while condemning European trade, the Republican-controlled Congress

25. Peter W. Rodman, "Mullah Moola" ["The Islamic Threat," pt. 2], *National Review*, 7 November 1994, p. 66; Shahram Chubin, *Iran's National Security Policy: Capabilities, Intentions and Impact* (Washington, DC: The Carnegie Endowment for International Peace, 1994), pp. 5–6.
26. Sciolino, "Christopher Proposes Tighter Curbs on Trade with Iran"; Shirley, "The Iran Policy Trap," pp. 78–81.
27. Eric Schmitt, "Republicans Warn Russia that Its Deal with Iran Threatens Aid," *New York Times*, 8 May 1995; Sciolino, "Calling Iran an 'Outlaw State,' Christopher Backs U.S. Trade Ban," *New York Times*, 2 May 1995.
28. Schmitt, "Republicans Warn Russia That Its Deal with Iran Threatens Aid." Secretary of State Christopher had already warned Russia that it "will rue the day it cooperated with the terrorist state of Iran if Iran builds nuclear weapons with Russian expertise and Russian equipment." Quoted in Steven Greenhouse, "U.S. Gives Russia Secret Data on Iran to Fight Atom Deal," *New York Times*, 3–4 April 1995.
29. Gary Sick, "A Sensible Policy Toward Iran: Consistency in American Policy Should Be a Top Priority," *Middle East Insight* (July/August 1995), p. 21.

and the powerful pro-Israel lobbying groups called for the administration to take firm action against Iran.[30] The Republicans were not mollified by the fact that Conoco dropped the plan after Clinton had issued a directive placing prohibitions on U.S. financing and management of the development of Iran's petroleum resources. New York Republican Senator Alfonse D'Amato, for example, introduced two bills in the Senate to prohibit American companies or their subsidiaries from doing business with Iran and to impose sanctions on foreign companies that were doing so.[31]

From Containment to Relentless Pursuit

Outflanked by the Republicans, and risking erosion of support from one of its most important domestic constituencies, the Clinton administration toughened its policy again.[32] Secretary of State Christopher, along with Martin Indyk, then senior Middle East specialist at the White House, recommended more assertive measures, including a trade ban, to isolate and punish the Iranian regime.[33] Christopher's move was motivated not only by the inefficacy of U.S. policy toward Iran but also by domestic politics – the fear that if the administration did not impose comprehensive sanctions, Congress would do so.[34]

Of all Clinton administration senior aides, Christopher seized the initiative on Iran, moving beyond the policy of dual containment to a more active approach – "relentless pursuit." According to some of his colleagues, Christopher saw in Iran "not a diplomatic abstraction

30. Sick, "The United States and Iran," pp. 69–70; Salpukas, "Conoco Signs Contract with Iran"; Sciolino, "U.S. Pressure Put on Iran and Iraq," *New York Times*, 5 April 1995.
31. Sciolino, "U.S. Pressure Put on Iran and Iraq"; Sick, "The United States and Iran," p. 70. A. M. Rosenthal criticized Clinton's Iran policy for failing to stand up against appeasement and empowerment of dictators. In the case of Iran, asserted Rosenthal, economic engagement "supports the terrorism, holy wars, arms and nuclear buildup that make Iran dangerous." See "How to Trade with Iran," *New York Times*, 24 March 1995.
32. Sick, "The United States and Iran," p. 70.
33. Sciolino, "Christopher Proposes Tighter Curbs on Trade with Iran"; Chris Hedges, "Iran May Be Able to Build an Atomic Bomb in 5 Years, U.S. and Israeli Officials Fear," *New York Times*, 5 January 1995.
34. Sciolino, "Christopher Proposes Tighter Curbs on Trade with Iran."

but a living menace, a terrorist state that if left to its own devices will soon have nuclear weapons and use them to bully its neighbors, subvert Israel and dominate oil transport routes essential to global commerce."[35] Iran energized Christopher almost to the point of "passion." His nightmare was that all his work in nursing Israel and its Arab neighbors toward peace was being endangered by Iranian-sponsored terrorism.[36]

Christopher's attitude toward revolutionary Iran was shaped in 1980, during which he was involved in grueling negotiations to obtain the release of Americans held hostage in Teheran. The hostage crisis had played a critical role in bringing down the Carter presidency and, with it, Christopher's hopes of becoming secretary of state in a second Carter term.[37] According to a State Department official, Christopher had had a bitter personal experience with Iran; he had been profoundly shaken by what the Islamic regime had done to Carter. Christopher's inflated rhetoric on Iran, added this ambassador, should be seen within this context; he simply did not want to have any contacts with the revolutionary Iranians.[38]

Foreign diplomats reported that when discussing Iran, Christopher's subtle and judicious manner vanished and his eyes flashed. Some European diplomats accused him of being motivated in part by vengeance.[39] Other Europeans criticized Washington for overreacting and for being obsessed with Iran's mullahs seventeen years after the hostage taking and spilt blood.[40] Indeed, Gary Sick, who had been a member of the Christopher's team that negotiated the

---

35. Quoted in Thomas W. Lippman, "No More Mr. Nice Guy: On the Subject of Iran, Warren Christopher Is the Hardest of the Hard-Liners," *Washington Post*, 15–21 May, 1995, National Weekly edition.
36. Ibid.
37. Ibid.
38. Interview, Princeton, NJ, 27 May 1995. In this regard, Christopher was the rule rather than the exception. According to Graham Fuller, a former intelligence official, "Washington policy makers are fearful of even touching the poisonous Iranian issue lest it infect them too. We were, it appears, born to hate each other – at least at this juncture in history." See "The Appeal of Iran," *National Interest* (Fall 1994), p. 92.
39. Sick, "The United States and Iran," p. 68; Lippman, "No More Mr. Nice Guy," p. 18.
40. Steve Coll, "The U.S. Case Against Iranian Nukes," *Washington Post*, 15–21 May, 1995, National Weekly edition, p. 23.

settlement of the hostage crisis during 1980–81, suspected that "the harsh criticism of Iran satisfied a desire for revenge against a regime that had humiliated the United Stated and contributed greatly to the electoral defeat of President Carter."[41]

The case of Christopher illustrates the impact that the Islamic revolution in Iran has had on the U.S. foreign-policy elite's views of revolutionary Iran and Islamic politics in general. As Graham E. Fuller, a former intelligence official, put it: "Iran is properly the most emotional foreign policy relationship to confront America since the Vietnam War."[42] Thus, Washington's thinking on political Islam appears to have been shaped by the U.S. experience with Iran.

The behavior of postrevolutionary Iran has not helped either, especially its attempt to export the revolution and its assistance to radical Islamic groups in Lebanon, Sudan, Algeria, and the West Bank and Gaza.[43] The clerical regime also remains hostile to the United States and committed to its revolutionary project. Teheran's antipathy toward Washington, asserts Shahram Chubin, stems from its position in the regional system, as well as its ambition to be the standard-bearer of Islam.[44]

Thus long before Christopher recommended a ban on U.S. trade and investment with Iran, some American officials were sounding the alarm. One NSC official said at the time that "the situation in Iran is gloomy and does not seem to improve as a result of our dual containment policy." The Clinton administration, added this official, was being forced to adopt a more aggressive approach: "The Iranian leadership are bastards, doing very bad things; they are personally implicated in assisting and sponsoring terrorism."[45] Senior administration aides are more convinced than ever that Iran's highest-ranking officials are directly involved in ordering and paying for terrorist operations abroad.[46] When asked whom he perceived as the greatest security threat to the United States, General John Shalikashvili, former Chairman of the Joint Chiefs of Staff, retorted quickly

41. Sick, "The United States and Iran," p. 71.
42. Fuller, "The Appeal of Iran," p. 92.
43. Bill, "The United States and Iran," p. 101.
44. Chubin, *Iran's National Security Policy*, pp. 1, 5.
45. Interview, Washington, DC, 29 March 1995.
46. Elaine Sciolino, "In World of Flux, a Constant: U.S. and Iran Still Foes," *New York Times*, Sunday, 29 December 1996.

that "we understandably worry most about our interests in the Middle East." Iran, added Shalikashvili, "is a threat to the whole region. Listening to the rhetoric coming out of Iran, it's hard to conclude anything other than they are very much opposed to the sort of things we and our friends stand for."[47]

In April 1995, Clinton announced a ban on all U.S. trade with and investment in Iran.[48] Senior U.S. policy makers made it clear that Iran must pay a price for flouting the norms of law-abiding nations. Of all the rogue states, Clinton said, Iran presented a particular problem to the peace process.[49] Christopher agreed: "Iran is the primary patron of terrorists trying to derail the Arab-Israeli peace process. Hamas, Islamic Jihad, Hizbollah, Ahmad Jibril's Popular Front – each of those organizations receives funds, training, and political support from Iran."[50]

47. See Claudia Dreifus's interview with General Shalikashvili, "Who's the Enemy Now," *New York Times*, Sunday, 21 May 1995, Magazine section, p. 37.
48. Some observers questioned the President's choice of venue and timing to announce his decision to impose a full economic embargo on Iran. He made the announcement at a World Jewish Congress dinner, while wearing a yarmulke, with Israeli Foreign Minister Peres sitting across the table. Thomas Friedman of the *New York Times* was one of those who criticized Clinton: "It left the impression with the Iranians, the Muslim world and the allies that the U.S. embargo was not a fundamental American and global interest, but was just pandering to a single U.S. interest group and therefore not to be taken seriously." See "Too Much of a Good Thing," *New York Times*, 18 June 1995. Another *New York Times* reporter, Todd S. Purdum, was more blunt: "Mr. Clinton's new announcement brings the United States policy on Iran more into line with Israel's." See "Clinton to Order a Trade Embargo Against Teheran," *New York Times*, 1 May 1995. Elaine Sciolino argued further that Clinton's decision was solely motivated by domestic politics: to preempt the Republicans from getting both houses to pass legislation to punish Iran and foreign companies that do business with Teheran. See "Calling Iran an 'Outlaw State,' Christopher Backs U.S. Trade Ban."
49. "Remarks by President Clinton at a Dinner of the World Jewish Congress," pp. 2–3. See also "Statement by Secretary of State Warren Christopher Regarding U.S. Sanctions Against Iran," p. 2; Pelletreau at the House "Hearing with Defense Department Personnel; U.S. Sanctions on Iran," p. 2.
50. "Statement by Secretary of State Warren Christopher Regarding U.S. Sanctions Against Iran," p. 1. In an editorial, the *Economist* found the

Clinton accused Iran of seeking to destabilize the region and destroy the peace by supporting terrorists and hungering for nuclear weapons. He rejected the arguments of some of his advisors who had argued that dialogue, not confrontation, is the best route to change Iranian behavior. In Clinton's view, "Iran has broadened its role as an inspiration and paymaster to terrorists." The President declared war on terrorism around the world, particularly on some Middle Eastern "rogue states who sponsor death in order to kill peace."[51]

Moreover, Clinton administration officials referred to U.S.–Iranian differences as a clash not only over national interests but also over values and the assertion of U.S. leadership abroad. Addressing the American-Israeli Political Action Committee (AIPAC) in May 1995, Clinton stated that Iran "seeks to undermine the West and its values by supporting the murderous attacks of the Islamic Jihad and Hizbollah and other terrorist groups." Clinton portrayed the conflict with Iran as part of a larger clash between open society and its enemies: "[T]he more open and the more flexible we are, the more vulnerable we are to the forces of organized evil."[52] A few days later, paying tribute to the generation that had won World War II and prevailed in the Cold War, Clinton warned that the nation is still confronting "forces of darkness" in different forms all around the world. As if to underscore his warning, Clinton's last official act before he delivered this speech was to sign an executive order formalizing the new embargo against Iran.[53]

Using similar language, Peter Tarnoff, under secretary for political affairs, said that Iran remains at the top of the Clinton administration's diplomatic agenda because its policies threaten our core interests and "values" as well. In explaining American policy, Tarnoff stressed Iran's active opposition to the Arab-Israeli peace process and its threat to Persian Gulf stability and security. He rejected the allies' advocacy that engagement, not confrontation, will alter Iran's objec-

administration's charge exaggerated, since outside Iran, the mullahs now do not control militant groups other than Hizbollah. See "Punishing Iran," 6 May 1995, p. 14.
51. "Remarks by President Clinton at a Dinner of the World Jewish Congress," pp. 2–4.
52. Cited in Todd S. Purdum, "Clinton Pays Homage to an Extraordinary Generation," *New York Times*, 9 May 1995.
53. Ibid.

tionable behavior, acknowledging a gap between American policy and that of most industrialized nations. Clinton himself acknowledged that difference: "I don't know that we're on the same wavelength" with the allies, adding, "the evidence is that constructive engagement with the Iranians has, at least so far, failed to produce any positive results." The President did not mention that he had not even consulted in advance with his closest allies regarding the economic embargo on Iran.[54]

Not satisfied even with the trade ban on Iran, the House of Representatives approved a sweeping sanctions bill, later signed by Clinton in August 1996, to punish foreign companies that invest $40 million or more in the oil resources of Iran. The new U.S. legislation has left the Clinton administration in sharp disagreement with its allies over policy toward Iran.[55] In response to the House bill threatening foreign companies, Washington's allies in Europe whose oil companies invested in Iran – such as French Total, which in 1997 signed a $2 billion gas field development with Iran, along with Russia and Malaysia – have threatened to retaliate if President Clinton acts on the bill. French Prime Minister Lionel Jospin said that the United States cannot impose its laws on the world; otherwise, "the world would be a different place, and we would no longer be the old independent nation that we are."[56] A German official called the U.S. initiative "wrong."[57]

54. Tarnoff, "Containing Iran," *U.S. Department of State Dispatch*, 13 November 1995, pp. 832, 834, and "Sanctions on Iran," *U.S. Department of State Dispatch*, 23 October 1995, pp. 768–70. Similarly, Christopher and his assistant secretary of state for Near Eastern affairs portrayed the President's decision to ban all U.S. trade and investment with Iran as a means of projecting American leadership abroad: "It sends an unmistakable message to friend and foe alike," emphasized Christopher and Pelletreau. See "Statement by Secretary of State Warren Christopher Regarding U.S. Sanctions Against Iran," pp. 2, 4; Pelletreau at the House "Hearing with Defense Department Personnel – U.S. Sanctions on Iran," p. 1.
55. Eric Pianin, "Clinton Approves Sanctions for Investors in Iran, Libya," *Washington Post*, 6 August 1996; Paul Blustein, "House Passes Measure Against Foreign Firms Investing in Iranian, Libyan Oil," *Washington Post*, 24 July 1996.
56. Cited by David E. Singer, "Two-Edged Sword: Anti-Terrorism Law Risks American Relations with Allies," *New York Times*, 30 September 1997.
57. Alan Cowell, "U.S. Fails to Enlist European Allies in Iranian Trade Embargo," *New York Times*, 3 May 1995.

Even the U.K., usually reluctant to confront the United States, expressed its opposition to the U.S. legislation. The greatest challenge to American policy so far came when NATO member Turkey, in defiance of the U.S. sanctions, signed a $20 billion contract with Iran for the supply of natural gas. The $2 billion contract signed by French-Russian-Malaysian companies with Iran has also put the United States in direct conflict with some of its allies and friends. Only two countries in the world thought the embargo strategy was a good idea: the United States and Israel.[58] Since mid–1996, the Clinton administration has found itself locked in a serious confrontation with its European partners (as well as with Canada), who seem to have no intention of following the United States down the path of active Iranian containment.[59]

Fortunately, not all U.S. officials share the alarmist view regarding Iran's subversive role in regional and Islamic politics. According to one NSC official, although Iran provides moral inspiration and some material support to various Islamists in the Middle East and North Africa, the Iranian connection is most apparent in the case of Sudan: "But Sudan is a peripheral state; we focus on the Sudan because it is a resting place for terrorists."[60] In Lebanon, some American diplomats note that the success of the peace process will sever Hizbollah's ties with Teheran.[61] It would be misleading, adds a member of the NSC, to blame Teheran for the Islamist challenges to the regional order. Nonetheless, this official concedes that "there is much obsession with Iran within and outside the U.S. government."[62] Another NSC official agrees that the domestic political atmosphere in Washington is "very agitated" against Iran, thus affecting Washington's behavior toward Teheran.[63]

58. Saeed Barzin, "Iran Rides High," *Middle East International,* 16 August 1996, pp. 4–5; Sick, "A Sensible Policy Toward Iran," p. 21.
59. Attempts by President Clinton to press the embargo at the Group of Seven Meeting in Halifax, Nova Scotia, in June 1995 failed. Privately, the Europeans and Japanese accused the United States of distorting the Iranian threat for domestic political reasons. See Sciolino, "U.S. Asserts Iranians Plotted to Disrupt Rally in Germany," *New York Times,* 25 June 1995.
60. Interview, Washington, DC, 29 March 1995.
61. Ibid., and interview with a State Department official, Princeton, NJ, 27 May 1995.
62. Interview, Washington, DC, 29 March 1995.
63. Interview, Washington, DC, 30 March 1995.

The frank assessment of U.S. officials interviewed contradicts the Clinton administration's portrayal of Iran as a nest of international terrorism and Islamist militancy. Their account also sheds light on the minor differences and divisions that exist within this administration and the effects of domestic politics on U.S. policy toward Teheran. According to William Quandt, several officials whose task focused on Iran were removed from their assignment because they had advocated a flexible, noninflammatory approach toward the Iranian mullahs.[64]

Some important members of the U.S. policy establishment have also criticized Clinton's dual containment policy for being ineffective, strategically unviable, and carrying a high financial and diplomatic cost. This strident U.S. campaign, noted two former national security advisers, Democrat Zbigniew Brzezinski and Republican Brent Scowcroft, and former Assistant Secretary of State Richard Murphy, has driven Iran and Russia together and the United States and its European allies apart. The three former policy makers call on the Clinton administration to review and correct current policy toward Iran.[65]

Although their views on Iran vary, American officials all agree that the mullahs must stop opposing the Arab-Israeli peace process and accept Washington's involvement in the maintenance of the security of the oil-producing Gulf region. As an NSC staff member said, "The United States would tolerate the Islamic revolution in Iran if its purpose was survival. But it will not allow the expansion of the Iranian revolution outside its borders."[66]

American officials also agree that containment of Iran is the safest option available to the Clinton administration, given the popularity of this strategy in the United States. In fact, as Gary Sick notes, the administration's confrontational strategy toward Iran has "played extremely well with the Congress and with the American public more generally, where the image of Iran was indelibly associated with terrorism and the hostage crisis of the 1980s."[67]

64. Interview with William Quandt, Washington, DC, 28 March 1995.
65. Zbigniew Brzezinski, Brent Scowcroft, and Richard Murphy, "Differentiated Containment," *Foreign Affairs* 76, no. 3 (May/June 1997), pp. 20–30
66. Interview, Washington, DC, 29 March 1995.
67. Sick, "The United States and Iran," p. 71.

After Clinton announced his decision to impose a unilateral embargo on Iran, Republican senators who had been critical of Clinton's Iran policy praised him for his boldness. "I applaud the President," said Senator John McCain, the Arizona Republican who has aggressively documented Iran's weapons programs over the years. "He did the right thing and I will support him however I can. The D'Amato legislation should certainly be held in abeyance."[68] Even Senator D'Amato felt the need to call the President's decision a "good first step."[69] Being particularly attentive to the domestic scene, Clinton recognizes the high political returns to be accrued from confronting the clerics in Teheran.

Washington's War on Revolutionary Islam

Over the course of its seven-year term of office, the Clinton administration has thus escalated the confrontation with Iran in an effort to isolate and reform its cleric-dominated regime. Although American officials assert that they have accepted the Islamic revolution in Iran, some of their pronouncements and actions indicate that their real hope is to destabilize the clerical regime. In a January 1995 interview with the *Washington Times*, Christopher called for the overthrow of the Iranian and Iraqi governments: "[W]e must isolate Iraq and Iran until there is a change in their governments, a change in their leadership."[70] Furthermore, President Clinton, bowing to pressure from the Republican leadership in Congress, authorized the CIA to mount a covert operation "to change the nature of the Government of Iran."[71]

68. Sciolino, "Calling Iran an 'Outlaw State' Christopher Backs U.S. Trade Ban."
69. Ibid. Confrontationalists also sang the praises of Clinton. Peter Rodman, for example, noted that unlike its three predecessors, the Clinton administration deserves credit for its firm resistance to Iran and rare display of strategic insight. In particular, Rodman credits Martin Indyk for being the principal architect within the administration of the hardline policy toward Iran, though he is critical of the Department of State for its complacent view of the Iranian threat. See "Mullah Moola," pp. 66–7, 84.
70. Quoted in Trude B. Feldman, "Christopher: Mideast Gains Will Hold," *Washington Times*, 18 January 1995.
71. Tim Weiner, "U.S. Plan to Change Iran Leaders Is an Open Secret Before It Begins," *New York Times*, 26 January 1996.

Although the administration rejects confrontationalists' claim regarding the existence of a coordinated Islamist network, it continues to suspect Iran of providing inspiration and assistance to "religious extremists" in the Middle East, North Africa, and beyond. America sees Iran as the driving force behind much of the Islamist militancy in the world. This fixation with clerical Iran stems not only from its humiliating experience during the hostage crisis but also from its fear of Iran's revolutionary Islamic ideology. First, Iran's revolutionary language is dangerous because it strikes directly at the generally accepted understanding of the quiescent role of religion in politics. Second, the Islamic revolution's clandestine modus operandi strikes terror at the heart of the United States and its regional allies as well.[72]

Hence, the theoretical distinction made by U.S. officials between "moderate" and "militant" Islamists does not apply in the Iranian case because the mullahs in Teheran, as President Clinton implied in his speech to the Jordanian parliament, represent "the forces of terror and extremism."[73] Revolutionary Islam as practiced by Iran is seen to be intensely anti-Western and clearly hostile to American interests, and the Clinton administration appears to be determined to wage war against this variant of political Islam.

The Iranian case sheds much light on the way in which the United States has approached Islamists elsewhere. Neither the ambiguity in U.S. thinking on the Islamic revival nor U.S. suspicion of Islamists can be understood without deciphering Iran's evocations of profound fears within the American foreign-policy establishment. Washington seems to use the Iranian revolution as the primary yardstick by which to measure resurgent Islamist movements throughout the Middle East and North Africa. In this context, U.S. policy toward Iran has broader implications for America's relations with Islamists elsewhere.

The Iranian Threat: Myth and Reality

The Clinton administration has a legitimate right to be alarmed about the clerical regime's repressive policies against Iranian dissi-

72. Shirley, "The Iran Policy Trap," p. 81.
73. See chapter 5 for Clinton's statements on Iran.

dents. The mullahs also are hostile to the United States and its allies, and Iranian leaders are on record as opposing the Arab-Israeli peace process. Clinton administration officials believe that Teheran undermines U.S. interests by providing material support for radical Islamist groups in Lebanon, Sudan, Algeria and the West Bank and Gaza.

The U.S. diagnosis of the Iranian threat, however, does not take into account the failings of the Islamic revolution at home and abroad. Far from being a model to be imitated, "the revolution," notes an Iranian analyst, "is a hollow shell that neither inspires nor animates its proponents."[74] Iran no longer constitutes an ideological or a cultural threat to the United States and its regional allies.

A classic example was Ayatollah Khomeini's failure to incite his Shi'ite coreligionists in Iraq to rise up against Saddam Hussein's regime during the Iran-Iraq war in the 1980s. The Islamic Republic's revolutionary rhetoric did find sympathy with some of Lebanon's Shi'ites. However, Hizbollah's rise to prominence was peculiar to the socioeconomic and political marginalization of the Shi'ite community in Lebanon, not to any social engineering by Teheran.

The fear that Khomeini's fiery sermons would destabilize the conservative, pro-Western monarchies in the Gulf proved to be exaggerated. Iran has failed to convert its ideology of revolutionary Islam into any discernible political influence. The riots in Bahrain in 1994 and 1995 are no exception. As a member of the NSC privately acknowledged, "The root causes behind the riots in Bahrain are basically local."[75]

Similarly, the political decay in Egypt and Algeria – as some U.S. officials acknowledge – is largely homegrown. Given the wretched socioeconomic and political conditions in these countries, Islamists' appeal is welcomed, with or without Iranian instigation. The same analogy applies to Sudan. The Sudanese are much more interested in obtaining Iranian oil, money, and logistics to bankroll their starved economy than in importing theological dogma. Hassan Turabi, leader of the Muslim Brotherhood and the power behind the pro-Islamist military regime in Sudan, has distanced himself from the

74. Chubin, *Iran's National Security Policy*, p. 76.
75. Interview, Washington, DC, 29 March 1995.

Islamic Republic, criticizing Iran's sociopolitical agenda for being "too abstract" and "sometimes wrong."[76]

Like their nationalist predecessors of the 1950s and 1960s, once Islamists in various countries come to power, they will end up dissipating much of their revolutionary energy in internal ideological and political rivalries. The Sunni-Shi'ite cleavage in Islam, coupled with the clashing egos of patriarchal leaders, works against the emergence and consolidation of a homogenous, internationalist Islamist movement.

The inability of the Islamic Republic to export its revolution is directly related to its conspicuous domestic political failure and dismal economic performance. The signs of decay are revealed by the ruling mullahs' increasing reliance on repression. High inflation and a soaring unemployment rate, coupled with rapid population growth – averaging 2.77 percent annually – have contributed to a stark deterioration in living standards. The mullahs, through mismanagement of the economy, corruption, social and political austerity, and costly military ventures abroad, have alienated large segments of society. Furthermore, despite the thin veneer of democratization introduced by the clerics, Iran is governed by a totalitarian regime that increasingly relies on repression to stifle dissent and maintain control.

The discontent was starkly revealed in May 1997 when Iranians defied their religious mullahs and overwhelmingly voted for Mohammed Khatami for president over the candidate favored by the ruling establishment. Since Khatami is well known for his reformist views, his election represents a rebuff of the conservative forces who have ruled Iran since 1979. Khatami's victory also shows that the religious conservatives have not been able to tame and subdue civil society. The latter is much more complex and resilient than some U.S. officials and observers would acknowledge. Despite considerable pressure by the conservative mullahs, Khatami has sent important conciliatory gestures toward the United States. At his first news conference, he said he hoped to reestablish a dialogue with the American people that has been virtually suspended since 1979. He declared "great respect" for the "great people of the United States"

76. Judith Miller, "Faces of Fundamentalism," *Foreign Affairs.*

and criticized the U.S. government for standing in the way of possible reconciliation. To show his seriousness, Khatami said it was "a source of sorrow" to him that the United States and Iran had not done more to reconcile: "Instead of talking with forked tongues, we want to have a rational dialogue."[77]

Since he assumed office in August 1997, Khatami has succeeded in patching up differences with the European Union that had resulted in the withdrawal of European ambassadors. Iran has also been working hard to rebuild ties with Arab neighbors like Saudi Arabia and Egypt. In December 1997, Teheran played host to the Islamic conference, which was attended by representatives of fifty-four countries. Slowly but steadily, Khatami has normalized Iranian foreign policy. This is no small achievement given the intense internal struggle for power that has turned violent at times.

President Clinton called Khatami's election "hopeful," and he recently said he hoped that the estrangement between the United States and Iran "can be bridged." Clinton quickly added, however, that Teheran's government would have to move first to change its policies. These include Iran's support for terrorism against Israel, its pursuit of chemical and nuclear weapons, and its effort to disrupt the Arab-Israeli peace process. The State Department's response to Khatami's warm and specific message to the United States was that "it's too early to tell whether this represents an offer or not."[78]

Although Clinton's comments represented a change of tone and were welcomed by the Iranian regime, they did not signal a fundamental shift in the U.S. approach. With the exception of Clinton's remarks and positive indications by other U.S. officials, the United States has not moderated its dual containment policy. The much awaited formal review of Clinton's second-term policy toward Iran has not yielded any major changes. Despite some positive predictions, it appears that the American-Iranian relationship is more

---

77. Cited in Douglas Jehl, "Iranian President Calls for Opening Dialogue with U.S.," *New York Times*, 15 December 1997.
78. Ibid. See also Alison Mitchell, "Clinton Sees Hope in the Election of Moderate as President of Iran," *New York Times*, 30 May 1997; Barbara Crossette, "Democracies Love Peace, Don't They?" *New York Times*, Sunday, 1 June 1997.

likely to remain hostile, at least during the second Clinton administration.[79]

Furthermore, the Clinton administration has found itself in a dilemma in the wake of the French Total oil deal with Iran. If Clinton imposes sanctions, that could alienate the European allies further and probably touch off a vicious trade war that could end up hurting the Western countries more than Iran. Even if the administration decides against sanctions, which it recently did, Clinton's dual containment policy – in addition to being costly to the United States – has caused friction with his European allies, disputes with Russia and China, and deep concern among some of the Gulf states, all this without success in isolating Iran.[80]

Also exaggerated is the administration's charge regarding the hegemonic ambitions behind Iran's massive military buildup. Iran spends much less on defense annually – $3 billion – than Iraq or Saudi Arabia, both of which bought almost $80 billion in arms between 1982 and 1992. Indeed, Iran has modest military capabilities in comparison with its two Gulf neighbors. Analysts agree that Iran presents no more than a "nuisance" militarily to U.S. friends.[81]

The U.S. government's more serious contention about Iran's drive to acquire nuclear weapons is also problematic. The United States has not produced any hard evidence to support its claims.[82] The director-general of the International Atomic Energy Agency (IAEA), Hans Blix, indirectly criticized Washington's allegation about Iran's trafficking in nuclear materials. He stressed that IAEA inspectors have never seen any diversion of materials for military

79. Sciolino, "In World of Flux"; Mitchell, "Clinton Sees Hope in the Election of Moderate as President of Iran"; Crossette, "Democracies Love Peace, Don't They?"
80. Donald Neff, "U.S. and Iran: Policy Under Fire," *Middle East International*, 2 May 1997, pp. 5–6, and "Agony in Washington," *Middle East International*, 10 October 1997.
81. Richard F. Grimmett, *Conventional Arms Transfers to the Third World* (Washington DC: Congressional Research Service, 1993), p. 9; Bill, "The United States and Iran," p. 103; Chubin, *Iran's National Security Policy*, p. 70.
82. Steve Coll, "The U.S. Case Against Iranian Nukes," *Washington Post*, 15–21 May 1995.

ends during regular visits to Iran and have had no difficulties in implementing safeguard agreements.[83]

Although some of the clerics would like to conduct research in the nuclear field, there is neither agreement nor debate within the Iranian leadership on nuclear weapons. A leading specialist on Iran's security policy argued that Iran has not yet made a definite decision on nuclear weapons and, as such, Teheran's "decision" to go nuclear could be reversed. The more isolated the Iranian rulers are, the more determined they become to pursue the nuclear option.[84] The Iranian leadership's conspiratorial mindset, coupled with a victimization mentality, appears to be the driving force behind its attempt to obtain nuclear weapons. Since his assuming the presidency, Khatami has lowered the profile of the nuclear bureaucracy by replacing its devoted and dedicated director with one of his supporters. The purpose seems to be to diffuse the nuclear issue that has poisoned U.S.–Iranian relations.

Treating Iran as an "international outlaw" and "rogue" state will reinforce its ruling elite's collective sense of paranoia. To prevent Iran from going nuclear, Washington should aim to assimilate the Islamic Republic into the international community, rather than treating it as an outcast. Iran's nuclear program should be seen more as a political, not a security or strategic, issue. Ironically, Washington has dealt quite differently with North Korea's nuclear potential than it has with Iran's.

The Clinton administration voices a legitimate concern about Iran's assistance to some revolutionary elements who engage in terrorism. Yet the charge that "Iran is the foremost sponsor of terrorism in the world" is far-fetched. As was noted in the *Economist*: "The mullahs may be uncomfortable to live with, and should be restrained. But, outside Iran, there is little hard evidence that they now control militant groups – other than the Hizbollah guerrillas in Lebanon."[85] Even Hizbollah, however, regularly laments the decline in Iranian aid. Although Hamas receives money from some Iranian clerics, the bulk of its support comes from Palestinian sources and citizens of the

83. Reported in *Jordan Times*, 4 July 1995.
84. Shahram Chubin, "Does Iran Want Nuclear Weapons," p. 101.
85. "Punishing Iran," 16 May 1995, p. 14.

Arab Gulf states. Hamas does not take its orders from Teheran. It has its own agenda.

It is, though, undeniable that Iran opposes the Middle East peace process and supports terrorism, particularly against its political opponents and dissidents at home. By early 1996, however, former President Ali Akbar Hashemi Rafsanjani tried to temper his country's opposition to the peace process by noting that Teheran would respect any peace deal between Israel and Syria. He also made it clear that Iran "opposes terrorism regardless of its perpetrators, even if it is committed by Hamas."[86] The 1996 parliamentary elections, as well as the 1997 presidential referendum in Iran, have strengthened the position of the reformist, technocratic camp.

Policy Recommendations

Given its bloody experience with the Islamic Republic since 1979, the United States cannot be blamed for being skeptical about Teheran's intentions. But there is good reason to doubt that blanket hostility will force political change in Iran. Twenty years of constant U.S. pressure have wrought little change. Clinton's confrontational approach may not fare better, given the lack of support by America's allies. Indeed, rather than changing Iran, it is more likely to provoke the hard-line clerics who have adamantly opposed resuming relations with Washington and who have depicted the United States as the Great Satan. Clinton's policy will also help weaken the remaining reformist forces within the mullah regime, especially the delicate position of the new president, Khatami. The latter has already came under fire by the conservative forces for appointing "moderates" to his cabinet, particularly Foreign Minister Kamal Kharazi, who has advocated talks with the United States.[87]

A more dynamic and selective American approach, combining both carrots and sticks, would be more effective in inducing Iran to

86. "Rafsanjani: We Support the Palestinian Struggle but We Reject Any Terrorist Act," *Al-Hayat*, 12 March 1996; "Iran Eases Stand on Peace Process," *Jordan Times*, 4 July 1995.
87. "Makeup of Iran's Cabinet Defies the Hard-liners," *New York Times*, 13 August 1997.

moderate its behavior. Although past U.S. attempts to open a dialogue with Teheran were rebuffed by the mullahs, the situation appears to be changing. While Iranian leaders are still divided over the question of dialogue with Washington, they have recently appeared more receptive to an opening. Iran, for example, deliberately chose a U.S. oil company (Conoco) over a European rival, stressing its desire to do business with the United States. This fact was confirmed by former President Rafsanjani: "We invited an American firm and entered into a deal for $1 billion. This was a message to the United States, which was not correctly understood."[88] According to a senior State Department official, Iran has also inquired about Washington's willingness for talks.[89]

Although Khatami has so far concentrated mainly on domestic politics, his administration has sent important signals to the Western countries about its desire to improve relations with its neighbors and the world at large. In his inauguration speech, Khatami promised that his government would avoid acting in any way that might cause discord abroad. Furthermore, in an address in Teheran, Khatami rejected the clash-of-civilizations hypothesis and called instead for dialogue between Islam and the West: "The Islamic revolution in Iran is ready to pursue dialogue on all levels with the Western civilization and the Christian world to achieve permanent peace."[90] Foreign Minister Kharazi said that establishing "normal" relations with the United States "does not conflict with the main principles of the Islamic revolution."[91]

Unlike the Americans, the Europeans claim that "critical dialogue" with Iran is more effective in moderating its behavior. They argue that Washington's confrontational approach toward Teheran has had the opposite effect – it has strengthened the hard-liners

88. Elaine Sciolino, "Iranian Leader Says U.S. Move on Oil Deal Wrecked Chance to Improve Ties," *New York Times*, 16 May 1995.
89. This point was made at an off-the-record meeting of a group of scholars, New York, April 1996.
90. Khatami, "The Dialogue of Civilizations and Its Difficulties," *Al-Hayat*, 11 July 1997. See also Ghassan Bin Jido, "Khatami Promises to Adhere to His Program: We Will Avoid Discord with the World," *Al-Hayat*, 5 August 1997.
91. Ghassan Bin Jido, "Kharazi: Relations with America Does Not Conflict with the Revolution's Principles," *Al-Hayat*, 16 September 1997.

within the mullah regime and escalated Iran's support for militant forces in the Middle East and North Africa. France and Germany argue that Iran's worsening economic conditions make it more willing to cooperate with the industrialized West: Hence economic ties, not containment or isolation, will bring the required changes in Iran's behavior. Although unproven, the European approach is not without merit. The weight of evidence indicates that Iranian leaders have been more sensitive to Europe's security concerns by reducing their aid to Hizbollah, tempering their country's opposition to the Arab-Israeli peace process, and stating their opposition to terrorism.[92]

Frustrated and bitter as they may be, U.S. officials should keep an open mind about any serious overtures from Teheran. Initiating dialogue with Teheran would give the reformist elements within the Iranian leadership an opportunity to make good on their promises: to be neutral vis-à-vis the peace process; reject terrorism, and cease bullying their smaller Gulf neighbors. By talking with Iran, the United States might be able to find some common ground, or at least parallel interests. These interests include avoiding incidents in the Persian Gulf, averting a crisis over the future of Iraq post–Saddam Hussein, cooperating on ways to end the bloody Afghan war, and agreeing on a set of implicit understandings regarding security issues, such as nuclear proliferation and humanitarian and political-economic cooperation in Bosnia, the Caucasus, and Central Asia.[93]

92. "Rafsanjani: We Support the Palestinian Struggle"; "Iran Eases Stand on Peace Process"; Barzin, "Iran Rides High," pp. 4–5. In April 1997, European-Iranian relations suffered a critical setback when a German court concluded after a three-year trial that the highest levels of Iran's "political leadership ordered the September 1992 killing of exiled Kurdish dissidents in Berlin." Although Germany and other European governments suspended the policy of "critical dialogue" with Teheran, they did not abandon the dialogue altogether, insisting that the policy served a purpose in moderating abuses of human rights by Iran. See Alan Cowell, "Berlin Court Says Top Iran Leaders Ordered Killings," *New York Times*, 11 April 1997, and "Mixed Responses from Europe on Ruling Linking Iran to Killings," *New York Times*, 30 April 1997.
93. The July 1996 prisoner exchange between Israel and Lebanon's Hizbollah is a case in point. Another example of U.S.–Iranian cooperation revolves around development and transport of oil in the Persian Gulf

Although the Iranian regime's behavior is worrisome, Iran's threat to U.S. interests is limited. Confronting Iran will not force political change in Teheran; on the contrary, it might have the opposite effect. The clerics, who pin the blame on Washington for all the miseries wrought by the revolution, might finally succeed in portraying their differences with Washington as part of a cultural clash between Islam and the Christian West.[94]

To his credit, President Clinton flatly rejected the clash-of-civilizations hypothesis. But the U.S. policy of blanket hostility is tilting the internal balance of forces in favor of the radical ruling mullahs. It also provides them with plenty of ammunition to use in their fight against the alien West and its "cultural threats." Paradoxically, Clinton's confrontational approach toward Iran's revolutionary Islam might result in the very clash of civilizations that he has decisively rejected.

and the Caspian Sea. See Steven Lee Myers, "White House Says Iran Pipeline Won't Violate Sanctions Act," *New York Times*, 28 July 1997; Barbara Crossette, "U.S. and Iran Cooperating on Ways to End Afghan War," *New York Times*, 15 December 1997.
94. Ghassan Bin Jado, "Khamenei Stresses the Need to Preserve Fundamentalism and Warns Against the 'Threat of Cultural Invasion,'" *Al-Hayat*, 11 December 1996.

7

Algeria

In spite of its leadership role within the nonaligned movement, Algeria historically has never figured prominently in U.S. thinking. Yet the current Algerian crisis touches on many sensitive questions that affect American interests and allies in North Africa and beyond. These questions include serious concerns about European security (floodtide of Algerian refugees, radicalization of Europe's Muslim communities, and disruption of economic trade); more contentious Franco-American relations; bolder Islamic movements in Egypt, Tunisia, Morocco, and Libya; and the potential for increased tensions between the worlds of Islam and the West.

Most importantly, however, the U.S. response to the bloody events in Algeria serves as a test case demonstrating the way American policy makers view political Islam and the affinity between Islam and democracy. Likewise, among many Muslims, Algeria is seen as an example of the ways in which the West could potentially reconcile itself with Islam and the United States could tolerate and coexist with a popularly elected Islamic government. Some Islamic leaders have warned that the West's support for the interruption of the democratic process in Algeria could alienate Muslims from Western values, driving them further away from democracy.[1]

Does the Clinton administration's stand on the Algerian crisis differ substantively from that of the Bush administration? In contrast

1. Rashid Ghannoushi, "Islamic Civilization Need Not Clash with Western Civilization," in *Islam: Opposing Viewpoints*, pp. 50–1; R. Scott Appleby, "Democratization in the Middle East Does Not Threaten the West," ibid, p. 229; Robin Wright, "Islam, Democracy, and the West," *Foreign Affairs*, p. 137.

to Bush, has Clinton adopted an accommodationist strategy toward the Islamist opposition in Algeria as represented by the Algerian Islamic Salvation Front (FIS)? If so, is the Clinton administration's position on Algeria an extension of its more nuanced and liberal approach toward Islamists in general? Or does the administration's response to the Algerian Islamists represent the exception rather than the rule?

Clinton's Initial Stand on Algeria: "Concerned Watchfulness"

Unlike the Bush administration, which initially deferred to France in its support of the military government and which sought to exclude "the radical fundamentalists," the Clinton administration from the start developed a "nuanced, sensitive" appreciation of the FIS and the realities of the political situation in Algeria. It attempted to strike a balance between the Islamists – as represented by the FIS – and the Algerian regime, seeking in a low-key manner to nudge the two warring parties into a reasonable compromise. Although the Clinton administration has refused to take sides in the Algerian civil war, it quietly pressed the Algerian government to proceed with the canceled elections, clean up its appalling human-rights record, overhaul its socialist economy, and begin serious negotiations with the mainstream Islamist opposition.[2]

Furthermore, between 1993 and 1994, the Clinton administration distanced itself from the Algerian regime by shunning high-level diplomatic contacts with the Zeroual government and criticizing the military's human-rights abuses. No senior U.S. official visited Algiers until after the 1995 Algerian presidential elections. American diplomats feared that high-level contacts with the Algerian regime would be viewed as a blank check of support for the "eradicators" – those who advocate a total war against the Islamists – within the military.[3]

In late 1993, the U.S. government also established discreet talks

2. Stephen S. Rosenfeld, "Through the Minefield of Political Islam," *Washington Post*, 31 March 1995; Christopher Dickey, "Islam Is Not the Issue," *Newsweek*, 30 May 1994.
3. Andrew J. Pierre and William B. Quandt, "Algeria's War on Itself," *Foreign Policy*, p. 147, *The Algerian Crisis: Policy Options for the West*

with an FIS representative, Anwar Haddam, who was permitted to take up residence in the United States. Some observers argued that the Clinton administration's contacts with the FIS should be seen more properly as an "insurance" policy to prevent the United States from becoming the "Great Satan" in Algerian eyes, as it did in the eyes of the Iranian mullahs, just in case the FIS should seize power.[4]

Some Clinton officials maintain that their new approach toward Algeria could be explained by the need to place things in time: "Time is a critical factor in policy analysis because it creates new contingencies and realities."[5] When Clinton assumed office in January 1993, the security situation in Algeria had rapidly deteriorated. There was a growing belief among U.S. officials and Western governments that the military regime was losing ground to Islamists, who were bound to seize power sooner rather than later. As a State Department official put it: "We faced a stalemate in Algeria. The longer the stalemate lasts the more dangerous the situation becomes. As a result, the moderate Islamic factions will be marginalized. Hence the Clinton administration advocated a compromise solution in Algeria out of pragmatism, not of any deep philosophical inclination."[6]

This feeling of urgency explained Washington's determination to bolster the moderate elements within the Algerian opposition. But far from attempting to undermine the Algerian government, U.S. initiatives were designed to prevent its collapse, and the ascent to

(Washington, DC: Carnegie Endowment for International Peace, 1996), p. 55; Charles Lane, "Rock the Casbah," *New Republic*, 27 February 1995, p. 13.

4. Daniel Williams, reporting in the *Washington Post*, 1 April 1995; Dickey, "Islam Is Not the Issue"; Haq Farhan, "Algeria–U.S.: Washington Reaches out to Muslim Moderates," *Inter Press Service*, 6 March 1995; James Phillips, "The Rising Threat of Revolutionary Islam in Algeria," *The Heritage Foundation: Backgrounder*, 9 November 1995, p. 11.

5. Interview with a State Department official, Washington, DC, 28 March 1995. A similar point was made by another member of the State Department's Policy Planning Staff, interview, Washington, DC, 27 March 1995.

6. Interview, Washington, DC, 28 March 1995. An NSC official in an interview on the following day was more blunt: "The Clinton administration had a strong feeling that it could not stand in the way of the inevitable because it was unwise."

power of Islamists, by calling for a power-sharing arrangement between the two warring parties.[7] In fact, the FIS–leaning policy was
largely devised by two junior State Department officials. This policy
came to an end in 1995 when Pelletreau moved these two junior
officials to other duties.[8]

Between 1993 and 1995, senior Clinton officials set out U.S.
thinking on Algeria in a series of testimonies before the Subcommittee on Africa of the House International Relations Committee. In
May 1993, former Assistant Secretary of State of Near Eastern Affairs Djerejian said that the current situation in Algeria had its roots
in the frustration of a populace whose basic economic and political
aspirations remain unmet. Djerejian repeatedly chastised the Algerian regime for its failure to implement real economic and political
reform: "[W]e cannot help but recognize gaps between official goals
and practice."[9]

Djerejian further criticized the Algerian government for making
little progress in restoring the democratic process and improving its
"disturbing" human-rights record. Algeria's problems, he noted,
cannot be resolved through security means, while political, economic, and social problems are not addressed.[10] Djerejian's testimony
was an explicit indictment of the military junta – an impressive,
substantive shift from the position of the Bush administration.

Almost a year later, the civil war escalated dangerously, claiming

---

7. Bruce Riedel, who was then responsible for long-term forecasting at the
   National Intelligence Council and a former director for Near East and
   South Asian affairs at the National Security Council, said that a political
   settlement was an urgent necessity to divert catastrophe in Algeria. For
   without a peaceful solution, warned Riedel, the Algerian crisis threatens
   the security and economic stability of the Maghreb and spurs regional
   tensions, endangering energy supplies for Southern Europe. See Riedel,
   Quandt, Richard Falk and Thomas Mattair in "The Middle East: What
   Is our Long-Term Vision," a discussion held by the Middle East Policy
   Council, in *Middle East Policy* 3, no. 3 (1994), p. 2.
8. Private correspondence with William Quandt, 7 October 1996.
9. Testimony in "Hearings and Recommendations for U.S. Foreign Assistance to Africa Before the Subcommittee on Africa of the House Committee on Foreign Relations," printed in *Foreign Assistance Legislation for
   Fiscal Year 1994*, pt. 7, 12 May 1993.
10. Ibid.

more than 40,000 lives.[11] As the fighting grew bloodier, militant elements, such as The Armed Islamic Group (GIA), eclipsed mainstream Islamists as represented by the FIS. The marginalization of the FIS was taken very seriously by the Algerian regime, as well as by the Clinton administration. To shore up its legitimacy, the military junta appointed Defense Minister Liamine Zeroual as president of Algeria in January 1994.

Mark Paris, acting assistant secretary for Near Eastern affairs, acknowledged the serious challenges facing the Algerian government and the danger that the country was coming apart. Fearing that "extremists" were gradually eclipsing "moderates" within the Algerian Islamist movement, Paris stressed the need for the Algerian regime to broaden political participation and to include Islamist leaders who reject terrorism. Paris was very vocal in his criticism of the Algerian government and its unwillingness to undertake real political and economic reforms. In his testimony he bluntly warned the Algerian authorities about the pitfalls of relying on repressive policies: "In the absence of serious political change, violence is likely to continue to escalate and threaten Algeria's stability."[12]

Paris' testimony was designed to send an unambiguous message to the military regime: The FIS could not and should not be crushed by force because it has become an important feature of Algerian politics. Paris also made an important distinction between "moderate" Islamists, as represented by the FIS, and other armed radical Islamist elements. Obviously, the Clinton administration viewed the FIS in a positive light and called for its co-option, rather than its exclusion. This recognition reflected the administration's nuanced approach toward the Algerian Islamists and the progressive evolution of American policy.

Despite their preoccupation with the security situation in Algeria, Clinton officials underscored the importance of the resumption of the democratic process and respect for basic human rights. In the Algerian case, initially, the administration was true to its principles by attempting to push the military regime into opening up the po-

11. *New York Times*, 6 March 1995.
12. "Update on the Crisis in Algeria," statement before the Subcommittee on Africa of the House Foreign Affairs Committee, 22 March 1994, pp. 196–7.

litical system. However, given the absence of U.S. bilateral aid programs with the Algerian government, Djerejian and Paris recognized the limits of Washington's influence and expressed their reluctance to take any concrete measures to help resolve the simmering crisis.[13]

Robert Pelletreau added new nuances to the U.S. interpretation of the internal struggle for power in Algeria. The rise of political Islam, stated Pelletreau, could be ascribed to socioeconomic inequities and "a search for a unique identity grounded in tradition."[14] Like his colleagues in the State Department, Pelletreau indirectly cautioned the Algerian government against reliance on security measures to end the crisis. He was also blunt about the need for the Algerian government to tackle social and economic issues and broaden political participation: The solution to the Algerian crisis "lies not in a strategy of repression, but in one of inclusion and reconciliation."[15]

Pelletreau noted further that the Clinton administration was trying to impress on the Algerian regime the need to establish a dialogue with both secular and Islamist opposition elements who were willing to work toward a nonviolent solution. Unlike Paris who did not foresee any spillover effects from the Algerian crisis, Pelletreau said that further "radical Islamist gains" in Algeria could embolden extremists in Egypt, Tunisia, and Morocco – key U.S. allies in the region. Instability in Algeria could also provoke an influx of refugees into France and other countries in Western Europe. Moreover, Pelletreau cautioned against making sweeping generalizations about the Islamic revival in North Africa. This revival, he stressed, was too diffuse and varied to be called a movement.[16]

In October 1995, echoing Pelletreau's concerns, Bruce Riedel, deputy assistant secretary for Near Eastern and South Asian affairs,

13. Ibid., p. 197, and Djerejian testimony in "Hearings and Recommendations for U.S. Foreign Assistance to Africa," pp. 92–3.
14. "U.S. Policy Toward North Africa; Statement Before the Subcommittee on Africa of the House Foreign Affairs Committee, 28 September 1994," *U.S. Department of State Dispatch*, 3 October 1994, p. 659.
15. Ibid., p. 660.
16. Ibid., pp. 659–60. See also Pelletreau, "Hearing of the House International Relations Committee; U.S. Assistance to the Palestinians," *Federal News Service*, 6 April 1995, p. 11.

said that the advent to power of a hostile Islamic government in Algeria carries very dangerous ramifications for U.S. defense and strategic policy throughout Europe, North Africa, and the Middle East. These include complicating Washington's military operations worldwide and possible chaos in neighboring states. According to Riedel, the United States must attempt to contain this radical Islamist insurgency in Algeria by supporting and strengthening its neighbors.[17]

Of all policy pronouncements made by Clinton administration officials on Algeria, the tone of Riedel was the most combative. This fact should not be surprising given the Defense Department's traditional focus on security issues. Riedel's statement reflected the heightened nervousness of the defense establishment, more than any real change in the U.S. approach toward Algeria. At the National Security Council, Riedel and another official pushed for more support for Zeroual and advocated a more assertive U.S. role in Algeria to assist the besieged Algerian regime.[18]

In the same month, Deputy Assistant Secretary for Near Eastern Affairs David Welch reiterated the main tenets of the U.S. approach toward Algeria: (1) condemning terrorism; (2) supporting economic reforms; and (3) calling for a broadening of the political process. Welch emphasized, however, as did Pelletreau and Riedel, the administration's fears regarding the repercussions of the Algerian crisis on key American allies. A victory by the most radical Islamists, stated Welch, could embolden extremists in neighboring North African states. Such an outcome could also provoke an influx of refugees into France and elsewhere in Western Europe.[19]

Welch hastened to add, however, that purely military means would not resolve the Algerian crisis; initiating a dialogue between the various segments of Algerian society and opening up the political field are the only viable alternatives to continued violence. In particular, Welch called on the Algerian regime to accept the national platform put forward by all major opposition parties, which had met

17. According to testimony before the House Subcommittee on Africa, 11 October 1995.
18. Private correspondence with William Quandt, 7 October 1996.
19. David C. Welch, "Terrorism in Algeria," *U.S. Department of State Dispatch*, 30 October 1995, p. 805.

in Rome under the auspices of the St. Egidio Society in 1995. He made it clear that the United States supported the spirit of the national platform as a basis to end the Algerian crisis.[20]

Several themes emerge from the various policy statements made by American officials. First, the Clinton administration admitted that the Algerian crisis was homegrown, rooted in frustration arising from political exclusion and economic inequality. Hence, the administration became convinced that security measures alone are inadequate to end the crisis. The alternative is to implement real economic and political reforms, among them liberalizing the economy and resuming the suspended electoral process. Second, the administration made a clear distinction between moderate Islamists (the FIS) and extremists (GIA). While U.S. officials supported the isolation and containment of the latter, they called for the integration of the former into the government. Finally, American diplomats recognized the potential spillover effects of the Algerian crisis on neighboring states, as well as on Europe.

Assessing the Clinton Administration's Initial Approach

Concerned as they were, U.S. officials did not accompany their public pronouncements on Algeria with any real incentives. A striking gap existed between official rhetoric and policy. During its first three years, the Clinton administration invested little political and economic capital in Algeria, deferring to its European allies instead. In other words, the United States did not engage politically or provide economic resources to help resolve the Algerian crisis. One sensed that American officials viewed Algeria as Europe's headache, that they believed Algeria's problems did not affect American interests enough to warrant a major U.S. investment.[21] Simply put, the Clinton administration did not have a policy toward Algeria; it had a "pose." Andrew Pierre and William Quandt aptly described the administration's stand as "concerned watchfulness."[22]

20. Ibid.
21. Morton I. Abramowitz, "Forward," in Pierre and Quandt, *The Algerian Crisis*, p. ix.
22. Pierre and Quandt, *The Algerian Crisis*, p. 1, and "Algeria's War on Itself," p. 146.

This pose reflected the American officials' belief that the United States could do little to bring about peaceful change in Algeria: first, because Washington has limited influence over the Algerian regime; and second, because Algeria – and North Africa in general – ranked low on the foreign-policy agenda. "Some U.S. officials go as far as to whisper this fact," intimated a State Department official.[23]

According to two knowledgeable U.S. diplomats interviewed by the author, North Africa's strategic importance was closely related to the Cold War. The Defense Department looked at this area as an alternative theater for military operations against the Soviet camp in case hostilities broke out. The end of the Cold War, coupled with the political opposition and turmoil in North Africa during the 1991 Gulf War, discredited that theory. The Defense Department is no longer interested in the area: "Events in North Africa, including Algeria, no longer have a big impact on American foreign policy."[24] An NSC official put it more bluntly: "Nobody cares about Algeria because our vital interests are not engaged there."[25]

Unlike Iran, Algeria does not evoke intense feelings, one way or another, among U.S. policy makers. It is not a hotly debated issue within the Clinton administration. In the words of a U.S. ambassador, "Although we are scared to death of militant Islamists in Algeria, we have taken a pragmatic stand toward them. We have kept some

23. Interview, Washington, DC, 27 March 1995.
24. Ibid.
25. Interview, Washington, DC, 29 March 1995. According to this source, junior officials are assigned to monitor events in Algeria. In a recent article in *Foreign Affairs*, Paul Kennedy listed Algeria as part of a small number of "pivotal states" whose future will profoundly affect their surrounding regions as well as international security. The accession of a radical Islamic regime in Algeria, argued Kennedy, would reduce political and economic security in the entire Western Mediterranean and threaten the survival of its immediate neighbors, Morocco, Tunisia, and even Egypt. It is in U.S. interests, concluded Kennedy, that the United States provide preventive assistance to the Algerian government to reduce the chance of its collapse. See Robert S. Chase, Emily B. Hill, and Paul Kennedy, "Pivotal States and U.S. Strategy," *Foreign Affairs* 75, no. 1 (January/February, 1995), pp. 34–5, 37, 46–7. Unfortunately, American officials interviewed for this book do not share Kennedy's assessment of Algeria's importance to U.S. interests.

distance."[26] Paradoxically, while the United States finds it easier to construct a sensible policy toward Algeria, it feels ambivalent about the country's strategic and political importance to U.S. primary interests; hence, the gap between Washington's impressive-sounding rhetoric and its actions.

According to some observers, the administration's perceived "neutrality" masks a hidden agenda. These critics accuse Washington of appeasing Islamists, grateful that no American oil men have been among the hundreds of foreigners killed by insurgents. Martin Kramer asserts that by talking to the FIS, the Clinton administration is buying protection for American diplomats and attempting to avoid the Iran trap: "It is quite obvious that U.S. citizens are not being harmed in Algeria."[27] Similarly, some angry Algerian officials attribute such protection to the dialogue intermittently maintained in Washington with members of the FIS and to the fact that many leaders of the latter were trained in Afghanistan at bases where the CIA once backed Islamic fighters against Soviet troops.[28]

A State Department official took issue with Kramer's assertions in an off-the-record interview: "We have been very realistic and balanced in our behavior and assessment of the sources of instability in Algeria. We have singled out the regime as well as the opposition for criticism. The Algerian regime is not innocent. The U.S. stand on Algeria is posited on the premise that the Algerian government has contributed to the escalation of violence."[29]

26. Interview with a senior U.S. ambassador, Princeton, NJ, 27 May 1995. It is not surprising, said another State Department official interviewed in Washington on 28 March 1995, that the Clinton administration's forward-leaning position on Algeria elicited a rebuke from the French.
27. Interview, Washington, DC, 31 March 1995. See also Lane, "Rock the Casbah," p. 13. Pierre and Quandt disagree with this "misplaced suspicion." Instead, they argue that Islamic groups in Algeria see no benefit in targeting American citizens and interests. See *The Algerian Crisis*, p. 26. Graham Fuller asserts that the FIS and other Islamists have consciously avoided killing American citizens to send a message to Washington. See *Algeria: The Next Fundamentalist State?* (Santa Monica, CA: Rand Corporation, 1996), monograph commissioned by the United States Army, p. 89.
28. Roger Cohen, "In Algeria, Oil and Islam Make a Volatile Mixture," *New York Times*, 28 December 1996.
29. Washington, DC, 28 March 1995.

Several other State Department officials dismiss the Iran analogy as well. They note that Clinton's position on Algeria is no longer conditioned by the polarized atmosphere of the 1980s and the fear of the Islamic Republic of Iran: Algeria is a different case from Iran; the Algerian Islamists are not as ideological as their Iranian counterparts.[30] According to these diplomats, the ideology of the Algerian Islamists is downplayed in favor of socioeconomic issues that makes sense in light of the FIS impressive showing at the polls.[31]

Furthermore, some Clinton administration officials criticized those commentators who call on Washington to support the beleaguered Algerian regime actively. How could the U.S. government, queried a State Department official, assist the Algerian regime – with arms, money, and training? Washington, added this official,

30. Both the Algerian government and the Islamist opposition attempted to exploit the Iran issue to enlist the United States on their side. The Algerian regime, for example, sent to Washington a Francophobic ambassador, who went on the lecture circuit preaching the evil deeds of all Algerian Islamists and their connection with Iran. In his campaign to alter U.S. policy by playing on the fears of Iran, the Algerian ambassador, Osmane Bencherif, accused Iran of fomenting trouble in Algeria and elsewhere, depicted Iran as the Comintern of the Muslim world. He also rejected the State Department's view that the FIS is a candidate for compromise: "It is a misguided policy to distinguish between moderate and extremist fundamentalists. The goal of all is the same: to construct a pure Islamic state, which is bound to be a theocracy and totalitarian." Cited by Daniel Williams in the *Washington Post*, 1 April 1995. Similarly, the FIS representative then in Washington, Anwar Haddam, also played on U.S. fears of Iran to influence Washington's policy toward Algeria. Haddam warned that Washington's support for the Algerian government would radicalize the struggle and make the United States unpopular, a sort of "Great Satan II." Ibid.

31. Interviews with a member of the State Department's Policy Planning Staff, Washington, DC, 27 March 1995; with a State Department official, 28 March 1995; with a senior State Department ambassador, Princeton, NJ, 27 May 1995. Jesse Helmes, chairman of the Senate Foreign Relations Committee, criticized the Clinton administration for looking for moderates among the Islamists in Algeria: "Whether you're killed by a 'moderate' fundamentalist or by a 'radical,' you're just as dead. It's too late to look for moderates in Algeria." Quoted in Daniel Pipes, "Interview with Jesse Helms," *Middle East Quarterly* (March 1995), p. 21.

has few options in Algeria: "Our policy is predicated on a realistic appraisal of our interest, influence, power, and limited leverage."[32]

In the final analysis, the U.S. stand on Algeria is a function of geopolitical and strategic interests. Although Algeria has plenty of oil and natural gas, it has had a closer relationship with Europe than with the United States. The latter has maintained a measured distance in its relations with Algeria. The farther away a country is from the main U.S. geostrategic concerns, the more nuanced American policy tends to be. This finding is consistent with one of the conceptual premises purporting to explain American foreign policy: When significant U.S. interests are not at stake in a country that is culturally and strategically distant, the United States tends to be less inclined either to rely on military might or to vigorously pursue negotiations to resolve major conflicts in that society.[33] Unlike its French counterpart, the Clinton administration can afford to be passive, or to take risks in Algeria by engaging Islamists, because of the country's geographical remoteness. The same cannot be said with regard to American policy toward Islamists in Egypt, Saudi Arabia, Iran, and the Arab-Israeli theater.

The U.S.–French Clash over Algeria

From the outset, the Clinton approach toward the Algerian Islamists has been much more liberal than that of its European ally, France. Unlike Washington, Paris does not distinguish between the various Islamists, all of whom are seen as extremists. The French have also not set any conditionality for their continuing economic aid to the Algerian government. France has provided direct aid to Algeria, totaling about one billion dollars annually.[34] In chilly meetings with their French counterparts, U.S. officials voiced their opposition to

32. Interview, Washington, DC, 28 March 1995.
33. Richard J. Payne, *The Clash with Distant Cultures*, p. xvi.
34. Pierre and Quandt, *The Algerian Crisis*, pp. 41–2; Mathew Connelly, "Déjà Vu All Over Again: Algeria, France, and U.S.," *National Interest*, no. 42 (Winter 1995–96), p. 35. Recently, France reduced its aid to Algeria by half ($600 million), according to Jean-Pierre Tuquoi in *Le Monde*, 26–27 June 1996.

the Algerian military's crackdown on Islamists and expressed their preference for a negotiated settlement.[35]

Throughout much of 1993 and 1994, the French attacked American motives for meeting with Islamists, suspecting the U.S. government of favoring the FIS over the Algerian regime. At one point in 1994, U.S.–French differences over Algeria captured newspaper headlines when French Interior Minister Charles Pasqua accused Washington of harboring Algerian "fundamentalist terrorists." Another French official said that Washington "lacks logic" by accusing Iran of sponsoring international terrorism, while urging a compromise with its proxies in Algeria. It was also reported that President Clinton and the late French President François Mitterrand clashed on the issue when they met in June 1995.[36]

The conflicting views on Algeria of Washington and Paris are compounded by historical, geopolitical, and domestic concerns. The French are upset because they see a repeat of the unwelcome U.S. involvement in their Algerian crisis of the late 1950s. French writers criticize the United States for, on the one hand, having let the Shah of Iran fall, yet now on the other, wanting to "play the FIS card" to secure preeminence in the Arab world. Furthermore, because France has a Muslim population of about three million, mostly from North African countries, the crisis there touches an important domestic nerve in Paris. France feels touchy about attempts by the Algerian Islamists to infiltrate its Muslim community and possibly inundate France with refugees.[37]

There is less to U.S.–French differences than meets the eye, however. Neither France nor Washington would welcome a victory by Islamists. As stated previously, the U.S. foreign-policy elite is very ambivalent about political Islam, especially in the Persian Gulf and the Arab East. American and French differences stem from their respective historical engagements in Algeria. American officials do not feel as strongly about Algeria as France does. Historically, the United States developed close links with Morocco and Tunisia, not

35. Lane, "Rock the Casbah," p. 13.
36. Pierre and Quandt, "Algeria's War on Itself," p. 145; Andrew Borowiec, "French–U.S. Clash over Algeria Policy Escalates," *Washington Times*, 5 August 1994.
37. Borowiec, "French–U.S. Clash over Algeria Policy Escalates"; Lane, "Rock the Casbah," p. 13.

with Algeria. The latter remained peripheral to American interests. Unlike France, the United States can afford to engage in discreet talks with the FIS – a low-risk strategy involving minimal costs.

Apart from this symbolic gesture, Washington has offered no tangible concessions to Islamists. Furthermore, U.S. contacts with Haddam, the FIS representative in Washington, were discontinued in 1995. In December 1996, the Immigration and Naturalization Service (INS) arrested Haddam for violating his residence status. However, he later accused the U.S. government of imprisoning him because of his political beliefs.[38] Indeed, by the time when Haddam was incarcerated in 1996, the Clinton administration appeared to have given up on the FIS and to have thrown its political weight almost entirely behind the Zeroual government. As the *New York Times* reported, presented with a choice between an authoritarian military-backed government and the violent currents of political Islam, the Clinton administration tended to side with the army and its repression – in a civil war that has already taken about eighty thousand lives since 1992.[39]

Thus, contrary to French and popular Algerian belief, American policy makers do not wish to see Islamists gain the upper hand in Algeria. The United States, along with France, has helped the Algerian regime stay afloat by assisting the Algerians to secure aid from international lending institutions. In 1994, the IMF granted Algeria a $1 billion standby credit for rescheduling its debt and in 1995, $1.8 billion to support its cautious free-market reforms.[40] The Export-Import Bank supplied $2 billion in loan guarantees for American projects in Algeria, and the U.S. government provided an additional $550 million in agricultural credits to Algeria.[41] Since 1995, Ameri-

---

38. Pierre and Quandt, *The Algerian Crisis*, p. 52; "Anwar Haddam Is on Food Strike: Grant Me Political Asylum or Hand Me in to Algeria," *Al-Hayat*, 16 May 1997.
39. Cited by Roger Cohen, "In Algeria, Oil and Islam Make a Volatile Mixture," 28 December 1996, and "25 Killed at Faked Roadblocks in Algeria," 30 November 1997.
40. Pelletreau's statement before the House subcommittee on Africa, "U.S. Policy Toward North Africa," p. 660; Phillips, "The Rising Threat of Revolutionary Islam in Algeria," p. 13; Lane, "Rock the Casbah," p. 13.
41. Jason F. Isaacson, "On the Threat of Islamic Extremism in Africa," prepared testimony before the Subcommittee on Africa, House Com-

can and European companies have signed billions of dollars worth of oil and gas contracts with the Algerian government.

By early 1995, U.S.–French differences over Algeria had narrowed considerably. The French came closer to Washington's point of view in their evaluations of the Algerian crisis. They joined Washington in welcoming talks between the FIS and secular opposition parties, expressing the hope that political dialogue might ease the crisis. Washington and Paris also gave verbal support to St. Egidio's national platform and hoped that it would lead somewhere. Unfortunately, nothing came out of the national platform, and the coalition that signed it did not work together very well. In a further sign full of symbolism, French aid to Algeria was reduced by half. The French also recognized the need for a limited involvement by their Western allies in Algeria to help restore peace. Although by 1997 French senior officials criticized the violence of both Islamists and the state, they still refused to link their economic aid to the pursuit of real democratization in Algeria.[42]

A New Policy: "Positive Conditionality"

By the end of 1995, a new U.S. approach toward Algeria appeared to be crystallizing. The Clinton administration viewed the outcome of the November 1995 presidential elections – Zeroual won a comfortable majority – as presenting a window of opportunity to resolve the Algerian crisis. American officials were concerned, however, that the "eradicators" within the Algerian military might interpret the election results as a mandate to intensify their crackdown against Islamists. To forestall such a possibility, the Clinton administration sent some signals to Zeroual, indicating a new willingness to become

mittee on International Relations," *Federal News Service*, 6 April 1995, p. 3.

42. Jean-Pierre Tuquoi in *Le Monde*; Heba Saleh, "The FIS Calls a Cease-Fire," *Middle East International*, 10 October 1997, p. 14. "Jospin Criticizes the Violence of the Government and the Islamists in Algeria," *Al-Hayat*, 1 October 1997; Randa Taqi al-Din, "France's Algeria Policy Is in Crisis," *Al-Hayat*, 1 February 1997; Roger Cohen, "A Chance to Try to End an Agony," *New York Times*, 2 February, 1997; Farhan, "Algeria–U.S.," p. 6; Pierre and Quandt, "Algeria's War on Itself," p. 145, and *The Algerian Crisis*, p. 30.

more actively engaged in Algeria on the condition that he follow through on his reform promises. In 1995 and 1996, Clinton wrote two letters to Zeroual, urging him to be inclusive – to reach out to as wide a spectrum of the nonviolent opposition as possible in seeking national reconciliation and economic reforms. Clinton also informed Zeroual that the U.S. government would support him as he took steps to broaden and accelerate that process.[43]

In March 1996 Pelletreau visited Algeria – the first senior U.S. official to visit the country since 1992. At a news conference in Algiers, Pelletreau said that the Clinton administration was prepared to strengthen its support for President Zeroual's efforts to end civil strife with Islamic fundamentalists. The assistant secretary applauded Zeroual for his intent to engage the opposition in dialogue and open up the political process. Pelletreau also praised Algeria for its participation in the "Summit of Peacemakers" at Sharm el-Sheikh, Egypt, in support of the Arab-Israeli peace process, and in the global fight against "terrorism."[44] The visit, concluded Pelletreau, gave him a better understanding of the challenges facing the Algerian government and its policies.[45]

Testifying before the Senate Foreign Relations Committee a month later, Pelletreau elaborated further on the administration's

43. Cohen, "In Algeria, Oil and Islam Make a Volatile Mixture."
44. In addition to using the Iran issue, the Algerian government has attempted to manipulate U.S. concerns for regional stability, such as the fight against terrorism, illegal immigration, and the proliferation of weapons of mass destruction, to obtain Washington's support in combating the Islamist opposition. The Algerian government tried to join the Arab-Israeli peace process as part of a broader public relations effort to obtain needed Western political, economic, and military assistance. See John Entelis, "Islamic Activism in North Africa: The View from Within – Algeria and Tunisia," unpublished paper given at the Institute for National Strategic Studies, National Defense University, Department of Defense, Washington, DC, 29 March 1996, pp. 31–2. Algeria's efforts seem to have borne fruit. Pelletreau and other U.S. officials praised Algeria's participation in the peace process and the fight against terrorism.
45. "U.S. Voices Support for Algeria Bid to End Civil Strife," *Reuters*, 12 April 1996. The Algerian press interpreted Pelletreau's visit and statements as a strong indication of U.S. support for Zeroual. Pelletreau said he was not surprised by the Algerian media's response to his visit because of the polarized situation in Algeria.

new thinking toward Algeria. The U.S. government, intimated Pelletreau, interpreted the 1995 presidential elections in Algeria as enhancing the legitimacy of the Zeroual government. He expressed "cautious optimism," however, warning that much remains to be done with regard to liberalizing the economy and consolidating progress toward political openness. The twin process of economic and political liberalization holds the key to stabilizing the situation over time, added Pelletreau. But this process, stressed the assistant secretary, "must be real. Words, however positive, will not be enough: actions are required."[46]

Thus, U.S. policy continued to emphasize the need for national reconciliation and political pluralism in Algeria. From the outset, the Clinton administration has been consistent in this stance. The 1995 presidential elections in Algeria have had two major implications for American policy. First, the election results legitimized Zeroual in U.S. eyes, making him a credible source with whom to discuss any prospects for finding a solution to the Algerian quagmire. During his visit to Algiers, Pelletreau told Zeroual that Washington would find ways to help him as he makes progress toward economic and political reforms: "[W]e state it as a positive conditionality."[47] Pelletreau added the word "positive" so as not to sound threatening or interventionist. (Algerians tend to be highly sensitive over any hint of foreign intervention, given their bloody colonial experience.)

The Clinton administration decided to use economic "conditionality" as a political instrument. It made its enhanced support conditional on the Algerian government's commitment to real political reforms. According to Pelletreau, political measures alone are not enough, "but must be coupled with vigorous pursuit of a policy of political inclusion, coupled with economic reforms."[48] In American eyes, Algeria must liberalize further and privatize state-owned companies and industries. The Algerian state plays a decisive role in

46. Testimony in *Situation in Algeria; Senate Foreign Relations Committee; Subcommittee on Near Eastern and South Asian Affairs* (Washington, DC: U.S. Government Printing Office, 16 April 1996).
47. Robert H. Pelletreau, "Dealing with the Muslim Politics of the Middle East: Algeria, Hamas, Iran," speech at the Council on Foreign Relations, New York, 8 May 1996, *Muslim Politics Report*, no. 7 (May/June 1996), p. 6.
48. Ibid.

managing the economy. This development reflected the administration's new confidence in Algeria and a new willingness to take risks: Risks to Western interests have been reduced considerably. Given Islamists' diminishing political fortunes, American officials no longer fear an Islamist victory in Algeria.[49]

Nevertheless, between 1993 and 1996, the Clinton administration was consistent in attempting to nudge the Algerian government toward political openness: resuming the normal electoral process and integrating pragmatic Islamist elements into the government. In the Algerian case, it appears that the Clinton administration hoped to advance the cause of pluralism by pressing the government to implement political reforms that are inclusive rather than exclusive.

Moreover, by the end of 1995, U.S. officials appeared to be interested in upgrading their low profile by playing a more active diplomatic role in the Algerian crisis. This strategy involved encouraging the Zeroual government to negotiate with the nonviolent opposition by offering economic inducements and political backing. A tactical shift occurred in U.S. pronouncements on Algeria. In testimonies and interviews, Pelletreau showered Zeroual with praise for promising to continue the process of liberalization. He also stressed Algeria's leadership role in North Africa, the Middle East, and the greater Mediterranean region. According to Pelletreau, the importance of Algiers lies in its support for the Middle East peace process, regional stability, and sizable U.S. public and private investments in the country's hydrocarbon sector.[50]

Pelletreau's statements represented a departure from previous

---

49. William Quandt asserted that Pelletreau managed to get support for positive conditionality, with support from Ambassador Ronald Newmann. But U.S. senior policy makers did not give much thought to the new policy; they wanted to wait and see how the constitutional reforms, electoral law reform, and then the local elections would go before making up their minds. According to Quandt, American officials were not very enthusiastic about Zeroual in October 1996, but they did not see any alternative Algerian leader who had the vision or will to resolve the Algerian crisis. Private correspondence with Quandt, 7 October 1996.

50. Pelletreau, "Dealing with the Muslim Politics of the Middle East," p. 6. See also a Pelletreau interview with *Al-Hayat*, 4 February 1996.

U.S. statements on Algeria, which had played down Washington's political and material investments there. In contrast, Pelletreau's recent testimonies underscored Washington's geopolitical and economic interests in the country, raising the possibility of a deeper U.S. engagement. Obviously, the Clinton administration saw a distinct opportunity for constructive change in Algeria and hoped to "play a positive role" in encouraging compromise among the contending parties.[51]

After the 1995 elections, British, French, and American companies concluded several major energy deals worth billions of dollars with the Algerian government for the development of its oil and gas reserves. These deals were certainly tied to Zeroual's victory in the country's first pluralistic elections since 1991, signaling a new readiness on the part of big business to invest in Algeria. As an observer of the oil industry put it: "You don't spend an average of $330 million a year for the next seven years in a country where you think the Government is about to fall."[52] Both the business community and the Western powers appear to be gaining confidence in Algeria. In their view, although the brutal massacres of civilians have intensified, the most violent Islamic factions have lost popular support and have been weakened by the military's crackdown and their own internal disputes.[53]

In 1996 ARCO invested more than $1.5 billion in Algeria, and the Anadarko Petroleum Corporation invested $100 million that year alone. Dozens of American entrepreneurs working in the Algerian oil and natural gas sectors have helped the cash-poor Zeroual government collect billions of dollars in revenues.[54] Western financial assistance has enabled the Algerian regime to fight a two-pronged war – against Islamists as well as against economic stagnation. This support has dramatically tilted the balance of power in favor of the Algerian ruling elite.

51. Pelletreau, "Dealing with the Muslim Politics of the Middle East," p. 6.
52. Youssef M. Ibrahim, "Algeria Gains a Vote of Confidence with Foreign Oil Contracts," *New York Times*, 12 December 1995; "ARCO to Produce Oil with Algerians," *New York Times*, 16 February 1996.
53. Ibrahim, "Algeria Gains a Vote of Confidence."
54. Cohen, "In Algeria, Oil and Islam Make a Volatile Mixture."

Institutionalization of Violence and Retreat in U.S. Policy

Throughout the Algerian crisis, the Clinton administration has moved cautiously, hoping that Zeroual would live up to his promises by broadening the government's sociopolitical base and liberalizing the economy. However, Zeroual appears to be disinclined both to incorporate the FIS into the government or even to include it in the ongoing national dialogue, which he initiated after the presidential elections, and to let the mainstream opposition play any meaningful role in government. Time and again, Zeroual and other senior Algerian officials have claimed the war is won and have described the FIS as a chapter of Algerian history that is now closed.[55] Yet American officials' hopes that the 1996 and 1997 legislative and local elections would be fair and representative of the complex political landscape were clearly dashed.

Unconcerned about the long-term implications, the Algerian government said that a new constitution banning Islamic political parties was overwhelmingly approved in a popular referendum held in November 1996. Although this charter allows the formation of political parties, it curtails the authority of their elected representatives in parliament and concentrates too much power in the hands of the president. The latter can block or overrule legislation passed by the parliament. Furthermore, opposition parties, along with independent Algerian and Western journalists, have called into question the vote count as being marked by "widespread fraud."[56]

Opposition parties and independent observers also questioned the government's vote count in both the parliamentary and departmental

55. Roger Cohen, "Islamic Front in Algeria Calls for Truce and Peace Talks," *New York Times*, 28 September 1997. During his visit to Algiers, Pelletreau pressed Zeroual to be flexible toward the FIS's moderate elements, but to no avail. Pelletreau made this point at an off-the-record meeting of a group of scholars, New York, April 1996.
56. Roger Cohen, "Algeria Says Charter Passes, But Critics Charge Vote Fraud," *New York Times*, 30 November 1996; "Algerians Seem Poised to Embrace Authority," *New York Times*, 29 November 1996; "With Leading Party Banned, Algeria Elects a New Parliament," *New York Times*, 6 June 1997.

elections in June 1997 and November 1997 respectively.[57] A *New York Times* editorial commented that "Algeria's sham elections were not a serious exercise in democratic governance," and called on the United States and France to pressure the Algerian regime toward dialogue.[58] Nonetheless, the United States maintained an official silence after the results of the elections were announced. It not only did not challenge the final outcome but also suggested that the elections could contribute to the growth of Algerian democracy. France went further than the United States and said the results of the elections showed that "Algerians want peace and a political solution to the crisis."[59]

The U.S. official stand on Algeria has evolved dramatically since 1992. Until early 1996, the United States, at least publicly, called on the Algerian government to engage the moderate, nonviolent elements within the FIS in dialogue and to co-opt them into the political field. This position is no longer attainable. The United States no longer subscribes to this position and it no longer links a resolution of the Algerian crisis to the integration of the FIS into the political process; it appears to have given up on the FIS after it was marginalized by the more violent splintered Islamist groups and the Algerian military as well.

Instead, U.S. officials consider the legal Islamic parties, such as the Movement for a Peaceful Society and the Nehda Movement, which participated in the elections and which won 103 seats combined in the new Parliament, the true representatives of Islamist sentiments. The Clinton administration had hoped that the legislative and local elections would enable Algerians freely to choose their representatives. These hopes were misplaced. As the military-dominated security state gained the upper hand against the insurgency, it has sought to consolidate its authority by creating a veneer of legitimacy involving a tightly controlled opening to, at best, only

57. Roger Cohen, "Military Tightens Grip in Algeria Election," *New York Times*, 7 June 1997. See also "Monitors Question Algeria's Vote," *New York Times*, 10 June 1997; "Algerian Elections Were Not Problem-Free," *New York Times*, 18 June 1997; Heba Saleh, " 'Rigged' Elections," *Middle East International*, 7 November 1997, p. 14.
58. "Algeria's Sham Election," *New York Times*, 7 June 1997.
59. Cohen, "Military Tightens Grip in Algeria Election."

the formal mechanisms of elective democracy. The Algerian state tolerates the participation of a minuscule, moderate opposition so long as it does not threaten its own monopoly on power. Zeroual and the generals have no interest in sharing power with the opposition, be it Islamic or secular. The most recent elections served as a smokescreen to augment their contested authority and confer legitimacy on it. In this context, the parliamentary and local elections were not meant to empower the opposition but rather to tame it through limited co-option.

To be sure, a genuine opening of the political process would most likely lead to an internal palace coup. Far from being cohesive and united, the secretive military-backed oligarchy that rules Algeria today is deeply divided over the future of Algeria. Two factions compete for hegemony: The so-called "eradicateurs," or hard-liners, are determined to crush Islamists through force of arms and consolidate their political monopoly. Again and again, the "dialoguistes" have intermittently favored negotiation and inclusion over exclusion. In the last year or so, tensions and divisions between the two factions appear to have deepened. Zeroual's hands are tied by this acute struggle for power within the ranks of the ruling military oligarchy.

In particular, the "eradicateurs" have succeeded in undermining and even sabotaging any serious attempt to come to an accommodation with the Islamist opposition. Over the past year and a half, many Western and local observers have attributed the meteoric escalation and intensification of violence in Algeria partly to this struggle for power within the Algerian ruling hierarchy. For example, in July 1997 the Algerian government released Abbassi Madani, a leader of the FIS, as a result of previous secret peace talks between the government and the Army of Islamic Salvation, the FIS's military wing. Two months later, the Army of Islamic Salvation declared a unilateral and open-ended truce by calling on its followers to lay down their arms. Instead of reducing violence, this window of opportunity precipitated a great deal of carnage and wholesale decapitations and massacres.

The intensity and brutality of the recent violence that accompanied the release of Madani and the subsequent truce prompted observers of the Algerian scene to suspect both the hard-liners in the military establishment and the Armed Islamic Group of waging a parallel, concerted campaign to discredit those inclined toward negotiation. The ambiguities in government circles was clearly apparent after Madani was placed under house arrest two months after his release. As a Western diplomat argued, "[T]o release him and then arrest him again suggests incoherence at best and perhaps extreme tension within the Government."[60] Furthermore, Amnesty International directly accused the Algerian government of responsibility for recent massacres near Algiers.[61]

The entire Algerian political landscape is fragmented and splintered. Neither the state security apparatus nor the Islamist opposition have absolute command over the actions of their various constituencies. This fluidity makes it extremely difficult to control the spiral of violence.[62] In fact, one can safely argue that violence has become institutionalized in Algeria. On the one hand, terrorism remains the only viable instrument in the hands of militant Islamists. On the other, low-intensity warfare, while not threatening the survival of the Algerian government, may serve its interests by enabling it to exercise near total political monopoly. In the name of "national security," any viable democratic project may thus be postponed indefinitely.

For all these reasons, Algeria may witness continuing strife for the foreseeable future. Although the Algerian regime has waged an increasingly effective war against the Islamic Front, some of the more militant elements that have split from the Front still have the means to terrorize the population, as the most recent bloodletting has clearly shown. The Algerian state's legitimacy was further undermined in the eyes of its citizens when it appeared to tamper with the results of legislative and local elections in 1996 and 1997. Despite the state of emergency in Algiers, Algeria's opposition parties sent thousands of their supporters into the streets to protest the "rigging" of the elections.[63]

60. Roger Cohen, "Divisions Deepen Among Algeria's Military Rulers," *New York Times*, 11 September 1997. See also Cohen, "Algeria's Main Rebel Faction Takes Risks and Calls Truce," *New York Times*, 25 September 1997; "85 Slain in New Attack Near Algiers, Setting Off Panic," *New York Times*, 24 September 1997; Saleh, "The FIS Calls a Cease-Fire." Rashid Kashana, "Algerian Massacres and the Reconciliation Project," *Al-Hayat*, 25 September 1997.
61. "Amnesty International Requests 'International Investigation' of Massacres in Algeria," *Al-Hayat*, 19 November 1997.
62. William A. Lewis, "Algeria at 35: The Politics of Violence," *Washington Quarterly* (Summer 1996), pp. 3–18.
63. Heba Saleh, " 'Rigged' Elections," p. 14.

Tragically, the mayhem and killings have become so random and brutal that it is very difficult for outsiders to determine who is responsible. As a leader of an opposition party put it: "We live between two terrors: one of the armed groups and the other the violent response of the state."[64] Complicating the situation is the Zeroual government's obsession with secrecy and its dogged refusal to entertain any external, be it regional or international, attempt to mediate among the warring factions. When in late 1997 U.N. Secretary General Kofi Annan suggested that the U.N. offer its good offices to help resolve the deadly stalemate, the Algerian government denounced all moves to "interfere" in its internal affairs or to "internationalize" the crisis.[65]

Zeroual and the generals have nothing to worry about. Neither the United States nor any other great power has the stomach to get entangled in the Algerian quagmire, because the flow of oil and gas from Algeria has not been affected by the war. In particular, it does not appear that the U.S. government has any plans to play an active role in Algeria. Responding to calls by some Algerian opposition leaders for President Clinton to name a mediator, the State Department said it could not act without a formal request from the Algiers government, and that no such request had been made.[66] Although American private corporations have increased their investment in the Algerian oil and gas sectors, U.S. foreign policy makers have kept their distance and a low-key approach – while expressing their horror at the escalating spiral of violence and reiterating their support for the Algerian government's efforts to put an end to "the outrageous

64. Cited by Youssef M. Ibrahim, "Algeria Votes, Recalling Fateful Election of 1992," *New York Times*, 24 October 1997.

65. Rhagida Dergham, "Annan Reserves Right to Call for Dialogue in Algeria," *Al-Hayat*, 12 September 1997; Heba Saleh, "The FIS Calls a Cease-Fire," pp. 13–14; Salim Nassar, "Zeroual Attempts to Clean the Reputation of the Military Institution," *Al-Hayat*, 18 October 1997. See also "Algeria Calls On France Not to Interfere in Its Affairs," *Al-Hayat*, 2 January 1997; "Ben Bellah: Nobody Knows Who Kills in Algeria," *Al-Hayat*, 19 November 1997. To their credit, in 1998, Zeroual and the generals finally agreed to a visit by a U.N. team as long as this team does not meet with any outlawed member of the FIS.

66. Roger Cohen, "Algerian Links Rebels to 'Foreign Interests,' " *New York Times*, 25 January 1997, and "85 Slain in New Attack Near Algiers, Setting Off Panic."

massacres."[67] In 1997, the departing American ambassador, Ronald Newmann, made it clear to the Zeroual government that the United States supports "military measures, consistent with the rule of law, to protect civilians." American officials said this statement amounted to an attempt by the Clinton administration "to give a gentle push to the army to do its job."[68]

Recently, the United States has also stopped using economic "conditionality" as a political instrument. Although the State Department is in the process of reviewing U.S. policy toward Algeria, no major shifts are expected. The United States seems to support Zeroual for the lack of a better alternative. Zeroual has kept Algeria's oil and gas flowing and has at least pursued the semblance of a democratic opening. The general view in Western capitals, including Washington, is that any replacement of Zeroual might turn out to be worse.[69] It remains to be seen how the Western powers would react to Zeroual's decision to step down soon. For Algeria, Zeroual's exit would be unlikely to change the domestic political equation.

Policy Recommendations

It remains to be seen if the United States would be willing to invest significant political and economic capital in Algeria, rather than simply delegate responsibilities to its European partners. Some U.S. officials interviewed for this book cautioned that the appearance of consistency on the part of the Clinton administration is misleading, because it has not been faced with the need to make costly, critical decisions on Algeria. As an NSC official put it, "by paying lip service to the Islamist opposition and the necessity for reforms, the Clinton administration has maintained consistency on the rhetoric level without taking any action."[70]

These same officials appeared to play down the external signifi-

67. "The Clinton Administration Condemned the Outrageous Massacres in Algeria," Al-Hayat, 4 September 1997.
68. Cohen, "85 Slain in New Attack Near Algiers, Setting Off Panic."
69. "America Reviews Its Policy in Algeria: No Fundamental Shift Is Expected," Al-Hayat, 19 October 1997; Cohen, "Divisions Deepen Among Algeria's Military Rulers." See also "Washington Supports the Algerian Government in Its Military Efforts," Al-Hayat, 11 September 1997.
70. Interview, Washington, DC, 29 March 1995.

cance of the Algerian crisis. In spite of recent statements by senior American diplomats, Algeria still occupies a peripheral place in the mind of America and is not seen as a "pivotal" state in the international system. It is not surprising, noted a State Department official, that "U.S. policy toward Algeria is mostly reactive."[71]

Zeroual's unresponsiveness and the spiral of violence should not deter the United States from pressing the case for a broadening of the Algerian political system. A viable solution to the Algerian crisis lies in the ability of the opposing parties to sit down and negotiate and conclude a political pact – a compromise settlement – that preserves their survival and minimal interests. Although the shape and nature of a final settlement depends on the Algerians themselves, the United States, along with its European partners, can play a constructive role in the resolution of the conflict. They should intensify their effort to mediate between the Algerian regime and the opposition by assuring Zeroual and the military of the West's support if they are willing to take some calculated risks.

American support should thus be made contingent, as the Clinton administration did in 1996, on the Algerian government's willingness to open up the political field and be inclusive. In return, the United States and its European allies might offer the Algerian government favorable rescheduling debt provisions, renewed and increased foreign investment, and political support. The United States could convert its backing by keeping open lines of communication with Zeroual and the would-be-elected president through regular contacts by senior American officials. Pelletreau's 1996 visit to Algiers is a case in point.

At the same time, the United States should impress on the Islamist opposition the need to renounce violence, condemn the GIA's terrorist methods, and commit itself unambiguously to a pluralistic political process. American officials should make it clear to the leaders of the Islamic and secular opposition that Western support for their political aspirations will be contingent on the opposition's flexibility, tolerance, and acceptance of the rules of democratic politics.

American mediation efforts should be accompanied by inducements and incentives. These should include a high diplomatic profile, reasonable financial aid, joint political and economic ventures with

71. Interview, Washington, DC, 27 March 1995.

its European partners, particularly France, and intellectual and educational resources assisting Algeria's transition to democracy and rebuilding bridges of trust between state and civil society. If there is one specific recommendation that this essay makes it is that U.S. official should become more diplomatically engaged in Algeria. By using its good offices and prestige to mediate among the warring factions, the United States would contribute considerable in helping to resolve the simmering crisis. Most of all, however, American officials should continue to talk to all parties about the need to respect human rights and encourage real democratic openings by integrating the rising social classes into the political process.

The material costs of such an active U.S. involvement would be minimal. American officials agree that Algeria has not been seen to be of critical importance to the United States. Those same officials acknowledge, however, that Algeria serves as a symbol that touches on U.S.–European dynamics and U.S. relations with the Muslim world. Algeria is a test case whereby a truly enlightened American policy could advance the cause of democracy and the coexistence between the West and Muslim societies.

The U.S. approach to the Algerian crisis is being watched very carefully by Muslims everywhere, as well as by governments facing similar, if less violent, upheavals. The lessons of Algeria are not lost on the Arab governments, whose fear of political liberalization has been reinforced as a result of the Algerian crisis. Many of these regimes, noted François Burgat, a reputable French scholar, concluded some years ago that parliamentary elections would not protect them from being defeated by their Islamist opponents. Accordingly, they have "strengthened the prohibition made to the Islamists to accede to the institutional system and intensified a very "preventive" repression against them."[72]

Islamists have drawn parallel lessons. To them, success at the ballot box has obviously not been a guarantee for achieving power. In Islamists' eyes, the cancellation of the 1991 elections discredited the entire democratic discourse – held both by the successive

---

72. François Burgat and William Dowell, *The Islamic Movement in North Africa* (Austin: Center for Middle Eastern Studies at the University of Texas at Austin, 1993), p. 306.

Algiers regimes and their foreign supporters – thus giving more influence to the backers of radicalization within the Islamic movements.[73]

In this respect, a successful U.S. mediation effort in Algeria may play a positive role in arresting the political decay infecting most Middle Eastern states and improve the form and structure of governance in the region. The potential returns on such a U.S. "investment" in Algeria are thus very high for Algeria itself, its neighbors, as well as for the United States.

73. Ibid.

8

Egypt

While world attention has focused on the protracted confrontation between the Islamists and the Algerian regime, observers have ignored a more momentous clash, that of the Egyptian government and the Islamist opposition. Since the early 1990s, Egypt has witnessed a low-level war of attrition between the regime and Islamists, costing more than a thousand casualties and billions of dollars in damage to the tourist industry. In the early 1990s, American officials became worried about the deteriorating security situation in Egypt and the polarization between state and society. According to an unconfirmed report in The *Sunday Times* of London, as early as 1993, a National Intelligence Estimate – which represented the collective input of all American agencies – suggested that "Islamic fundamentalist terrorists will continue to make gains across Egypt, leading to the eventual collapse of the Mubarak government."[1]

Although several U.S. officials denied such an estimate, the fact remains that the United States is terribly concerned about the turn of events in Cairo.[2] In few other countries of the Middle East are American interests as involved as they are in Egypt. Egypt serves as the gate to the Arab world and the anchor of American Middle East policy because of its proximity to the oil-producing Gulf region and its active involvement in the Arab-Israeli peace process. The United States has invested heavily in Egypt, providing it with more than $2

---

1. James Adams, "Mubarak at Grave Risk of Being Overthrown by March of Islam," 20 February 1994.
2. Interview with two National Security Council officials, Washington, DC, 29 and 30 March 1995.

billion in economic and military aid each year. Since 1979 Cairo has been a close ally of Washington – initiating the peace process, facilitating Arab-Israeli negotiations, and legitimizing the U.S.-led coalition against Iraq.[3] For all theses reasons, U.S. officials have hoped that Egypt would remain a beacon of stability in a dangerous regional environment.

The American stand toward the Egyptian Islamists should be seen within this context. Unlike its posture toward Algeria, the United States cannot afford to remain distant or disengaged in the face of grave challenges to the Egyptian government, a close ally. From the outset, U.S. officials have recognized the gravity of the Egyptian crisis and the need to be engaged so as not to be caught completely off guard in case Islamists gained power. Washington has not had the luxury to reflect on how the Egyptian struggle for power would unfold. Thus, in this examination of American policy on political Islam, the situation in Egypt serves as a counterpart to Algeria.

The Internal Struggle for Power

The Mubarak regime has succeeded in containing the threat from fringe Islamist elements, like al-Jama'a al-Islamiyya and Jihad. It has scored major successes in suppressing Jama'a's and Jihad's seven-year-old campaign of violence.[4] The Egyptian state has failed, however, to win the battle for the hearts and minds of middle-class Egyptians who are alienated from the government. Al-Jama'a's and Jihad's success lies in exposing the weakness of the political system and highlighting the government's economic ineptitude and inefficacy, its dependency on foreign handouts and servitude to the United States, and, therefore, its lack of legitimacy.

This bloody clash between militant Islamists and the Egyptian regime has played into the hands of the mainstream Islamist opposition, particularly the Muslim Brotherhood. The latter tried to capitalize on the precarious security situation by pressing Mubarak to open up the political field and share power. The combina-

3. Fawaz A. Gerges, "Egyptian-Israeli Relations Turn Sour," *Foreign Affairs* 74, no. 3 (May/June 1995), p. 78.
4. Douglas Jehl, "Egypt Is Playing Down Sheik's Jail Term in U.S.," *New York Times*, 20 January 1996.

tion of security and political pressures has augmented the Egyptian state's siege neutrality. Mubarak has responded in a two-pronged way.

Internally, the Mubarak regime retreated from secular politics and culture by Islamisizing sociopolitical space. The official discourse is becoming more Islamic, with the government emphasizing the virtues of religion.[5] Nowhere is this more evident than in the domain of education and communication, particularly in television, a critical medium for shaping public opinion.[6] Islamization from within is slowly but steadily changing the character of Egypt. On a more superficial level, a visitor to Cairo easily encounters religious symbols throughout over the city, from numerous bearded men to women wearing the Islamic head covering. Unable to tackle Egypt's mounting socioeconomic problems, Mubarak also slowed down the liberalization program, which was initiated in the 1980s, and widened his crackdown on Islamic activists.[7]

Furthermore, the Egyptian state no longer distinguishes between Islamists who espouse violence and the vast majority who do not. Mubarak has unleashed the security apparatus against moderates and militants alike.[8] He accused the Muslim Brothers of collusion with al-Jama'a in undertaking "terrorist activities." When asked why he does not initiate dialogue with moderate Islamists, Mubarak re-

5. Mustapha K. Al-Sayyid, "A Civil Society in Egypt," *Middle East Journal* 47, no. 2 (Spring 1993), pp. 241–2; Sana Hasan, "My Lost Egypt," *New York Times*, Sunday, 22 October 1995, Magazine section, p. 63; Fouad Ajami, "The Sorrows of Egypt," *Foreign Affairs* 74, no. 5 (September/ October 1995), p. 77.
6 A poll conducted by a research center in Egypt showed that an overwhelming number of Egyptians, 73 percent, rely on television for news, as well as entertainment. It is worth noting that there are no television stations owned privately in Egypt. The government controls the airways. See "Sixty-Six Percent of Egyptians Do Not Pay Attention to Politics," *Al-Hayat*, 19 April 1997.
7. Douglas Jehl, "Islamic Militants' War on Egypt: Going International," *New York Times*, 20 November 1995, and "In the Face of Criticism, Egypt Sentences 54 Muslim Leaders," *New York Times*, 24 November 1995.
8. "Where Islam Recruits," *Economist*, 12 November 1994, p. 14; Fahmi Howaidi, "Political Thinking!" *Al-Ahram*, 2 March 1993; Ahmed Abdallah, "Egypt's Islamists and the State," *Middle East Report* (July/August 1993), p. 29.

torted: "Who are the moderates? Nobody has succeeded in deline-ating them for me."[9] In the aftermath of the November 1997 Luxor terrorist attack in which sixty-eight foreigners and Egyptians were killed, Mubarak dismissed the possibility of initiating a dialogue with militant Islamists: "Dialogue with whom? It will be the dialogue of the deaf. We had had a dialogue with them for fourteen years, and every time we engaged them, they became stronger . . . Dialogue is old-fashioned. The ones who are asking for dialogue do not know [Islamists]. We know them better."[10]

In August 1995 Egyptian authorities arrested and put hundreds of the Brotherhood's leading figures on trial in a special military court formerly reserved for terrorist suspects.[11] Egyptian courts also or-dered the closure of some professional syndicates controlled by the Brothers so as to restrict their political activities.[12] The Mubarak regime went further by restricting the activities of Egyptian human-rights and nongovernmental organizations.[13]

Externally, Mubarak accused Iran, Sudan, and veterans of the Afghan war of sponsoring terrorism and fueling Islamic violence in Egypt and elsewhere in the region. He has tried to portray the internal struggle for power in Egypt as part of an international campaign orchestrated and financed by Islamic Iran and Sudan: "We are confronting foreign plots and attempted intervention."[14]

9. Mohammed Saleh, "Mubarak: 'The Brothers' Practice Terrorist Activ-ities," *Al-Hayat*, 27 September 1995.
10. Jihan al-Husseini and Ishraf al-Fiqi, "Mubarak: The Terrorists in Brit-ain and No Dialogue with Them Because It Strengthens Them," *Al-Hayat*, 24 November 1997.
11. Mohammed Saleh, "Egypt: The Moment of Reckoning for the Muslim Brothers," *Al-Wasat*, 7 August 1995, pp. 14–17.
12. *Al-Hayat*, 29 January 1996; Wahid Abd al-Majid, "A Fundamentalist Threat?" *Al-Hayat*, 28 July 1997.
13. Mohammed Saleh, "Egypt: Confrontation Between the Government and Human Rights Organizations," *Al-Hayat*, 10 August 1995, p. 7; Denis J. Sullivan, "State and Civil Society in Conflict in Egypt," *Journal of Middle East Affairs* 3, no. 1–2 (Winter/Spring 1997), pp. 72–7.
14. "U.S.–Egyptian Search for Peace and Stability in the Middle East: President Clinton and President Mubarak's News Conference," *U.S. Department of State Dispatch*, vol. 4, no. 15, 12 April 1993, p. 227. See also *Al-Hayat*, 11 August 1995, p. 5, and *Al-Hayat*, 28 August 1995, p. 1.

Mubarak felt assured that his attempt to implicate Iran and Sudan in the internal violence in Egypt would find receptive ears in the United States, which has branded the two countries as "rogue" and "terrorist" states. But Mubarak's difficulties have proved to be much more complex than trying to pin the blame on a few neighbors. For example, after al-Jama'a's devastating attack on Luxor, Mubarak lashed out angrily against Britain and other European states for granting political asylum for Egyptian "terrorists" under the pretext of human rights: "I believe that if the world had cooperated against terrorism, the Luxor strike would not have happened. The terrorists have protection in Britain and other European countries, while they commit their crimes, collect money, and plan with the Afghani elements, who are all killers."[15] Mubarak had earlier warned European countries that granted asylum to Islamist militants, cautioning that such countries would "one day pay a very high price."[16]

Mubarak's strategy is designed to divert world attention from Egypt's simmering internal difficulties and its crisis of political legitimacy. He also hopes to enlist U.S. assistance in the fight against Islamic activists in Egypt and beyond. Besieged and frustrated in his effort to get Washington to support him fully, however, Mubarak criticized the Clinton administration for failing to take a more active role in the war against international terrorism. He also accused the U.S. administration of having secret contacts with "terrorists" from the Muslim Brotherhood: "You think you can correct the mistakes that you made in Iran, where you had no contact with the Ayatollah Khomeini and his fanatic groups before they seized power. But, I can assure you, these groups will never take over this country; and they will never be on good terms with the United States."[17]

Mubarak blamed the United States for creating the basis for an international Islamic network by supporting the Afghan mujaheden

---

15. "Mubarak: The Terrorists in Britain; no Dialogue with Them Because It Strengthens Them."
16. "Egypt Is Upset by Britain's Noncooperation in Combatting Terrorism," *Al-Hayat*, 30 November 1997; Jehl, "Islamic Militants' War on Egypt."
17. Mary Anne Weaver, "The Battle for Cairo," *New Yorker*, 30 January 1995, p. 69. See also *New York Times*, 3 and 5 April 1993 and 20 November 1995.

against the Soviet invaders: The United States should play "a tough role" in putting the Islamic genie back into the bottle again.[18] After the 1993 World Trade Center blast, Mubarak declared that that attack might have been prevented had U.S. officials heeded his country's warning about the existence of an "Islamic fundamentalist" network in the United States.[19] Mubarak called on the United States to commit itself in the fight against international terrorism, particularly Islamic fundamentalist groups and their state sponsors – Iran, Sudan, and the mujaheden in Afghanistan.[20]

Mubarak wanted to influence U.S. policy on political Islam as well as belittle the importance of the Islamist opposition to his beleaguered regime. He also felt anxious about U.S. openings to the Algerian Islamic Salvation Front (FIS) and the implications for American policy toward Islamists in the whole region.

The Clinton Administration's Initial Flirtation with Islamists

As mentioned previously, in the first half of the 1990s U.S. officials became worried about the precarious situation of the Mubarak regime. While the Egyptian government was battling al-Jama'a, Jihad, and other fringe groups, the Muslim Brotherhood was positioning itself as an alternative political force and moderate voice. Indeed, the Brotherhood was the main beneficiary of the bloody confrontation between the state and al-Jama'a. The Mubarak government's harsh

18. Elaine Sciolino, "Egypt Warned U.S. of Terror, Mubarak Says," *New York Times*, 5 April 1993. Another official echoed Mubarak's accusation by blaming U.S. security services for creating the "Arab Afghani" phenomenon. See Hussam Kamal, "Egyptian Official Blames America for the 'Arab Afghani' Phenomenon," *Al-Hayat*, 26 May 1997.
19. When asked to comment on Mubarak's remarks, Laurence Pope, acting coordinator for counter-terrorism at the Department of State, disputed Mubarak's account. Pope said that Egypt did not provide any "information concerning possible terrorist acts to be carried out in the United States." See *Hearing of the Senate Judiciary Committee, Terrorism and America: A Comprehensive Review of the Threat, Policy, and Law, 21 April 1993*, p. 32.
20. *New York Times*, 5 April 1993.

crackdown against the Brotherhood has failed to stem the latter's popularity, however.[21]

The Brotherhood remains politically the most effective opposition force in Egypt. As one informed Egyptian writer already noted five years ago, the Muslim Brotherhood "is becoming a pole of power for a radical but non-violent Islamist alternative in Egypt. If free elections were held now, a repetition of the Algerian episode would be a serious prospect."[22] The more the Egyptian state attempts to suppress the Brotherhood, the more it plays into the latter's hands. Exclusion and suppression have failed to tame or weaken the main-stream Islamist opposition.

Although they are sensitive to Mubarak's difficulties, U.S. officials do not buy his assertion that al-Jama'a's attacks are part of a foreign plot or a scheme coordinated with the Muslim Brothers. Hence, in the early 1990s American diplomats stationed in Egypt established discreet contacts with some of the Brotherhood's leaders in order to collect information and keep diplomatic channels open to moderate Islamists.[23] Mubarak misread Washington's flirtation with the Brothers. Neither the Bush nor the first Clinton administration was giving up on the Egyptian regime; rather, the United States wanted to be ready to absorb any potential reverberations of a sudden political earthquake in Egypt.

A National Security Council official expressed his frustration over this Egyptian misunderstanding of Washington's behavior toward

21. Egyptian authorities have asserted that al-Jama'a and the Brotherhood represent two sides of the same coin. They claim further that both organizations coordinated their activities so as to maximize the political payoff. See Mohammed Saleh, "Mubarak: 'The Brothers' Practice Terrorist Activities." Some Egyptian writers accuse the Brothers of believing in the use of violence as a legitimate instrument in their political struggle. See, for example, Hala Mustapha, "The Brothers and the Egyptian State: New Confrontation," *Al-Wasat*, 7 August 1995, pp. 18–19. See also her book in Arabic, *The State and the Islamic Opposition Movements: Between Truce and Confrontation During the Sadat and Mubarak Administrations* (Cairo: Markaz Al-Mahrousa Lilnasahr, 1995); Joseph Kechichian and Jeanne Nazimek, "Challenges to the Military in Egypt," *Middle East Policy* 5, no. 3 (September 1997), p. 133.
22. Abdallah, "Egypt's Islamists and the State," p. 30.
23. Several U.S. officials acknowledged holding such contacts with some Egyptian Islamists.

Islamists: "Meeting with Islamic leaders is distinct from policy. Incumbent regimes are not the only actors with whom the U.S. government maintains relations. Opposition actors have a role to play. Islamists are important players in the Middle East and North Africa."[24] This NSC official did not discern any contradiction between holding discussions with some Islamists who use violence, and U.S. policy statements, which make clear distinctions between moderate and extremist Islam: "Collecting information is traditional diplomacy. This is true of American contacts with other non-Islamic organizations. The United States seeks neither protection nor the establishment of close ties with Islamists, only information gathering."[25]

Another NSC official provided a more perceptive justification for continuing U.S. contacts with certain Egyptian Islamists. The existing Middle Eastern regimes, said this official, are bound to disappear in the future because change is inevitable; one of Washington's major policy objectives is to manage the transition to a new Middle Eastern political order with minimal cost. The United States views Islamists as integral players among the broad social forces operating in the region. Thus, to survive, the dominant ruling elites will have to broaden their social base by integrating Islamists into the political field. This reality explains the rationale for the first Clinton administration's early decision to initiate a discreet dialogue with Algerian and Egyptian Islamists. The challenge facing Washington, noted this NSC official, was to maintain contacts with Islamists without antagonizing its allies: "It is a delicate thing. But we need to be in touch with the opposition."[26]

For America, resolving Egypt's crisis depended on Cairo's ability to effectively manage its pressing socioeconomic and political problems. Responding to a question about the escalation of the confrontation between the Mubarak regime and al-Jama'a in the early 1990s, Clinton said that Egypt's problems, along with those of other states, could not be seen solely in political terms but in the context of the challenge of "sustainable development, of balancing a rapidly growing population with all the pressures and problems that creates with

24. Interview, Washington, DC, 30 March 1995.
25. Ibid.
26. Interview, Washington, DC, 29 March 1995.

the need to provide for them food and shelter and education and a stable set of opportunities."[27]

In the same context, Vice President Al Gore stated that the challenge facing Egypt in the new Middle East was to rise and lead the region economically in the same manner that it had earlier led the region politically.[28] To show its commitment, the first Clinton administration created three committees on growth and development, co-chaired by Al Gore and Mubarak, that were meant to enhance and strengthen the private sector.[29] This joint partnership reflected the administration's belief that privatization and liberal capitalism would help cure Egypt's socioeconomic and political ills.

U.S. diplomats reportedly made several private demarches in the early 1990s, and Clinton himself urged Mubarak to address the underlying causes of Islamist militancy: unrepresentative government, high unemployment, social inequality, overpopulation, corruption, and the steady decline of civility in public life. Mubarak successfully resisted these discreet suggestions by U.S. officials. Looking at the Algerian crisis, he feared the destablilizing effects that would accompany a process of political liberalization in Egypt. According to an Egyptian writer, the sweeping victory of Islamists in Algeria in 1991 had sounded the death knell for democracy in Egypt: The former Egyptian minister of the interior, General Musa, declared that he would never permit an Islamist victory at the ballot box.[30]

The "Algerian complex" has not only fueled the Cairo regime's sense of insecurity toward all social groups with an Islamist bent but has also intensified the secular leaders' fears of Islamist extremists. Secular leaders have become largely dependent on the Mubarak regime for protection from religious zealots. Therefore, the government has capitalized on the support it had gotten from both right and left to crack down on Islamists of all shades – and the secular

27. "Transcript of Remarks by President Clinton and King Hassan II of Morocco in Press Conference," *U.S. Newswire*, 15 March 1995. p. 4.
28. *Al-Hayat*, 16 January 1996.
29. "U.S.–Egypt Partnership for Economic Growth and Development," text of joint communiqué issued at the inaugural meeting of the U.S.–Egyptian Sub-Committee on Economic Policy, Trade, Investment, and External Finance, Washington, DC, 2 June 1995, *U.S. Department of State Dispatch*, vol. 6, no. 24, 12 June 1995, p. 501.
30. Hasan, "My Lost Egypt," p. 61.

opposition as well. The result is that civil society and democratization suffer considerably.[31]

Reversing American Policy: Full Support for Mubarak

Mubarak felt confident that U.S. policy makers would not exert any effective pressure on Egypt lest the country plunge into a full-scale civil war with the Islamists. And such has been the case. After some initial hesitation, by 1994 the Clinton administration appears to have accepted Mubarak's version by reaffirming Washington's backing for his government. In this context, as early as 1993 American officials had accused the Sudanese government of aiding "Egyptian extremists with military training and explosions."[32] Subsequently, President Clinton voiced his support for Mubarak's fight against "religious extremism" and terrorism, saying that both countries were "absolutely determined to oppose the cowardly cruelty of terrorists wherever we can."[33]

Given Cairo's political and strategic importance to the United States, it was unlikely that the Clinton administration would say or do anything to jeopardize Egypt's internal security or Washington's close relationship with Cairo. The State Department seemed reluctant to criticize publicly the arrests and show trials of many leaders of the Muslim Brotherhood since 1995 or the increasingly abysmal human-rights situation in Egypt. American officials remained ambivalent about the Egyptian regime's increasing reliance on repression.[34]

By 1994 some Clinton administration aides were expressing their satisfaction that the Egyptian government has finally achieved some important successes in its battle against "terrorism," hastening to

31. Mona Makram-Ebeid, "Democratization in Egypt: The 'Algeria Complex,'" *Middle East Policy* 3, no. 3 (1994), pp. 119, 121, 124; Abdallah, "Egypt's Islamists and the State," p. 29.
32. See Laurence Pope testimony in *Hearing of the Senate Judiciary Committee; Terrorism and America*, p. 31.
33. "U.S.-Egyptian Search for Peace and Stability in the Middle East," p. 227; "An Arab-International Consensus on Condemning the Luxor Attack," *Al-Hayat*, 19 November 1997.
34. See the Lawyers Committee for Human Rights' annual *Critique: Review of the U.S. Department of State's Country Reports on Human Rights Practices* (Washington, DC: Lawyers Committee for Human Rights, July 1990–6).

add that democratic values and respect for human rights might become casualties.[35] Such statements reveal Washington's anxiety about political developments in Cairo, as well as its hope that the Egyptian authorities would neutralize and even eliminate the threat posed by radical Islamists.

It is not surprising that human-rights organizations are not impressed by U.S. officials' expressions of concern about the Egyptian regime's human-rights abuses. Some of them have criticized the American government for appeasing Mubarak and downplaying his government's pervasive violations of human rights. These include arrest without charge or trial, torture, killing of suspects under interrogation, and other bloody measures, according to reports by Middle East Watch and Amnesty International. The Egyptian Organization for Human Rights says it can document more than seventeen thousand people who were arrested in connection with militant violence or political opposition between 1989 and 1997. Human-rights organizations stress that the human-rights situation in Egypt is deteriorating with each passing year.[36]

Human-rights organizations also criticize U.S. policy makers for regarding Mubarak's third term as a genuine reelection, and not as a predetermined reappointment.[37] For example, the Lawyers Committee for Human Rights asserted that the State Department report on Egypt is "often ambiguous and equivocal in tone, as if reluctant to hold the Egyptian Government responsible for its human rights commitments."[38]

35. Robert H. Pelletreau, "Recent Events in the Middle East," statement before the Subcommittee on Europe and the Middle East of the House Foreign Affairs Committee, Washington, DC, 14 June 1994, *U.S. Department of State Dispatch*, vol. 5, no. 25, 20 June 1994, p. 411.

36. See the reports by Middle East Watch, *Egypt: Hostage-taking and Intimidation by Security Forces* (New York: Human Rights Watch, January 1995); *Egypt: Trials of Civilians in Military Courts Violate International Law* (New York: Human Rights Watch, July 1993); *Behind Closed Doors: Torture and Detention in Egypt* (New York: Human Rights Watch, 1992). See also the 1995 *Critique* by the Lawyers Committee for Human Rights, p. 70; Douglas Jehl, "Killings Erode Cairo's Claim to 'Control' Militants," *New York Times*, 15 March 1997.

37. See, for example, the 1996 *Critique* by the Lawyers Committee for Human Rights, pp. 61–2, and the 1993 *Critique*, pp. 88–9.

38. Ibid., for 1995, pp. 67, 71.

Several reasons account for the Clinton administration's apparent decision to cease its contacts with Islamists and side fully with Mubarak. Although weak and unpopular, the Mubarak regime had shown its resolve by crushing the military capabilities of al-Jama'a and Jihad and killing most of their effective leaders. Observers of the Egyptian scene agree that the government had succeeded more or less in disarming the most violent fringe groups, and it exacted heavy losses from the armed al-Jama'a, Jihad, and other Islamists. The security situation appeared to be stabilizing, particularly in Cairo, the nerve center of politics and economics. By 1995 U.S. decision makers no longer seemed alarmed by the Islamist phenomenon as they had been in the early 1990s.

With hindsight, it is clear that American and Egyptian officials appeared overly confident in their assessment of radical Islamists' fortunes. In effect, the Egyptian government seemed on the verge of declaring victory in its war against Islamist militants: In 1996 Hassan al-Alfi, then Egyptian interior minister, asserted that the security forces had regained "full control" over its internal affairs in the face of the bloody campaign begun by the militants more than five years ago to topple Cairo's mostly secular regime and replace it with an Islamic state.[39]

What Egyptian and U.S. officials did not take into proper account was the further splintering of the Islamist movement into more radical factions. This fragmentation would make the Cairo government's efforts to exercise "full control" almost untenable. Egyptian officials were rudely awakened to this fact in the spring and summer of 1997 when al-Jama'a and Jihad launched a series of terrorist attacks in Central Egypt, Luxor, and Cairo itself that left more than one hundred Western and Egyptian civilians dead.[40]

The importance of these renewed attacks lay not only in undercutting the Cairo government's claims of victory but also in demonstrating the staying power and extended reach of the Islamists. From 1992 until 1996, nearly all the violence had been confined to gun battles between security forces and militants in central and upper

39. Jehl, "Killings Erode Cairo's Claim to 'Control' Militants."
40. Ibid. See also Steve Negus, "Copts Massacred," *Middle East International*, 7 March 1997, p. 11, and "Tourists Slain in Cairo," *Middle East International*, 26 September 1997, p. 11.

Egypt. The Mubarak government had succeeded in isolating the parameters of the confrontation far away from Cairo and most tourist sites. But in September and November 1997, respectively, the militants successfully and brutally assaulted Western tourists in front of the Egyptian Museum in the heart of Cairo and at Luxor, killing almost one hundred civilians.

These two attacks were a painful reminder that the destruction of al-Jama'a and Jihad as organized movements did not mean an end to politically inspired violence in Egypt. The attacks also showed that the government's admittedly powerful crackdown on the militants would not by itself eliminate terrorism so long as the Mubarak regime did not address the broader issues of social reforms and political participation. To be potent, the security track must be accompanied by political measures to expand the social base of the regime and give the rising social classes new hope in the future. Otherwise, the army of the young unemployed – marginalized and alienated – will be tempted by heavenly rewards and revolution, thus keeping al-Jama'a and Jihad in business.[41]

The Beginning of the End of al-Jama'a and Jihad?

The power of the militants should not be exaggerated, however. They have suffered devastating military blows. One of the difficulties facing al-Jama'a and Jihad now is their inability to maintain lines of communication among the rank and file. Recently, several developments and incidents have exposed the existence of serious divisions, tensions, and contradictions within the two militant groups. In July 1997 the so-called historic leaders of al-Jama'a and Jihad, who are incarcerated, declared a unilateral and unconditional cease-fire and called on the leaders overseas and their followers in Egypt to refrain from armed attacks. Although dozens of the leaders of al-Jama'a and Jihad agreed to join the call for a cease-fire, their colleagues in exile refused to accept this initiative. The latter rationalized their decision by challenging the incarcerated leaders' authority and free will while being in prison.[42]

41. Wahid Abd al-Majid, "Reform to Confront Terrorism," *Al-Hayat*, 23, 7 November 1997; Negus, "Tourists Slain in Cairo," p. 11.

42. Mohammed Saleh, "Egypt: Leaders of the 'al-Jama'a al-Islamiyya' Decide to Cease Hostilities," *Al-Hayat*, 6 July 1997. Saleh, "Egypt: Two

The subtle but bitter debate engendered by the call for a cease-fire revealed a chasm in the militants' rank and file. Paradoxically, the Mubarak government joined the hard-liners in al-Jama'a and Jihad by rejecting the offer of the cease-fire. Former Interior Minister al-Alfi said the government "rejects initiating any dialogue with illegal groups." He also stressed Cairo's determination to fight and defeat the militants.[43] One would have expected the authorities to use the cease-fire offer to isolate the Islamist hard-liners further. Not only did the government fail to do so but it also undermined those leaders in al-Jama'a and Jihad who might have had seconds thoughts about terrorism. In this context, the government's shortsighted response strengthened the hard-liners and may have contributed to the prolongation of the confrontation.

Furthermore, the attack on Luxor also deepened the cleavages between al-Jama'a's incarcerated leaders and those in exile. It is reported that the imprisoned leaders "were shocked at the Luxor incident" and considered the strike a "dangerous violation of the safety vow which they extended to tourists following their call for cease-fire."[44] The fugitive leaders also questioned the usefulness of such terroristic means and gave strict orders against attacking tourist targets. A statement from al-Jama'a expressed its horror at the brutality of the massacre and said that it "has decided to stop targeting either the tourism industry or foreign tourists."[45]

Leaders of Jihad Join the Declaration of Cease-Fire," *Al-Hayat*, 10 July 1997. Saleh, "Egypt: Leaders of 'al-Jama'a' and 'Jihad' Join the Cease-Fire," *Al-Hayat*, 13 July 1997. Saleh, "Members in 'al-Jama'a and 'Jihad' Join the Cease-Fire," *Al-Hayat*, 25 July 1997. Saleh and Hussam Kamal, "Leaders of 'al-Jama'a' and 'Jihad' Overseas Reject the Cease-Fire," *Al-Hayat*, 12 July 1997. Saleh, "Egypt: Failure of Attempts to Convince Leaders of 'al-Jama'a' and 'Jihad' Overseas to Support the Cease-Fire," *Al-Hayat*, 4 August 1997. Saleh, " 'The Case of Big Assassination' in Egypt: The Accused Support the Cease-Fire," *Al-Hayat*, 25 September 1997.

43. Hussam Kamal and Mohammed Saleh, "Al-Alfi: No Dialogue with al-Jama'a al-Islamiyya in Egypt," *Al-Hayat*, 7 September 1997.
44. Mohammed Saleh, "Egypt: Imprisoned Leaders of 'al-Jama'a' Considered the Luxor Operation a Violation of the Safety Vow," *Al-Hayat*, 23 November 1997.
45. Mohammed Saleh, "Egypt: 'al-Jama'a al-Islamiyya' Decides to Stop Operations Against Tourism," *Al-Hayat*, 8 December 1997. Saleh, "Inves-

Indeed, no incident has mobilized Egyptian public opinion and
that of the Arab/Muslim world against al-Jama'a as the Luxor massacre has. In Egypt, political parties, religious leaders, and civil society organizations of all orientation condemned this deadly act and
called on the government to escalate the confrontation against terrorism. The Muslim Brotherhood described the attackers as having
no "conscience or religion."[46] Islamist governments and groups were
unequivocal in their denunciation of al-Jama'a's attack. Iranian President Mohammed Khatami wrote to Mubarak and denounced the
attack as inhuman and cowardly. So did Sudanese President Omar
Hassan al-Bashir. Mohammed Fadllalh, spiritual head of Hizbollah,
criticized the "criminal and savage" attack which can never be justified from an Islamic perspective. Palestinian Hamas denounced the
attack in the strongest possible terms. The Algerian FIS also reiterated its opposition to all crimes against civilians.[47]

Repulsive and bloody as it was, the Luxor massacre may enable
the Egyptian government to seize the political initiative from Islamists and repair broken bridges with civil society. Will Mubarak deal
with the political and social factors that fuel frustration, alienation,
and terrorism, rather than concentrate on the security aspects, as
most Egyptian opinion makers, civil and political leaders have urged
him to do? Early indications do not seem promising. Mubarak responded to the Luxor attack by dismissing his interior minister, al-
Alfi, and administering a security shake-up that he clearly hopes will
help salvage the tourist industry. For the first time, the army will

tigations Inside the 'al-Jama'a al-Islamiyya' Looks at Irregularities in the
Luxor Operation," *Al-Hayat*, 29 November 1997. See also "Rebel
Group Forswears Tourist Attacks in Egypt," *New York Times*, 9 December 1997. One ought to be suspicious of al-Jama'a's declared motives
behind its decision to stop attacking tourists and the tourist industry.
One thing is clear, however. The Luxor bloodbath has left al-Jama'a
naked and exposed it in the eyes of local, regional, and world opinion.
It has dug its own grave.
46. "An Arab-International Consensus on Condemning the Luxor
Attack."
47. Daoud Hasan, "Iranian President to Mubarak: Foreign Powers Conspire Against Egypt," *Al-Hayat*, 20 November 1997. "Condemnation of
the Luxor Massacre Continues and Consensus Regarding Its Harm to
Islam," ibid.; "Fadllalh Accuses Israel and America in the Luxor Operation," *Al-Hayat*, 21 November 1997.

participate in policing vital tourist and historical sights, a mission that had been reserved solely for the police.[48]

The deepening and intensification of security measures was not accompanied by any political signals to the opposition. In fact, Mubarak rejected dialogue in favor of escalating the confrontation against the militants.[49] Opposition sources also do not expect the Luxor attack to bring any qualitative shift in the government's approach toward the mainstream Islamists. They fear more intimidation and repression.[50] On a much smaller scale than that of Algeria, the spiral of violence appears to be institutionalized in Egypt.

Assessing U.S. Policy toward Egypt and Its Islamists

Despite these problems, both the Algerian and Egyptian regimes have proved to be much more resilient than initially feared. The difference in the Clinton approach to the two countries is striking, however. The U.S. administration has publicly and privately impressed on the Algerian regime the need to implement political and economic reforms and integrate nonviolent Islamists into the government. In the case of Egypt, the Clinton administration has by and large refrained from making any public statements, let alone exerting real pressure, that may be construed as being critical of the Mubarak regime. It has made no public mention of Mubarak's crackdown on the Muslim Brothers or of his assault on professional associations. When asked why Washington has kept silent, a senior State Department official said that the United States cannot interfere in Egypt's internal affairs.[51] This aide did not seem to be concerned

48. Mohammed Saleh, Hussam Kamal, and Hazem Mohammed, "Egypt: The Army Participates for the First Time in the Protection of Tourist Areas," *Al-Hayat*, 23 November 1997. Douglas Jehl, "Shake-Up in Cairo Follows Tourists' Killings," *New York Times*, 20 November 1997.
49. Al-Husseini and al-Fiqi, "Mubarak: The Terrorists in Britain; No Dialogue with Them Because It Strengthens Them."
50 Hazem Mohammed, "Changes in the Egyptian Security Apparatus Highlights the Role of 'Political Security,'" *Al-Hayat*, 21 November 1997.
51. This point was made at on off-the-record meeting of a group of scholars and officials, New York, April 1996.

that locals interpret Washington's inaction as clear support for the Mubarak regime. In U.S. eyes, the stability of the Egyptian state clearly overrides other considerations.

According to William Quandt, American policy makers believe that "the achievements of the past could be lost if, for example, the regime in Egypt changed suddenly, [or] if radical Islamic movements gained ground."[52] Historian Paul Kennedy asserts further that the Mubarak government has provided a "bulwark against perhaps the most significant long-term threat in the region – radical Islamic fundamentalism." Kennedy adds that the collapse of the Mubarak regime might damage American interests more than the Iranian revolution.[53]

American officials are apt to share Mubarak's interpretation of Islamists because they see a fundamentalist victory in Egypt as the first and most significant falling domino, after which the rest of the Arab world might well succumb to revolutionary Islam.[54] Egypt also continues to play a critical role in the Arab-Israeli peace process, a vital American concern. For all these reasons, such experts as former Undersecretary of Defense for Policy Paul Wolfowitz advises the United States and its partners to support the Egyptian government in a period of extreme danger by showing some understanding for the harsh measures the Egyptian government has taken to combat "terrorism."[55]

Not all American officials share these sentiments, however. Some fear that the Egyptian government's crackdown against the mainstream Islamic movement could "backfire," endangering the survival of the Mubarak regime. This minority view within the U.S. govern-

52. William B. Quandt, *Peace Process: American Diplomacy and the Arab-Israeli Conflict Since 1967* (Berkeley and Los Angeles: University of California Press, 1993), p. 418.
53. Chase, Hill, and Kennedy, "Pivotal States and U.S. Strategy," *Foreign Affairs*, p. 40.
54. Zachary Karabell, "The Wrong Threat: The United States and Islamic Fundamentalism," *World Policy Journal* (Summer 1995), pp. 44–5.
55. Paul Wolfowitz, "Challenges to U.S. Interests in the Middle East," in Mirsky, Ahrens, and Sultan, eds., *Challenges to U.S. Interests in the Middle East: Obstacles and Opportunities*, p. 19.

ment wants Mubarak to show greater respect for human rights and to promote political reforms.[56] According to an NSC official, "we have impressed on our friends, including the Egyptians, the need to be more inclusive, to broaden their political base, and integrate the major opposition forces, which are reform-minded, into the political process."[57]

The dilemma facing U.S. policy makers in Egypt today is how to best balance a concern for human rights and democratization with the need to take account of the larger issues of regional stability and the condition of a comprehensive Arab-Israeli peace settlement. For example, a study commissioned by the Senate Foreign Relations Committee in 1993 cautioned against taking any hasty measures that would compromise Egypt's internal stability and undermine American interests.[58] Five years later, a relative consensus exists among students of the Egyptian situation that human-rights issues have not featured prominently in U.S.–Egyptian relations despite the pattern of serious violations that have existed there.[59]

The Clinton administration appears reluctant to criticize Egyptian government violations of human rights. Even when it does, it frequently implies that the Mubarak government's actions are primarily an unfortunate but necessary response to "extremist" violence. Yet the fear among neutral observers is that by adopting an unconditional hostile position toward Islamists or Islamic extremists, the U.S. government inadvertly helps Mubarak feel justified in disregarding the human rights of its Islamist opposition, thus contributing to the general decline of the rule of law.[60]

56. *The Battle Looms: Islam and Politics in the Middle East*, study commissioned by the Senate Committee on Foreign Relations, p. 19.
57. Interview, Washington, DC, 29 March 1995.
58. *The Battle Looms*, p. 19.
59. See for example, "Human Rights in the Middle East," testimony of Neil Hicks, before the Subcommittee on Europe and the Middle East of the House Committee on Foreign Affairs, 15 September 1992; various issues of *Critique* by the Lawyers Committee for Human Rights, especially 1996 and 1997; Cassandra, "The Impending Crisis in Egypt," *Middle East Journal* 49, no. 1 (Winter 1995), pp. 25–6.
60. Lawyers Committee for Human Rights, *Critique*, 1992, 1995, 1996, 1997.

Policy Recommendations

The violence of opposition groups does not justify the pervasive violations of human rights committed by Egyptian authorities. As one of the oldest nation–states in the world, Egypt does itself much harm if it continues to breach the rule of law and behave like al-Jama'a. Unfortunately, the Egyptian government has acted like its nemesis and has tried to justify its abuse of human rights by citing the violence perpetuated by extremist Islamist elements. This short-sighted behavior is counterproductive and unnecessary as well. Unlike Algeria, Egyptian political and legal institutions are highly developed and well equipped to deal with the threat of radical Islamists. Time and again the Egyptian state has survived paramilitary challenges, proving its staying power and resiliency. Mubarak appears to be playing into the hands of al-Jama'a and other fringe groups by narrowing the avenues of legitimate political participation and protest.[61]

The danger is that the more the Egyptian government acts brutally, the more it alienates the middle classes, long the bedrock of its legitimacy. The draconian measures adopted by the Mubarak regime have already contributed to the further polarization and radicalization of Egyptian politics. The mainstream Muslim Brotherhood has also gained much sympathy and influence by calling for national dialogue and condemning al-Jam'a's violence.[62] The Brotherhood's moderate public tone has made it look more and more like a responsible shadow government.

The Clinton administration must balance its support for Mubarak with the needs to safeguard and advance human rights, the rule of law, and more representative government. Sadly, the United States has allowed its short-term security calculations to prevail over its commitment to liberal and democratic values. Although the State Department's Country Reports on Human Rights Practices accurately document the Egyptian government's human-rights abuses,

61. Cassandra, "The Impending Crisis in Egypt," pp. 10, 15, 17–8.
62. See the interviews with a leading figure of the Brotherhood, Seif Al-Islam Bana in *Al-Hayat*, 14 November 1995, p. 5; *Al-Wasat*, 7 August 1995, pp. 16–17. *Al-Hayat*, 20 November 1995, p. 5; *Al-Hayat*, 21 November 1995, pp. 1, 6.

these reports have not guided or influenced American policy. American policy makers not only steer away from criticizing Mubarak's harsh actions but also seem implicitly to condone them. Egyptians view official silence in Washington as giving Mubarak a carte blanche to suppress the legitimate opposition.

The Clinton administration's distinction between "moderate" and "extremist" Islamists does not seem to apply in the case of Egypt. Initially, U.S. officials recognized Islamists' important role and influence and engaged them in some sort of dialogue. They suddenly ceased such contacts, however, when Mubarak accused the United States of double-crossing him and undermining his regime. By giving in to Mubarak's pressure, Clinton administration officials, whether they agree or not, appear to share his fear that Islamists are irredeemably anti-Western and antidemocratic. The result is that Mubarak has been emboldened in his drive to marginalize and silence all opposition.

Mubarak's confrontational strategy is a recipe for protracted social conflict. Several U.S. officials have privately expressed their concern that Mubarak seems to be taking Egypt in the same direction as the Algerian hard-line generals. They worry that the Egyptian regime is substituting force for politics and antagonizing large segments of the Egyptian population. These officials' warnings do not appear to be taken seriously or acted upon by the Clinton administration. The latter does not want to offend Mubarak and threaten the survival of a pivotal ally.

Current American policy toward Egypt, however, might produce the opposite results. The more Mubarak concentrates power in his hands, the more he will prolong Egypt's crisis of legitimacy. The Egyptian political order appears on the brink of reaching a stalemate. It can either maintain the status quo and court disaster or move forward, liberalize, open up the political field, and create a more inclusive, democratic community. The latter option carries the potential of rejuvenating Cairo's institutions and mending the rifts between state and civic society. Egyptian civil society is vibrant and dynamic, and it can easily withstand any political shocks.

The key to stability and progress in Egypt lies in a more inclusive, rather than exclusive, sociopolitical and economic structure. The mainstream Islamists, as well as other opposition elements, should be co-opted, not repressed, and given an opportunity to participate in the political process. Expanding political space and participation would reduce popular pressure on the government, especially as it attempts to implement its economic austerity program, which has important social costs. Political reforms, coupled with positive economic indicators that have recently been recorded, might help end the spiral of violence.[63]

Egypt's problem lies in its one-party system, which is unwilling to share power. Militant Islamists can be easily reduced to insignificance if the Egyptian state mobilizes all civil and political segments of society. Mubarak has a golden opportunity to act and heal political rifts in the country, especially after the Luxor slaughter and the overwhelming good will and support expressed by civil and political organizations toward the state. The United States needs to confront its Egyptian ally about the long-term costs if he fails to reform: Egypt will not only fail "to join the world economy" but will sink further into more poverty and disorder.

63. The Egyptian economy has made some impressive gains. Egypt's foreign debt has been reduced from $50 billion to around $34 billion. Trade reform has removed import restrictions. Interest rates are now freely determined by banks and have remained above the inflation rate for the past three years. Foreign reserves, in 1995, totaled $16 billion, giving the government a one-year to two-year cushion of foreign exchange to meet import needs. Inflation has been cut from a high of more than 20 percent in 1989 to 8.4 percent in 1995. The budget deficit has also been cut from 18 percent of the GDP to under 3 percent. See Sullivan, "State and Civil Society in Conflict in Egypt," pp. 80, 86. As importantly, the psychological mood regarding the economy inside and outside Egypt is positive, thus promising more progress.

9

Turkey

For the first time in the modern history of Turkey, Islamists, as represented by the Refah (Prosperity or Welfare) Party, achieved a major political victory when they garnered more than 21 percent of the popular vote and 158 seats in the 550-member National Assembly in the December 1995 parliamentary elections. Initially, the two largest secular center-right parties, the Motherland and True Path, pressured by the powerful military, denied Islamists the fruits of their electoral triumph by forming a minority coalition government. However, after three months of political paralysis, the forced marriage between the two leaders of the Motherland and True Path, Mesut Yilmaz and Tansu Ciller, respectively, collapsed in June 1996, opening the way for the Refah to form a government jointly with the True Path. Necmettin Erbakan, leader of Refah, was finally allowed to assume the position of prime minister.[1]

The unthinkable had happened: The most secular state in the Middle East had succumbed to the Islamist surge. Mustafa Kemal Ataturk's vision of a secular, modern state in the West's image lay in near ruins. In hindsight, like all visionaries, Ataturk failed in his quest to craft a new man who is unencumbered by the historical legacy of the five-hundred-year-old Ottoman empire. The Turks joined, though belatedly, their religious Persian and Arab cohorts in the quest for a synthesis between modernity, religion, and cultural au-

---

1. Jenny B. White, "Pragmatists or Ideologues? Turkey's Welfare Party in Power," *Current History* (January 1997), p. 27; Kelly Couturier, "Short-Lived Coalition Out in Turkey," *Washington Post*, 7 June 1996; Sami Kohen, "Turkey's Shaky Coalition Keeps Islamic Party Out," *Christian Science Monitor*, 4 March 1996.

thenticity. But unlike their Muslim neighbors, the Turks did so through constitutional avenues and the institutions established by the Kemalist state. What distinguishes Turkey in this sphere is its pluralism, which may account for the marginality of violent Islamist groups in Turkey, as compared with the armed Islamist opposition in Egypt and Algeria.[2]

Unlike Iran, Algeria, and Egypt, Turkey represents a unique case in the attempt of a secularist Muslim country to reconcile religion and secularism in a democratic context. Islamists and the dominant secular ruling elite made an effort, albeit short-lived, to coexist politically and share power as well. The implications for Turkey and other Muslim states on both pragmatic and theoretical levels are critical: striking a balance between religion and secularism; determining the proper relationship between military and civilian establishments in democratic societies; examining the compatibility between Islam and democracy; and balancing ideology in domestic and international relations.[3]

Furthermore, the rise of an Islamist party raises critical questions for Turkey's relations with the Western powers, particularly the United States. How does the U.S. foreign-policy elite view the Islamist phenomenon in Turkey? How did the United States react to the Islamist-based government in Ankara? To what extent was Washington's response to Islamists in Turkey dramatically different from its response to Islamists in Algeria and Egypt? Did American officials and policy specialists draw any parallels between the Turkish case and other Islamist movements? Would the Turkish case, which found a reformist Islamist leader in power, reveal a radically alternative U.S. perspective on Islamic revivalism? In other words, U.S. reaction to the Islamist-led government in Turkey illuminates another important aspect of the relationship between the United States and political Islam. The Turkish case also shows the extent to which the United States is willing to come to terms with a constitutionally elected Islamist government in a vitally strategic country.

2. Sami Zubaida, "Turkish Islam and National Identity," *Middle East Report* (April/June 1996), p. 11–13.
3. "Focus – Islam and Turkey: The Regional Impact," *Bulletin of Regional Cooperation in the Middle East* 6, no. 2 (Summer 1997), p. 11.

The importance of Turkey lies in the fact that U.S. officials have often referred to it as a model of coexistence between the world of Islam and the West. In the words of Deputy Secretary of State Strobe Talbott, Turkey, being both a Western and a Muslim country, refutes the dire prediction of a global clash of civilizations and clearly shows "how productive and enduring cooperation among 'the peoples of the book' can be."[4] President Clinton had sounded a similar theme: "Our relationship with Turkey proves that diverse people – East and West, Muslim, Christian, and Jew – can work closely together toward shared goals."[5]

U.S.–Turkish Relations after the End of the Cold War

Since the end of World War Two, Turkey has played a pivotal role in American foreign policy toward the Middle East, the Balkans, and Europe. As a member of NATO, Turkey has acted as one of the first lines of defense against the Soviet Union. Ankara's strategic significance has been unquestioned. Turkey has also served as a gateway to the Muslim world.[6]

The 1979 Islamic revolution in Iran, coupled with the Soviet invasion of Afghanistan, increased Turkey's importance as a "strategic asset" to the United States. Furthermore, Ronald Reagan's victory in 1980 and the triumph of Papandreou's socialist party in Greece in 1981 enhanced Turkey's value in Washington's eyes. Secretary of State Alexander Haig saw Turkey as "absolutely irreplaceable" and worth supporting at virtually any price. American support for Turkey manifested itself in forthcoming loans by the International Monetary Fund (IMF) and other financial institutions. Be-

4. "U.S.–Turkish Leadership in the Post–Cold War World," address at Bilkent University, Ankara, Turkey, 11 April 1995, *U.S. Department of State Dispatch*, 24 April 1995, p. 360.
5. "The United States and Turkey," opening statements at a news conference by President Clinton and Turkish Prime Minister Ciller, Washington, DC, 15 October 1995, *U.S. Department of State Dispatch*, 1 November 1993, p. 767.
6. Patricia Carley, *Turkey's Role in the Middle East: A Conference Report* (Washington, DC: United States Institute of Peace, 1995), background. "Delicate Relations with Turkey," editorial, *New York Times*, 8 March 1997.

tween 1980 and 1987, Turkey received $13 billion and enjoyed a growth rate of almost 5 percent in those years.[7]

The end of the Cold War further reinforced Turkey's strategic relevance in U.S. eyes. As former Assistant Secretary of State Richard Holbrooke noted, "Turkey after the Cold War is equivalent to Germany during the Cold War – a pivotal state, where diverse strategic interests intersect."[8] U.S. officials view Turkey as a frontline state in a global struggle between the forces of reform, modernization, and secularism and those of backwardness, intolerance, and anti-Westernism; between religious obscurism and civic modernity.[9] In geostrategic terms, U.S. leaders and policy pundits regard Turkey, with its secular political system, as a model for Muslim countries and as a bulwark against the spread of revolutionary Islam.[10]

American officials hoped that Central Asian countries and the Balkans would imitate Turkey rather than the Iranian version of Islamic radicalism. Presidents Bush and Clinton stressed Turkey's indispensable stabilizing role in a particularly sensitive region like the Middle East and in the Muslim republics of the Caucasus and Central Asia. In particular, Bush and Clinton cited Turkey as "a

7. Feroz Ahmad, *The Making of Modern Turkey* (London: Routledge, 1993), pp. 206–7. Simon V. Mayall, *Turkey: Thwarted Ambition*, Paper 56 (Washington, DC: National Defense University, January 1997), p. 92; William Safire, "Sending in Marines," *New York Times*, 14 February 1980.

8. Quoted in Henry J. Barkey, ed., *Reluctant Neighbor: Turkey's Role in the Middle East* (Washington, DC: United Institute of Peace Press, 1996), p. vii.

9. Colonel W. Mountcastle, "Forward," in Stephen J. Blank, Stephen C. Pelletiere, and William T. Johnson, *Turkey's Strategic Position at the Crossroads of World Affairs* (N.C.: Strategic Studies Institute, U.S. Army War College, 1993), p. v; Talbott, "U.S.-Turkish Leadership in the Post–Cold War World," p. 362.

10. *A National Security Strategy for a New Century* (Washington, DC: White House, May 1997), p. 22; Talbott, "U.S.-Turkish Leadership in the Post–Cold War World," p. 360; Graham E. Fuller and Ian O. Lesser, *Central Asia: The New Geopolitics* (Santa Monica, CA: Rand Corporation, 1992. p. vi. John Pomfret, "Turkey's Identity Crisis," *Washington Post*, 17 April 1995. Turkey's secular officials play to the fears of regional upheaval and a new global religious schism to enhance Ankara's status as a broker. See John Darnton, "Discontent Seethes in Once-Stable Turkey," *New York Times*, 2 March 1995.

secular democratic model" that could be influential in predominantly Muslim former Soviet republics. The 1997 National Security Strategy report stressed that U.S. strategic interests were well served by a "democratic, secular, stable and Western-oriented Turkey. . . . Its continued ties to the West and its support for our overall strategic objectives in one of the world's most sensitive regions is critical."[11] Clinton added further that "Turkey's secularism acts to deflect the rising tide of fundamentalism."[12] Washington's goal was to bring the Muslim republics of Central Asia "into our larger community of values and nations and institutions."[13]

Moreover, Turkey's importance after the Cold War also stems from its capacity to participate in the U.S.–dominated world economy. American officials are aware of Ankara's economic potential. The United States now ranks second among Turkey's trading partners, with roughly a 10 percent share in Turkish imports and a 9 percent share in exports. Turkey is also one of the few countries with which the United States has a favorable trade balance. The U.S. Department of Commerce classified Turkey as one of the world's ten most promising big emerging markets.[14]

Turkey provides a major market for U.S. goods and is "a funnel

11. *A National Security Strategy for a New Century*, p. 22.
12. "The President's News Conference with Prime Minister Tansu Ciller of Turkey, 15 October 1993," *Weekly Compilation of Presidential Documents*, U.S. Government Printing Office, 18 October 1993, p. 1750. See also Bruce Kuniholm, "Turkey and the West," *Foreign Affairs* (Spring 1991), p. 47.
13. "Enhanced U.S.–Turkish Partnership," excerpts from press briefing, the White House, 11 February 1992, *U.S. Department of State Dispatch*, 17 February 1992, p. 109; Talbott, U.S.–Turkish Leadership in the Post–Cold War World," p. 362.
14. U.S.–Turkish Leadership in the Post–Cold War World," p. 360; Morton I. Abramowitz, "Dateline Ankara: Turkey After Ozal," *Foreign Policy*, no. 91 (Summer 1993), pp. 179–80; Duncan L. Clarke and Daniel O'Connor, "U.S. Base-Rights Payments After the Cold War," *Orbis* 37, no. 3 (Summer 1993), p. 451; "Turkey: The Emerging Market Bridging East and West," *Foreign Affairs* 75, no. 3 (May/June 1996); Philip Robins, "Between Sentiment and Self-Interest: Turkey's Policy Toward Azerbaijan and the Central Asian States," *Middle East Journal* 47, no. 4 (Autumn 1993), pp. 595–6.

of investment" and the principal gateway to markets in the independent states of the former Soviet Union and the Middle East.[15]
Turkey's continued stability and leadership role also represents a
vital strategic link for Washington in promoting greater regional
stability. The late Secretary of Commerce Ron Brown stated that
"the United States has never lost sight of the great importance of
Turkey, both strategically and economically. Turkey is a key NATO
partner, and its future as a democratic, secular, Muslim state in a
volatile region has never been more important."[16] For all these reasons, Turkey can have a decisive impact on U.S. interests in a large
swath of the world.[17]

The 1991 Gulf War: Deepening of U.S.–Turkish Relations

The end of the Cold War confronted Turkey with the most serious
challenge since the end of World War Two. Turkey's political establishment feared the effects of the collapse of the Soviet Union on the
West's perception of Turkey's geostrategic role, including a lessen-
ing of the likelihood of its becoming a full member of the European
Union. The NATO alliance has been Turkey's key institutional and
psychological link to the West.[18] The principle – anticommunism,

15. "Building U.S.–Turkey Economic Cooperation," address by Assistant
Secretary Alan P. Larson before the U.S.–Turkey Business Council, 20
February 1997, printed in *Turkish Times*, 1 March 1997; "U.S.–Turkish
Leadership in the Post–Cold War World," p. 360; *Turkey Confidential*
newsletter (London, March 1992). "Turkey: The Emerging Market
Bridging East and West."
16. "Turkey: The Emerging Market Bridging East and West"; Carley,
Turkey's Role in the Middle East, chapter 3; "Turkey, Star of Islam,"
Economist, 14 December 1991.
17. "U.S.–Turkish Leadership in the Post–Cold War World," p. 362;
Mountcastle, "Forward," in Blank, Pelletiere, and Johnson, *Turkey's
Strategic Position*, p. v.
18. Ziya Onis, "Turkey in the Post–Cold War Era: In Search of Identity,"
Middle East Journal 49, no. 1 (Winter 1995), p. 49; Abramowitz, "Date-
line Ankara," p. 166; Carley, *Turkey's Role in the Middle East*, p. 12;
Ahmad, *The Making of Modern Turkey*, p. 223.

fear of the Soviets – that had defined the political life of Turkey's ruling elite, has largely evaporated. However, far from diminishing Turkey's role, the end of the Cold War increased Turkey's foreign-policy options.[19]

The 1990 Gulf crisis presented President Ozal with the opportunity, despite dissension among some military and civilians circles, to align Turkey decisively with the United States against Iraq.[20] Ozal hoped to make Turkey indebted to the United States, a goal which in his view was critical to Ankara's economic and technological development and also for the modernization of the Turkish armed forces. Bush also agreed that Ankara should play a pivotal role in the Arab-Israeli peace process and in Washington's proposal for a new security arrangement for the region. In Ozal's eyes, participation in the Gulf War provided Turkey with an opportunity to escape marginalization and revitalize its role as a regional power.[21]

Turkey's Ozal supported the United Nations sanctions against Iraq, shut down the pipeline that carried 1.5 million barrels of oil a day, allowed coalition planes to launch missions from bases in Turkey, later mobilized troops on Iraq's northern border, and permitted foreign troops on Turkish soil. "After the crisis," stressed Ozal, "the map of the Middle East will change completely. If there is a better

19. Carley, *Turkey's Role in the Middle East*, Introduction; Onis, "Turkey in the Post–Cold War Era," pp. 48–9; Abramowitz, "Dateline Ankara," p. 165; Paul B. Henze, *Turkey: Toward the Twenty-First Century* (Santa Monica, CA: Rand Corporation, 1994), p. 31; Ahmad, *The Making of Modern Turkey*, p. 226.
20. Carley, *Turkey's Role in the Middle East*, pp. 25–6; Stephen C. Pelletiere, "Turkey and the United States in the Middle East: The Kurdish Connection," in Blank, Pelletiere, and Johnson, *Turkey's Strategic Position*, pp. 38–9; Malik Mufti, "Daring and Caution in Turkish Foreign Policy," unpublished paper presented at the Middle East Studies Association, Providence, RI, November 1996, p. 23; Ahmad, *The Making of Modern Turkey*, p. 201.
21. Chanan Naveh, "Foreign Policy of Regional Powers in the 1990s: The Cases of Israel and Turkey," unpublished paper delivered at the 35th Annual Convention of the International Studies Association, Washington, DC, 29–31 April-May 1994, p. 21; Abramowitz, "Dateline Ankara," pp. 166, 179; Mayall, *Turkey*, p. 78; Mufti, "Daring and Caution in Turkish Foreign Policy," p. 21; Clarke and O'Connor, "U.S. Base-Rights Payments After the Cold War," pp. 453–4.

place for us in the world, we must take it."[22] This active posture was reaffirmed by Ozal's successors.[23]

Determined to contain and deter any threats to its primary inter-ests in the Gulf and to assert its control, the Bush administration needed a committed regional ally to be a cornerstone of its anti-Iraqi coalition. Turkey's Ozal was an ideal partner. Bush, who described Turkey as America's "staunchest ally," wooed Turkey and praised Ozal's courageous stand against Iraq. The U.S. government pledged new economic assistance, trade concessions, and a sharp increase in military aid. Between 1991 and 1993, Turkey, taking full advantage of the NATO cascade program, received nearly $8 billion worth of U.S. and German military equipment. Turkey, the third largest re-cipient after Israel and Egypt of U.S. assistance, is also Washington's fifth largest client, with arms purchases amounting to $7.8 billion from 1984 to 1994. Washington now provides 85 percent of Tur-key's arms imports and 90 percent of its military aid.[24]

In this sense, the Gulf War deepened and consolidated U.S.–Turkish relations. Turkey became a partner of the United States in its regional policies. As former Assistant Secretary of State Hol-brooke put it, Turkey stands at the "crossroads of almost every issue of importance to the U.S. on the Eurasian continent."[25] Deputy Secretary of State Talbott reiterated this sentiment: "Turkey is yet again on the front line of the world's most important struggles just as it was during the Cold War."[26]

22. *Turkey Confidential*, newsletter No. 16 (London, February 1991), p. 1; Ahmad, *The Making of Modern Turkey*, p. 200.
23. Reported by *Reuters*, 18 November 1993 and 13 December 1994.
24. Mayall, *Turkey*, pp. 79–80. Abramowitz, "Dateline Ankara," p. 179; "America Arms Turkey's Repression," *New York Times* editorial, 17 October 1995; Eric Rouleau, "Turkey, Beyond Ataturk," *Foreign Policy*, no. 91 (Summer 1993), pp. 93–4; Ahmad, *The Making of Modern Turkey*, pp. 200, 226; Kurkcii, "The Crisis of the Turkish State," *Middle East Report* (April/June 1996), p. 3; Naveh, "Foreign Policy of Regional Powers," p. 21.
25. Quoted in *U.S. Department of State Dispatch*, 20 May 1995, p. 215. See also Darnton, "Discontent Seethes in Once-Stable Turkey."
26. "U.S.–Turkish Leadership in the Post–Cold War World," p. 360. See also Sabri, Sayari, "Turkey: The Changing European Security Environ-ment and the Gulf Crisis," *Middle East Journal* 46, no. 1 (Winter 1992), p. 13; *Turkey Confidential*, newsletter (London, January 1991), p. 1.

AMERICA AND POLITICAL ISLAM

AMERICA AND POLITICAL ISLAM

Turkish leaders have aimed to strengthen coordination of post–Cold War strategic and economic policies with the United States.[27] The Arab-Israeli peace process, coupled with other changes in Middle Eastern politics, opened up another foreign-policy opportunity for Ankara. Fearful of being left behind, Ankara rushed to deepen its relations with Tel Aviv.[28] Several military agreements have been signed between Tel Aviv and Ankara that call for cooperation between the air and naval forces of the two countries. U.S. naval forces have taken part in joint Turkish-Israeli naval maneuvers.[29] Turkey's generals want to be useful to the United States, and the Israeli card appears to be the safest course for appealing to the U.S. foreign-policy apparatus.[30]

The United States has blessed the Turkish-Israeli marriage and has lent its political and military weight to consolidating it. U.S. officials appear to have designated Turkey and Israel as the new "Regional Policemen" of the Middle East, with the former replacing Iran in this capacity.[31] The Turkish-Israeli alliance contributes to

27. Naveh, "Foreign Policy of Regional Powers in the 1990s," p. 9; Ahmad, *The Making of Modern Turkey*, pp. 225–6; Sami Kohen, "Regional Conflicts on U.S.–Turkey Agenda," *Christian Science Monitor*, 18 October 1993.
28. Naveh, "Foreign Policy of Regional Powers," p. 12; Carley, *Turkey's Role in the Middle East*, p. 20; Eric Rouleau, "The Challenges to Turkey," *Foreign Affairs* 72, no. 5 (November/December 1993), p. 114; Scott Peterson, "Mideast Balance of Power Shifts as an 'Axis' Is Born," *Christian Science Monitor*, 29 August 1996.
29. Mufti, "Daring and Caution in Turkish Foreign Policy," p. 7; Sami Kohen, "Who Runs Turkey?" *Christian Science Monitor*, 9 May 1997.
30. Alan Makovsky, "Israeli-Turkish Relations: A Turkish 'Periphery Strategy'?" in Barkey, ed., *Reluctant Neighbor*, pp. 153–7, 170; Muhammad Muslih, "Syria and Turkey: Uneasy Relations," in ibid., pp. 113–29; Murhaf Jouejati, "Water Politics as High Politics: The Case of Turkey and Syria," in ibid., pp. 131–46; Kelly Couturier, "Turkey, Israel Launch a Military Partnership," *Washington Post*, 16 April 1996; Peterson, "Mideast Balance of Power Shifts as an 'Axis' Is Born"; Hugh Pope, "Attempt on Demirel's Life," *Middle East International*, 24 May 1996, p. 13; Robert Olson, "The Turkey-Israel Agreement and the Kurdish Question," *MEI*, 24 May 1996, p. 18; Olson, "An Israeli-Kurdish Conflict?" *MEI*, 5 July 1996, p. 17; Olson, "PKK the Target," *MEI*, 21 February 1997, p. 14.
31. Naveh, "Foreign Policy of Regional Powers," p. 12; Carley, *Turkey's Role in the Middle East*, chapter 3; Robert Olson, "The Turkey-Israel

U.S. efforts to contain the so-called "rogue states," such as Iraq, Iran, and possibly Syria, and to support pro-Western regimes in the region; it also increases Israel's dominance over the eastern Mediterranean.[32]

As a reward, the United States has lobbied the European Community hard to admit Turkey to this exclusive club; strongly supported Turkey's bloody campaign against the Kurdistan Workers' Party (PKK); played down Turkey's violations of human rights; supplied Ankara with arms, and shown an indulgent understanding of the Turkish army's twenty-two-year occupation of northern Cyprus. The various U.S. administrations have also resisted appeals by members of Congress to censure Turkey for escalating its war against the Kurds.[33]

Thinking the Unthinkable: Refah in Power and U.S. Reaction

It is within this context that U.S. response to the rise to power of Islamists in Turkey should be framed. The electoral victory of Islamists in 1995 aroused considerable concern in the United States, where the Islamic revolution in Iran was still fresh in policy makers' minds. U.S. officials were unsure how to react to the Islamist surge in Turkey. Initially, a high degree of uncertainty, nervousness, and skepticism colored U.S. views toward Refah. This ambivalence and tension partly explain why officials were very circumspect in their response to the electoral victory of the Refah Party and then to the formation of the Islamist-based government a year later. Some in the Clinton administration quietly hoped that the Islamist-led govern-

Agreement and the Kurdish Question," p. 18; Hugh Pope, "Turkey's Generals Behind the Israel Axis," *MEI* (16 May 1996), p. 3.

32. Robert Olson, "Israel and Turkey – Consolidating Relations," *Middle East International*, 4 April 1997, pp. 16–17; "The United States and Turkey," opening statements at a news conference by President Clinton and Turkish Prime Minister Ciller, p. 767; Mayall, *Turkey*, p. 92; Rouleau, "Turkey Beyond Ataturk," pp. 84–5, and "The Challenges to Turkey," p. 116; Abramowitz, "Dateline Ankara," p. 180; Darnton, "Discontent Seethes in Once-Stable Turkey."

33. Rouleau, "Turkey Beyond Ataturk," p. 85; Steven Greenhouse, "U.S. Support for Turks' Anti-Kurd Campaign Dims," *New York Times*, 29 March 1995.

ment would fail, discrediting the fundamentalists and leaving Ciller to pick up the pieces. But other officials also recognized that the means of Refah's departure could serve to strengthen Refah and undermine Turkey's long-term stability.[34]

Unlike their reaction to the situation in Iran, Algeria, and Egypt, U.S. policy makers did not panic. Washington adopted a wait-and-see, pragmatic approach toward Refah's ascendance to power. State Department spokesman Nicholas Burns said that Washington would be "listening to the rhetoric as well as watching the actions" of the new government.[35]

Ignoring the advice of some working-level officials at the State Department, the Clinton administration authorized Peter Tarnoff, then undersecretary of state, to meet with the newly appointed Prime Minister Erbakan, thus arguably giving him a U.S. approval just before the Turkish parliament's own vote of confidence. Tarnoff told Erbakan that the United States was willing to work with him so long as he respected American security interests in the region. In particular, Tarnoff expressed the U.S. wish for renewal of the mandate of Operation Provide Comfort – a linchpin in U.S. strategy toward Iraq.[36] Shortly after the vote of confidence, the State Department spokesman Burns said, "I don't think we've ever said that secularism is something that we feel must continue for us to have a relationship with Turkey."[37]

Although Madeleine Albright, then U.S. ambassador to the United Nations, later rejected it, Burns's statement was significant because it revealed Washington's muddled thinking toward the Islamist-based government; it also showed the extent to which the United States was willing to tolerate and coexist with Islamists so

34. Jim Hoagland, "Political Con Game in Turkey," *Washington Post*, 11 July 1996; Rouleau, "Turkey Beyond Ataturk," p. 97; Robert Marquand, "Religious Right Elbows Way onto World's Political Stage," *Christian Science Monitor*, 13 June 1996; D. Migdalovitz, "Turkey's Unfolding Political Crisis," in *Congressional Research Service Report for Congress* (Washington, DC: The Library of Congress, 11 April 1997), p. 1.
35. *Turkish Daily News*, 10 July 1996; Mayall, *Turkey*, p. 11.
36. Hoagland, "Political Con Game in Turkey"; Couturier, "Islamic Leader Wins Approval Vote in Turkey," *Washington Post*, 9 July 1996; Lally Weymouth, "Saddam's New Friend," *Washington Post*, 30 July 1996.
37. Weymouth, "Saddam's New Friend."

long as the latter's foreign-policy orientation did not endanger U.S. security interests. Some policy circles in Washington even viewed the Islamist-led government as offering a unique opportunity to engage Islamists who had risen to power by democratic means. Lines of communication were kept open with Erbakan. Tarnoff and Albright's meetings with Erbakan were widely interpreted by Turks as demonstrating support and conferring legitimacy on his government.[38]

Unlike their nervous response to Islamists elsewhere in the Middle East, U.S. officials recognized the inherit limits of Islamists in Turkey. Refah's narrow electoral victory (21 percent of the popular vote) did not allow Islamists to form a government alone. Refah's coalition with the True Path Party served as a check on the former's ambitions. More important in U.S. eyes was the fact that the Kemalist ruling establishment, especially the army, seemed determined to prevent Islamists from exercising real power, with the generals constituting the major deterrence to any attempted establishment of an Islamic state in Turkey. During his visit to Ankara in June 1997, Deputy Secretary of State Talbot had lunch with Turkey's powerful Deputy Chief of Staff General Cevik Bir.[39] This gesture could not be lost on either the military or the Islamist-based government.

Since the late 1940s, the United States has exercised much leverage in Ankara, and U.S. officials need to be reminded that their every move and public pronouncement are taken very seriously by most Turks. Thus, Turkey's political establishment looked at initial U.S. reactions to the Erbakan government with care. When U.S. officials met with Erbakan before a parlimentary vote of confidence in the summer of 1996, the meeting was interpreted as a U.S. endorsement of the Refah-based coalition. Similarly, in February 1997, the State Department was perceived to be sending a further message of support to the coalition government when it said that "We believe that Turkey is stable politically. We believe that its secular democracy is going to continue."[40]

38. Migdalovitz, "Turkey's Unfolding Political Crisis," p. 21.
39. Zeynep Alemdar, "Turk Military on Anti-Islam Offense," *Associated Press*, 10 June 1997.
40. Zeyno Baram, "Too Little Stability in Turkey," *Christian Science Monitor*, 18 February 1997; see also Migdalovitz, "Turkey's Unfolding Political Crisis," p. 21.

From the outset, the Turkish military kept a close watch on the new government, hoping for an opportune moment to apply political pressure, even physical force if necessary, to topple it. After their suppression of the leftist forces in the 1980s, the generals were unwilling to tolerate the existence of a rival ideology that might represent a serious challenge to the Kemalist state. In their fight against Islamists, Turkish generals knew that there are effective ways to appeal to Washington's latent fears of Islamists. For example, the military listed Kurdish terrorism and Islamic fundamentalism as "No. 1 threats" to Turkey, citing Iran and Syria as the countries having "links" with local groups involved in such activities.[41]

The military brass believed correctly that they could count on the Western powers' implicit backing. Some members of the European Union suggested putting Turkey at arms' length because of its "Islamist" prime minister. According to various reports, EU policy makers commented privately that the rejection of Turkey's membership in the EU had to do with the rise of Muslim sentiments in the country and the problems this poses for Europe.[42] Although U.S. officials did not take any concrete steps to reveal their irritation with the turn of events in Ankara, Turkish generals knew that the United States would support the military's pressure tactics so long as they fell short of a coup d'état. These generals were well aware of the anti-Islamist sentiments in various policy circles in Western and Middle Eastern capitals.

The Campaign Against Islamists

The campaign against Islamists in Turkey began in earnest in the late 1980s, led by three camps: The first camp included "radical" secularists in Turkey who represented an integral part of the ruling

41. Zeynep Alemdar, "Turkey to Combat Islam Influence," *Associated Press*, 11 June 1997; Sami Kohen, "Who Runs Turkey?"
42. White, "Pragmatists or Ideologues?" p. 30; Rouleau, "Turkey Beyond Ataturk," p. 83; Celestine Bohlen, "European Parliament Admits Turkey to Its New Customs Union," *New York Times*, 14 December 1995; Shada Islam, "Cautious EU Response," *Middle East International*, 5 July 1996, p. 12, and "Turkey and NATO," *Middle East International*, 21 February 1997, pp. 15–16.

political establishment. The second encompassed pro-U.S. Middle Eastern allies, such as Israel and Egypt, who feared the effects of Islamism in Turkey on Islamist groups in their own countries and on Ankara's foreign-policy alignment. The last camp consisted of Western observers who distrusted Refah and called for its isolation.

Long before Refah scored its 1995 electoral victory, the secular political establishment had raised alarm bells about the "challenge to secularism." Former President Kenan Evren warned the public that the dangers facing Turkey were "communism, fascism and religious reaction."[43] Radical secularists see a zero-sum relationship between secularism and Islam, and reject the idea of reconciliation between the two. Long before Islamists won in the polls, a Turkish journalist put the confrontation between Islamists and secularists in apocalyptic terms: If Turkey should be lost to the Sharia, to Islamic radicals, it would be the end of the struggle in the world between secularists and religious radicals.[44]

Like their Israeli and Egyptian counterparts, Turkey's secular elite have tried to manipulate U.S. fears of Islamic militancy by portraying the country as an enclave of stability in a volatile neighborhood. They continue to justify Ankara's importance to the United States and Europe in terms of the "immense influence" over the region that it can deploy against religious radicalism. No one had been more apt at this game than former Premier Ciller before she joined the coalition with Erbakan. Before the 1995 elections, Ciller toured Europe and the United States, appealing for foreign support on the grounds that she was the only politician who could prevent the

43. Ronnie Margulies and Ergin Yildizoglu, "The Political Uses of Islam in Turkey," *Middle East Report* (July/August 1988), pp. 12–13. This alarmist language is strikingly similar to that used by some Reagan administration officials. Vice-President Dan Quayle compared the "rise of Communism, the rise of Nazism [with] the rise of radical Islamic fundamentalism."
44. Mehmet Ali Birand in Carley, *Turkey's Role in the Middle East*. See also Metin Heper, "Islam and Democracy in Turkey: Toward a Reconciliation," *Middle East Journal* 51, no. 1 (Winter 1997), p. 42; Scott Peterson, "Turkey's Army Keeps the Faith at Bay," *Christian Science Monitor*, 9 April 1996; Hugh Pope, "The Erbakan Whirlwind Sweeps Through Turkey," *Middle East International*, 19 July 1996, p. 3; Henze, *Turkey*, p. 7.

fundamentalists from "dragging the country back to the dark ages."[45] As an editorial in *New York Times* noted, "Turkish politicians now reflexively brandish the Islamic threat to silence Western criticism. That gives them a free hand to pursue repressive policies that play into the hand of Islamic and other antidemocratic forces at home."[46]

Regionally, pro-U.S. Middle Eastern allies, who are under assault by Islamist opposition forces, feared that Erbakan, by proving that Islamism need not be synonymous with militancy, would give the Islamic movements new respectability among their middle classes and in the West. In particular, Israel and its U.S. friends worried that Erbakan, given his previous anti-Israeli pronouncements, would reverse the close security collaboration between Tel Aviv and Ankara that had begun in the early 1990s. President Mubarak also worried that Refah's close ties to the Egyptian Muslim Brothers might strengthen the Islamist opposition in Cairo.[47] America's Middle Eastern allies made their views clear to their U.S. counterparts in order to impress on Washington the need to confront Erbakan's Islamists.

Similarly, some Western policy confrontationalists encouraged the Turkish military in its fight against the Islamists. Commentators found Washington's seemingly calm official response disturbing, since, in their view, an Islamist-based government "would spell dis-

45. "The United States and Turkey," opening statements at a news conference by President Clinton and Turkish Prime Minister Ciller, p. 768. Blank, Pelletiere, and Johnson, *Turkey's Strategic Position at the Crossroads of World Affairs*, p. 2; Baram, "Too Little Stability in Turkey"; Couturier, "Conservative Islamic Prime Minister Named in Turkey," *Washington Post*, 29 June 1996; Stephen Kinzer, "Turkish Ex-Premier's Comeback Hits a Snag," *New York Times*, 2 July 1997, "The Islamist Who Runs Turkey, Delicately," *New York Times*, Sunday 23 February 1997, Magazine section, and "Brussels Meeting Dims Turkey's Bid to Join European Union," *New York Times*, 11 March 1997; Weymouth, "Saddam's New Friend"; Sami Kohen, "Secular Turks Hope to Check Nation's First Islamist Leader," *Christian Science Monitor*, 1 July 1996; Darnton, "Discontent Seethes in Once-Stable Turkey"; Richard C. Hottelet, "Turkey, NATO's Eastern Hinge, Is Far from Breaking Loose," *Christian Science Monitor*, 19 November 1996.
46. "Washington and the Kurds," 4 April 1995.
47. Migdalovitz, "Turkey's Unfolding Political Crisis," p. 21; Kinzer, "The Islamist Who Runs Turkey, Delicately," pp. 30–1.

aster for Turkey's relations with the West."[48] These confrontation-alists urged Turkey's secular leaders and their Western allies, partic-ularly the United States, to keep Islamists at "bay" and unequivocally support secularism; they also called on the U.S. government "to abandon the idea that is trendy in some [Washington] circles that it can tame the radical Islamists."[49]

Jim Hoagland, an influential Washington commentator with close contacts to senior U.S. officials, advocated a more "active and con-sidered" U.S. role in undermining the Islamist-led government; he said that the United States should not just wait for Erbakan to fail but rather wake up to the regional pressures that are building and draw "red lines" around Turkish behavior. The red lines, added Hoagland, require using the threat of withholding U.S. economic and military aid to bring about desired change in Turkey.[50]

Some Western diplomats worried that Turkey was becoming a threat and might one day turn into an Iran or Algeria. One diplomat raised serious concerns about the rise of Islam in Turkey, warning that it should not be taken lightly. Another former high-ranking U.S. official went so far as to say, "We're witnessing the destruction of the Turkish political system."[51]

The media joined the chorus of alarmist voices in the United States by portraying Refah's victory as strengthening Islamic extrem-ists and as demonstrating strong opposition to the West, including

48. Lally Weymouth, "Turkey: The Search for a Deal," *Washington Post*, 27 February 1997. See also Alan Makovsky, "Erbakan on the Ropes," *Policywatch*, no. 239 (published by the Washington Institute for Near East Policy, 12 March 1997), and "Assessing the Intentions of Turkey's Refah Party," *Muslim Politics Report*, published by the Council on For-eign Relations, New York, November/December 1996, p. 5. Makovsky, "How to Deal with Erbakan," *Middle East Quarterly* 4, no. 1 (March 1997), pp. 6–7.
49. Weymouth, "Saddam's New Friend." See also Weymouth, "Turkey: An Anti-Western Tilt?" *Washington Post*, 23 January 1996; Hoagland, "Political Con Game in Turkey"; Makovsky, "How to Deal with Er-bakan," pp. 7–8.
50. Hoagland, "Political Con Game in Turkey."
51. Weymouth, "Saddam's New Friend." See also Weymouth, "Turkey: The Search for a Deal"; Kelly Couturier, "Conservative Islamic Prime Minister Named in Turkey"; Sami Kohen, "Islamic Party Jumps Out Front," *Christian Science Monitor*, 29 November 1995.

the United States, Israel, and the European Union. Leading American newspapers described Erbakan as "anti-Western, pro-Islamic" and cautioned that Refah might throw out the pro-West state ideology and replace it with an anti-West Islamic order, such as practiced in Iran and Sudan.[52]

A convergence of views and interests among the three camps – Ataturkists' secularists, some Middle Eastern regimes, and Western confrontationalists – represented a powerful coalition that lobbied the United States to keep its distance from and exert pressure on the Erbakan government. As importantly, this coalition reinforced and fuelled the Turkish military's drive to remove Erbakan from power.

Refah's Record and the American Role

By the end of February 1997 Turkish generals, using the National Security Council (NSC), the military-civilian body in charge of sensitive security matters as their instrument, waged a full offensive against the Erbakan government. They demanded a crackdown on all aspects of Islamic education in particular. The military's goal was not only to humiliate and discredit Erbakan but also to force him to resign. Initially, Erbakan attempted to assert his constitutional authority and stand up to the military. However, he subsequently reversed course and tried to accommodate the military's demands.[53]

Despite his Islamic rhetoric during the election campaign, Erbakan proved to be fiercely nationalistic and pragmatic, a voice of

52. Sami Kohen, "Turkey's Islamists Gain Strength in Local Vote," *Christian Science Monitor*, 30 March 1994, and "Islamic Party Win Worsens Turkey's East vs. West Woes," *Christian Science Monitor*, 27 December 1995; Kelly Couturier, "Pro-Islamic Party Leads in Turkey," *Washington Post*, 25 December 1995, and "Turkish Parties Vow Coalition to Keep Islamists Out of Power," *Washington Post*, 26 December 1995; Celestine Bohlen, "Turkish Army in New Battle," *New York Times*, 30 March 1996.
53. Kohen, "Turkey's Military Tries Political Moves to Squelch Premier's Islamic Ambition," *Christian Science Monitor*, 3 July 1997; Kinzer, "Turkish Generals Raise Pressure on Premier," *New York Times*, 13 June 1997, and "Turkey's Prime Minister, About to Step Down, Defends Record," *New York Times*, 17 June 1997; Nicole Pope, "Turbulent Times," *Middle East International*, 7 March 1997, p. 19.

"moderation," and "remarkably mild," as Stephen Kinzer of the *New York Times* acknowledged.[54] Internally, Erbakan bowed to the wishes of the NSC by accepting the expulsion of hundreds of military officers, increasing military salaries, and recanting previous anti-Semitic statements. Erbakan and his allies in the party's central leadership dismissed the leaders of eight of seventy regional committees, whom they accused of being too radical. He reiterated his support for pluralism and political democracy, and pledged to "fight against the threat of religious fundamentalism." Erbakan also pursued mainstream free-market economic policies, disregarding Islamist campaign promises to do away with interest rates and introduce a pan-Muslim currency. His government negotiated with the International Monetary Fund (IMF) for a resumption of support for economic reform and stabilization programs. Erbakan also sanctioned the establishment of a new security zone in northern Iraq.[55]

Externally, Erbakan stressed that he was not against the Customs Union Agreement with the European Union, which he had earlier opposed, and supported the security forces' campaign against terrorism, as well as Turkey's international treaties, including the military accords with Israel.[56] Although Erbakan toyed with the idea of forging a new Islamic organization called the "Developing Eight" – Turkey, Pakistan, Indonesia, Iran, Bangladesh, Egypt, Malaysia, and Nigeria – his orientation toward the Muslim world was motivated

---

54. "The Islamist Who Runs Turkey, Delicately," p. 28, and "Islam and Liberty: Struggles in Two Lands," *New York Times*, 22 June 1997.
55. Baram, "Too Little Stability in Turkey"; Stephen Kinzer, "Turks' Chief Surprisingly Silent on Iraq," *New York Times*, 14 September 1996, "Turks March in Campaign to Preserve Secularism," *New York Times*, 16 February 1997, "The Islamist Who Runs Turkey"; p. 31, and "Turkey's Islamic Leaders Vow to Keep Secularism," *New York Times*, 14 March 1997; Hugh Hope, "The New Middle: Turks Add their Voices to Contest of Generals and Fundamentalists," *Wall Street Journal*, 14 March 1997; Kelly Couturier, "Islamic Leader Wins Approval Vote In Turkey"; Nicole Pope, "Turkey Goes Back into Iraq," *Middle East International*, 30 May 1997, p. 4; James M. Dorsey, "With Friends Like Qaddafi, Islamist Erbakan Doesn't Need Enemies," *Washington Report on Middle East Affairs* (November/December 1996), p. 37.
56. Zubaida, "Turkish Islam and National Identity," p. 10; Heper, "Islam and Democracy in Turkey," pp. 43–4.

more by a desire to make Turkey the leader of a bloc instead of remaining a second-rate power within a U.S.-led military and political alliance. Erbakan wanted to demonstrate his independence from the United States. His yearning was to lead rather than be led.[57]

According to Abdullah Gul, minister of state, Erbakan's multidimensional foreign policy, his embrace of both Iran and strategic ties with Israel, shows that "We want to maintain good relations both with the West and with the East."[58] But some Western officials and policy circles viewed Refah's balancing act in a negative light because, they believed, it endangered Turkish-Western relations. Initially, Washington feared that Erbakan, slowly but steadily, would push the traditional secular-leaning country away from its traditional pro-Western orientation and seek new, anti-American alliances with radical Muslim states, particularly Iran.[59] This perception showed the extent to which Iran has a firm grip on the American imagination. Consciously or unconsciously, U.S. officials used Iran as the yardstick by which to compare other Islamist movements, including mainstream Islamists in Turkey.

The American officials' trepidation proved to be unjustified. Historically, Refah had supported NATO during the Cold War years and was as anticommunist as it was anti-Soviet. Refah viewed itself as a reliable partner of the West.[60] After assuming power, Erbakan dealt pragmatically with the United States and assured visiting U.S.

57. Kinzer, "The Islamist Who Runs Turkey, Delicately"; Yalman Onaran, "Muslim Leaders Pledge Cooperation," *Associated Press*, 15 June 1997. Onaran, "Muslim Nations Meet at Summit," *Associated Press*, 14 June 1997.
58. "Turkey Is a European Country," interview with the Minister of State Abdullah Gul, *Turkish Times*, 1 March 1997. See also Kohen, "To U.S., Turk Leader's Tour Goes to all the Wrong Places," *Christian Science Monitor*, 3 October 1996; Margulies and Yildizoglu, "The Political Uses of Islam in Turkey," pp. 14–15; Henry J. Barkey, "Turkish Politics after the Elections," unpublished paper presented at the Commission on Security and Cooperation in Europe, 25 January 1996, pp. 2–3, 5; Kelly Couturier, "Conservative Islamic Prime Minister Named in Turkey."
59. "Delicate Relations with Turkey," *New York Times* editorial; Sami Kohen, "Pro-Islamic Premier Stays in Power, but the Future of Turkey Still Murky," *Christian Science Monitor*, 10 October 1997; Scott Peterson, "Turkey Ties Trade Knot with Iran, Sparks Alarm," *Christian Science Monitor*, 24 December 1996.
60. Rouleau, "Turkey Beyond Ataturk," p. 79.

officials that he wanted better relations with Washington. He sent several friendly signals to American officials, such as upholding the military accord with Israel and supporting the extension of Operation Provide Comfort to protect the Kurdish areas in Iraq. He confirmed that he wanted amicable ties with the United States, saying "Turkey and the U.S. have always been friends and they will always stay friendly."[61] Of course, Refah needed U.S. support on many fronts, and its social program was unattainable without the continuing assistance of the U.S.-dominated World Bank and IMF.[62] Turkey's dependence on Western markets and finance to bankroll its development precludes a dramatic shift in its foreign relations. There is simply no market like Europe and the United States, which offers such potential for Turkey.[63]

As mentioned, soon after coming to power, Erbakan stopped his anti-Western and anti-Israeli rhetoric; he upheld the military accord with Israel; and he supported the extension of Operation Provide Comfort after the United States promised in return not to sanction the establishment of an independent Kurdish state in Iraq. Although Erbakan extracted a few concessions from the United States, his support of Provide Comfort shows that, when it really matters, Turkey's elite, both secular and religious, is still ready to do Washington's bidding. Although some U.S. commentators criticized Erbakan's cynical bargaining tactics, one Western diplomat begged to differ: "Erbakan has proved to be a skillful Oriental bargainer. He knows . . . the value of what he is offering – a military presence and political influence in the Gulf that the U.S. cannot afford to relinquish."[64]

61. Sami Kohen, "In a First Test, Pro-Islamic Turkey Stays the Course on Western Ties," *Christian Science Monitor*, 26 July 1996; Stephen Kinzer, "Meeting U.S. Envoy, Turkish Premier Takes Pro-Arab Stance," *New York Times*, 3 July 1996; Kelly Couturier, "New Turkish Leader's Islamic vision Clouded by Political Reality," *Washington Post*, 25 July 1996.
62. Mayall, *Turkey*, p. 112.
63. Ibid., pp. 110, 112; Mufti, "Daring and Caution in Turkish Foreign Policy," pp. 17, 21–2; White, "Pragmatists or Ideologues?" pp. 27–8.
64. Weymouth, "Saddam's New Friend." See also Kohen, "In a First Test, Pro-Islamic Turkey Stays the Course on Western Ties," and "To U.S., Turk Leader's Tour Goes to All the Wrong Places"; Hottelet, "Turkey, NATO's Eastern Hinge, Is Far from Breaking Loose"; Nicole Pope,

After his first meeting with Erbakan in mid-1996, Tarnoff said that he had found the prime minister committed to working with the United States on all issues that have been important to U.S. intersts in recent decades: "We found a disposition in all of our conversations to respond to all of our security cooperation concerns."[65] Erbakan kept his word. When the United States attacked Iraq in September 1996 after the latter had challenged the cease-fire terms imposed by the U.N. in 1991, Erbakan refused to denounce the U.S. action and cooperated with the United States in ferrying and then airlifting thousands of Iraqi dissidents in northern Iraq across Turkey's border. By doing that, Erbakan opened himself up to a barrage of criticism from Islamist supporters at home, who disapproved of Refah's "soft" Islam. One Istanbul newspaper printed a caricature of him wearing a yarmulke bearing a Jewish star and a tie designed to look like an American flag.[66]

Turkish foreign-policy priorities remained much the same as they had been before Erbakan assumed office. Once in power, he toed the Turkish government's traditional line on almost every important issue and discarded virtually all his campaign promises. As the Islamist Minister of State Gul noted: "It's not easy to take radical steps in international relations. Because realities put constraints on you. Foreign policy and international relations demand realism."[67] Thus the alleged shift in Turkish foreign policy was more noticeable for its style than substance. Erbakan's visits to Iran and Libya were cases in point.

In August 1996, Erbakan set off alarm bells in Washington by visiting Iran against U.S. warnings, just days after Clinton had signed an "antiterrorism" law to prevent foreign firms from investing more than $40 million a year in Iran's oil and gas sectors. He also signed a

---

"Long Live Provide Comfort," *Middle East International*, 10 January 1997, p. 12.

65. Quoted in Kinzer, "Meeting U.S. Envoy, Turkish Premier Takes Pro-Arab Stance."

66. Ibid; Kinzer, "Turks' Chief Surprisingly Silent on Iraq"; Thomas W. Lippman, "U.S. Prepared to Airlift Dissidents," *Washington Post*, 12 September 1996; Hugh Pope, "The Erbakan Whirlwind Sweeps Through Turkey," p. 4.

67. "Turkey Is a European Country." See also "Focus – Islam and Turkey," p. 11.

$23 billion gas deal with Teheran. Far from heralding a radical change in Ankara's orientation, however, Erbakan's visit to and deal with Iran was backed by the ruling secular elite which has long-standing commercial interests.[68]

Similarly, his October visit to Libya – which turned into a fiasco and almost split his ruling coalition – and other Muslim states should be seen as a diversification of economic interests, rather than the birth of an Islamic trading bloc. Given his postelection acceptance of strategic links with the United States and Israel, Erbakan felt the need to play a Muslim card to retain credibility with his followers.[69]

The United States expressed "very serious reservations" about the rapprochement between its NATO ally and Iran and Libya. The State Department warned Erbakan to stop making "objectionable" remarks and "taking potshots" at the United States: "When other countries, especially friends of the United States, like Turkey, consider normalizing or treating on an equal basis countries like Libya, of course we have some concerns. . . . It is up to allies to be good allies and to understand you can't pick and choose places where you are going to support us or not support."[70] Some congressional lead-

68. James M. Dorsey, "Erbakan Striking Balance Between Islamic Neighbors and Secular Army," *Washington Report on Middle Eastern Affairs* (October 1996), p. 28; Aydin Nurhan, "Turkey and Middle Eastern Stability, pp. 131–2; Kelly Couturier, "Ignoring U.S., Turkey and Iran Sign Trade Accords," *Washington Post*, 22 December 1996; Kohen, "Pro-Islamic Premier Stays in Power, but the Future of Turkey Still Murky."
69. "U.S. Criticizes Turkish Leader for Libya Trip and Trade Deal," *New York Times*, 8 October 1996; Kohen, "Who Runs Turkey?" and "Dollars vs. Diplomacy: Turks Differ with U.S.," *Christian Science Monitor*, 25 May 1995, and "To U.S., Turk Leader's Tour Goes to All the Wrong Places"; Kelly Couturier, "Turk's Libya Trip Causes Political Crisis at Home," *Washington Post*, 8 October 1996; Thomas W. Lippman, "Turkish Official Cautions U.S. on Cyprus Pressure," *Washington Post*, 1 March 1997; Dorsey, "With Friends Like Qaddafi, Islamist Erbakan Doesn't Need Enemies," p. 37. Peterson, "Mideast Balance of Power Shifts"; "Fehim Adak: Erbakan Seeks Cooperation with America," interview, in *Middle East Quarterly* (March 1997), p. 66.
70. Kinzer, "Turkey Sending Envoy to U.S. to Clear up 'Misunderstanding,'" *New York Times*, 27 December 1996, and "The Islamist Who Runs Turkey, Delicately," p. 31; Couturier, "Ignoring U.S., Turkey and Iran Sign Trade Accords"; Kohen, "To U.S., Turk Leader's Tour

ers pressed then Secretary of State Warren Christopher to either prevent Turkey from signing the deal with Iran or place sanctions on Ankara.[71]

It is worth remembering that in 1994, former Prime Minister Ciller visited Libya with little outcry from the United States. Turkey's gas deal with Iran had also been negotiated under the auspices of Ciller in 1995, while she was prime minister. In this context, the U.S. response to Erbakan's visits to Iran and Libya was indicative of the deep doubts and suspicions that U.S. officials entertained about where Refah was taking Turkey. Nevertheless, the United States' tense diplomatic response was not matched by any hostile action against the Islamist-based government. The State Department even expressed understanding of Turkey's need for Iranian natural gas. American officials also insisted that Erbakan's signing of the gas deal with Iran would not cause a rift in relations between Washington and Ankara.[72]

On balance, the U.S. relationship with the Islamist-led government was cordial, though strains, which were reflected in occasional public pronouncements by Washington and Ankara, persisted between the two partners. These sources of friction involved Cyprus (and Greek-Turkish relations in general); ties to Iran, the seemingly insoluble Kurdish issue; and congressional criticism of Turkey's human-rights record.[73] However, most of these disagreements predated

Goes to All the Wrong Places"; "U.S. Criticizes Turkish Leader for Libya Trip and Trade Deal."

71. Shirl McArthur, "Turkey Defies Iran Sanctions," *Washington Report on Middle Eastern Affairs* (October 1996), p. 21.
72. Dorsey, "Erbakan Striking Balance Between Islamic Neighbors and Secular Army," p. 28; Migdalovitz, "Turkey's Unfolding Political Crisis," p. 21; Thomas W. Lippman, "Turkish Official Cautions U.S. on Cyprus Pressure"; M. M. Ali, "Refah Foreign Affairs Expert: Turkey's Outreach to Muslim States 'Realistic,' " *Washington Report on Middle Eastern Affairs* (April/May 1997), p. 15; Stephen Kinzer, "Turkey Sending Envoy to U.S. to Clear up 'Misunderstanding' "; Kohen, "Pro-Islamic Premier Stays in Power, but the Future of Turkey Still Murky"; Richard C. Hottelet, "Turkey, NATO's Eastern Hinge, Is Far from Breaking Loose."
73. Barkey, "Turkish Politics after the Elections," pp. 5–6; Lippman, "Turkish Official Cautions U.S. on Cyprus Pressure."

Refah's coming to power. The United States thus chose not to antagonize the Islamist-based government and avoided an open rhetorical confrontation with Ankara. U.S. officials even acknowledged – and praised – the "positive" efforts made by the Erbakan government to improve human-rights conditions in Turkey.[74]

Washington's nuanced approach also manifested itself in the State Department's announcement that it would seek a "private dialogue" with Erbakan.[75] According to a senior U.S. official, the U.S. ambassador to Turkey was given great latitude to pursue dialogue with Erbakan on a broad range of questions. This U.S. diplomat emphasized that the American approach was pragmatic and devoid of cultural or religious residues of hostility toward Islamism.[76] Each side "must respect the roles, capabilities and values of the other," stressed Assistant Secretary Alan Larson.[77]

Several factors account for Washington's subtle and complex approach to the Islamist-based government in Ankara. American officials had more confidence in Turkey's institutions than they had in Algeria's and Egypt's. In the worst circumstances, the U.S. foreign-policy elite could count on the Turkish military to step in and undo any radical changes implemented by Refah. Turkish generals are well seasoned in the art of intervention in domestic politics, and they have shown resolve in using their power to pacify and punish dangerous challengers. In other words, the United States counts on the Turkish military to preserve order and Ankara's foreign-policy alignment. Also important in U.S. eyes was the fact that Erbakan proved to be much more cooperative and pragmatic once he assumed office. The prime minister showed respect for Washington's security interests, particularly regarding Iraq and Israel. Although U.S. officials never completely trusted the Islamist-led government, they managed to have a businesslike relationship with it.

74. Jonathan Ewing, "Long Hunger Strike in Turkey Speeds Prison Reforms," *Christian Science Monitor*, 30 July 1996.
75. *Reuters*, 9 October 1996.
76. This point was made at on off-the-record meeting of a group of policy makers and scholars in New York in September 1997.
77. Larson, "Building U.S.–Turkey Economic Cooperation."

The Military's Final Assault and Removal of Erbakan

The Turkish military establishment was not impressed by Erbakan's new realism, however. Military brass viewed the confrontation between secular and religious forces as a "matter of life or death" for Turkey.[78] Furthermore, as the political struggle intensified, the military's appetite expanded. Nudged by the army, a senior public prosecutor filed charges in the spring of 1996 to outlaw Refah on the grounds that it endangered the basic tenets of secularim and fomented a "civil war atmosphere."[79] Indeed, the military enjoyed its new active role in politics that was qualitatively different from past behavior. Although from the foundation of modern Turkey the army had involved itself, overtly or covertly, in politics, it kept a low profile and played a subtle, complex role. In the 1990s, the army threw caution to wind and acted like any other party, thus exposing its political ambitions and inherent strengths and weaknesses. Between 1960 and 1980, the military overthrew three elected governments. However, an outright coup was no longer feasible in the 1990s because of the strength of Islamists and a changed world environment.[80]

Europe and the United States also opposed a coup d'état. The United States impressed on Turkish generals the danger of staging a putsch. American officials issued discreet warnings and privately told Turkish generals that the NATO alliance would have great difficulty tolerating a military-led regime. When the struggle intensified between the military and the Islamist-based government, Secretary of State Madeleine Albright stressed that "whatever changes people are thinking about they [should pursue them] in a democratic context," and that civilian rule in Turkey is an important part of democracy. Albright also noted that all sixteen NATO members are ruled by

78. Yalman Onaran, "Turkey's Military Boycotts Islam," *Associated Press*, 7 June 1997; Stephen Kinzer, "Turkish Generals Raise Pressure on Premier."
79. "Turkish Prosecutor Seeks to Outlaw Islamic Party," *New York Times*, 22 May 1997; David Swanson, "Secular Turkey Teeters over Plan to Close Islamic Schools," *Christian Science Monitor*, 12 June 1997. Nicole Pope, "Turkey Goes Back into Iraq," p. 4.
80. Sami Kohen, "With Islam's Crescent Rising over Turkey, the Army Howls," *Christian Science Monitor*, 2 June 1997.

civilians, a pointed message against a military putsch. At the same time, Albright balanced her message to the military by saying that it was essential that Turkey remains a secular democracy.[81]

The United States tried hard to balance its stance by walking a fine line between the two opposing factions – the secularist military and the Islamist-based government. On the one hand, the United States wanted the generals to keep Erbakan on his toes so as to prevent him from realigning Turkey's traditional pro-Western policy. On the other, American officials feared the effects of a military coup on the long-term political stability of Turkey. The administration felt it had learned valuable lessons from the Algerian case, and it was reluctant to condone or give the impression of support to any military putsch in Ankara. When asked if the U.S. government sanctioned the military's moves in Ankara, the State Department spokesman gave a response that reflected Washington's predicament: "Certainly, the military has a role to play in Turkish political life, if you look at the Turkish constitution and look at Turkish history. But we believe in secular democracy. That is the foundation of our policy. We actually believe that Turkey has great inner strength, that its democratic institutions have survived crises in the past."[82]

81. U.S. State Department Daily Briefing, *Reuters*, 4 March 1997. See Barry Schwed, "Albright Backs Secular Turkey," *Associated Press*, 13 June 1997; Kinzer, "Turkish Generals Raise Pressure on Premier"; Susan Frazer, "Turkey Islamic Leader Cedes Power," *Associated Press*, 13 June 1997; Nicole Pope, "Turkey: Erbakan Versus the Generals," *Middle East International*, 2 May 1997, p. 3.
82. Schwed, "Albright Backs Secular Turkey." In editorials, the mainstream U.S. media impressed on American officials the need to take a firm and unambiguous stand against a military putsch. For example, the *New York Times* urged the United States to make clear to the Turkish generals that it favors civilian governance and would be obliged to distance itself from any military-dominated regime; it warned U.S. officials that a putsch would probably radicalize Turkey's Islamists and send the wrong signal to friend and foe; the United States should support democratic solutions to Turkey's problems, rather than those imposed by force. In another editorial, the *Times* accused the military of fabricating charges against the Islamist-based government to "club the opposition." See "Outlawing Islam," *New York Times*, 19 June 1997. See also "Turkey's Meddlesome Generals," editorial, 25 March 1997, and "Military Meddling in Turkey," editorial, 14 June 1997. Likewise, the *Washington Post* cautioned those policy circles in Washington who sympathize with the

For all these reasons, military brass had to play the political game by using all instruments of pressure at their disposal, short of a coup d'état, including the implicit threat to employ force. Turkey's generals and their secular allies used comparisons with Iran and Islamic militancy to impress on their Western allies the urgency of the situation.[83] As 1997 progressed, the generals stepped up their pressure and considered a "civilian coup" that would bring down the coalition.[84] Responding to the military's pressure, Ciller threatened that her party would quit the coalition if she were not made prime minister immediately. In June 1997 Erbakan yielded to pressure from the military and resigned after nearly a year in power.[85]

The generals and their secular allies rejoiced for saving the country from fundamentalism and making sure that Turkey was no longer in danger of becoming "another Iran" or "another Algeria." Yet in some quarters in Turkey and the United States, disquieting questions were raised about the wisdom of the "soft coup" engineered by the military. Was not the latter, by implicitly using the threat of force to overthrow the Islamic-led government, following the same policy as the late Shah of Iran and more recently the Algerian military? Was the military driving the mainstream Islamists underground, thus laying the groundwork for more serious trouble in the future?[86]

military's aggressive tactics, since short-circuiting democracy now is likely only to exacerbate the problem. "What Turkey Needs," reprinted in the *International Herald Tribune*, 21–2 June 1997.

83. Alemdar, "Turkey to Combat Islam Influence"; Kinzer, "Turkish Generals Raise Pressure on Premier," and "In Defense of Secularism, Turkish Army Warns Rulers," *New York Times*, 2 March 1997; Kohen, "With Islam's Crescent Rising over Turkey, the Army Howls"; Pomfret, "Turkey's Identity Crisis."

84. Kohen, "Turkey's Military Tries Political Moves to Squelch Premier's Islamic Ambition."

85. Suzan Frazer, "Turkey Islamic Leader Cedes Power"; Kohen, "Secular Turks Hope to Check Nation's First Islamic Leader."

86. Many Turks also criticized the military for overstepping its mandate and acting as a partisan political force, with lasting damage to constitutional democracy. Even the Turkish Industrialists and Businessmen Association, a bastion of the ruling establishment, issued a report calling for quicker democratization and advocating the assertion of civilian control over the military by abolishing the NSC. See Stephen Kinzer, "Islam and Liberty: Struggles in Two Lands," and "Pro-Islamic Premier Steps Down in Turkey Under Army Pressure," *New York Times*, 19 June 1997;

As expected and in deference to the military, President Demirel asked Mesut Yilmaz, a center-rightist, to form the next government. After doing so at the end of June 1997, Yilmaz said that he would put a definite end to Turkey's year-long experiment with Islamic rule. His first act was to propose and have the parliament successfully pass a bill that increased compulsory secular education from five to eight years, in effect shutting down the junior high school sections of Islamic secondary schools. The generals and their allies have also initiated a concerted effort to ban Refah from playing a role in the political process.[87] In November 1998 their efforts bore fruit when Turkey's highest court yielded to military pressure and banned Refah from all participation in the political process.

Although the State Department stressed its commitment to secular democracy in Turkey, it did not utter a word in support of the constitutionally elected government or in criticism of the military's aggressive tactics. American officials might have been pleased with the final turn of events in Ankara. Once again the military proved to be the guardian of the Kemalist state and its Western-leaning foreign policy. Islamists were undermined in their attempt to balance Ankara's relations with the Western powers and Muslim states. Turkey remains firmly anchored within the U.S. orbit. Although American policy makers did not panic or take a hostile stand toward the Islamist-based government, they hardly approved or felt easy about this new, unpredictable experiment.

On the whole, suspicion and fear marked U.S. perceptions and views of Refah's ideology and policies, particularly when Erbakan appeared to challenge American security concerns in the Gulf and the Middle East. However, U.S. officials did not allow such fears to cloud and damage relations with their NATO ally. To their credit, they learned how to coexist with the Refah-led government by initiating a high-level dialogue with Ankara. Accommodation, not con-

Nicole Pope, "The Crisis Drags on," *Middle East International,* 13 June 1997, p. 10; James M. Dorsey, "Turkish Military 'Advice' Reins in Islamist Erbakan Government," *Washington Report on Middle East Affairs* (June/July 1997), p. 93.
87. Stephen Kinzer, "A Centrist in Turkey Gets Chance to Govern," *New York Times,* reprinted in the *International Herald Tribune,* 21–2 June 1997, and "Turkey's Islamic Rule Ends as Secular Leader Takes Over," *New York Times,* 1 July 1997.

frontation, typified the U.S. approach toward Turkey's Islamists. The result was that the U.S. and the Islamist-based government avoided rhetorical confrontations and maintained correct relations as well. In this sense and as a first step, American foreign policy toward Refah might serve as a model to apply to other cases where Islamists participate in the political process.

The Islamic Threat: Myth or Reality?

How real was and is the Islamist threat in Turkey? Will Islamists grow powerful enough to restore an Islamic state ruled according to the law of Islam, the sharia? The consensus among scholars of Turkey is that there are many barriers to the establishment of an Islamist state in Ankara. To begin with, public surveys show that while the Turks are religious, they are far from being fanatical. In a 1986 survey, only 7 percent of a national sample approved of a statement that Turkey should be ruled by sharia. For the majority of the urban middle class, religion has also become a private affair. Another poll conducted in 1995 shows that two-thirds of Turks support strong ties with the West. Simply put, popular support does not exist for constructing either an Islamist state or qualitatively reorienting Turkish foreign policy.[88]

Islamists knew the public mood and behaved accordingly. Although some of the leaders of the Refah Party say that a state based on the sharia is "theoretically possible," they stress their wish for a Muslim society but not for an Islamist state. Erbakan stressed that Turkey is neither Algeria nor Iran, and Refah will always submit to the popular will out of its respect for pluralism. Militant Islamists who oppose the secular democratic state constitute only a small minority among Islamists. The majority of Islamists are inclined to pursue peaceful means to further their objectives.[89]

88. Ilter Turan, "Religion and Political Culture in Turkey," in Richard Tapper, ed., *Islam in Modern Turkey* (London: I. B. Tauris, 1991), p. 55; Jeremy Salt, "Nationalism and the Rise of Muslim Sentiment in Turkey," *Middle East Studies* 31, no. 1 (January 1995), p. 22; Heper, "Islam and Democracy in Turkey," pp. 35, 43. Ahmad, *The Making of Modern Turkey*, p. 223; Henze, *Turkey*, p. 7.
89. Sayari, "Turkey's Islamist Challenge," *Middle East Quarterly* 3, no. 3 (September 1996), p. 37; Heper, "Islam and Democracy in Turkey," pp. 38, 43; Henze, *Turkey*, pp. v, 8; Barkey, "Turkish Politics After

Next, Islam in Turkey is diverse and multicentered. Far from being monolithic, Islamists are divided along liberal, left-leaning, and scriptural fundamentalist lines.[90] Turkey's mainstream Islamists are much more open to political pressure than their counterparts elsewhere due to the pluralist nature of Turkish politics. Turkey has proved resistant to Islamic militancy from abroad, such as the Persian and Arab variants. Islamists in Turkey are a product of different historical and material circumstances. Hence, an Islamist course for Turkey may involve only a recognition of Turkey's historical role and rediscovery of Turkey's Islamic roots, with restoration of Islamic traditions ignored or rejected as from the past.[91]

Furthermore, Turkish Islam retains the central core of Turkish nationalism and statism. Turkish Islamists do not perceive a contradiction between being Muslims and having an attachment to the Kemalist secular state, viewing both as integral to national identity. Secularization has shaped the identities and practices of new Islamists. A 1994 survey indicated that only 7 percent of the Refah Party's voters voted for the party primarily because it was an Islamic party. Like their counterparts in the Arab world and Iran, the Turkish Islamists have adopted the science and technology of the West – while rejecting its cultural values – and modern models of the nation–state as centralized and bureaucratized.[92]

the Elections," pp. 2–3; Rouleau, "Turkey Beyond Ataturk," p. 79.

90. Salt, "Nationalism and the Rise of Muslim Sentiment in Turkey," p. 21; Henze, *Turkey*, p. 7; Nilufer Gole, "Secularism and Islamism in Turkey: The Making of Elites and Counter-Elites," *Middle East Journal* 51, no. 1 (Winter 1997), p. 53; Sencer Ayata, "Patronage, Party, and State: The Politicalization of Islam in Turkey," *Middle East Journal* 50, no. 1 (January 1995), p. 55; Margulies and Yildizoglu, "The Political Uses of Islam in Turkey," p. 17; White, "Pragmatists or Ideologues?" p. 30; Sayari, "Turkey's Islamist Challenge," p. 39.

91. Graham E. Fuller, "Alternative Turkish Roles in the Future Middle East," in Barkey, ed., *Reluctant Neighbor*, pp. 212–15; Margulies and Yildizoglu, "The Political Uses of Islam in Turkey," p. 13; Zubaida, "Turkish Islam and National Identity," p. 15; Heper, "Islam and Democracy in Turkey," pp. 35, 42; Carley, *Turkey's Role in the Middle East*, p. 24; Kohen, "Islamic Party Jumps Out Front"; Kinzer, "Islam and Liberty."

92. Ergun Ozbudun, "Islam and Politics in Modern Turkey," in Barbara Freyer Stowasser, ed., *The Islamic Impulse* (Washington, DC: Center for

Erbakan's hands were also tied by two political realities. First, his coalition with Ciller imposed constraints on their joint government. On several occasions Ciller succeeded in moderating Erbakan's politics. Second, the military constitutes the major deterrent to the establishment of an Islamic state in Turkey. Islamists were well aware of this fact and acted accordingly. In fact, Islamists underwent a gradual change of attitude from an antiregime stance to a proregime one.[93] The short experience of the Refah Party in power is illuminating in this respect. Inclusion and participation in the political process breed moderation. On balance, Islamists have proven to be pragmatic in coping with political realities. While in power, Refah worked within a pluralist political framework.[94]

Islamist militancy might represent a danger to the existing order if politicized religion becomes a vehicle for the expression of discontent among the have-nots, whose numbers have multiplied since the 1980s. The real threat to the Kemalist state comes not from political Islam but from the rapid transformation of socioeconomic and urban conditions in Turkey and from the continuing war against the Kurdish insurgency. Thus, the Islamic impulse in the political process will

Contemporary Arab Studies, Georgetown University, 1987), p. 144; James Brown, "Islamic Fundamentalism and Turkey," *Journal of Political and Military Sociology* 16 (Fall, 1988), p. 239; Ayata, "Patronage, Party, and State," p. 56; Heper, "Islam and Democracy in Turkey," pp. 33, 45; Gole, "Secularism and Islamism in Turkey," p. 48; Feroz Ahmad, "Politics and Islam in Modern Turkey," *Middle Eastern Studies* 27, no. 1 (January 1991), p. 17; Richard Tapper and Nancy Tapper, " 'Thank God We're Secular!' Aspects of Fundamentalism in a Turkish Town," in Lionel Caplan, ed., *Studies in Religious Fundamentalism* (London: Macmillan, 1987), pp. 51–78; Zubaida, "Turkish Islam and National Identity," pp. 10, 14; Pomfret, "Turkey's Identity Crisis."

93. Heper, "Islam and Democracy in Turkey," p. 33; Stephen Kinzer, "Once the Hope of Secular Turks, Ex-Leader Is Now Widely Reviled," *New York Times*, 6 April 1997; Kohen, "To U.S., Turk Leaders' Tour Goes to All the Wrong Places," and "Pro-Islamic Premier Stays in Power, but the Future of Turkey Still Murky."

94. Ahmad, "Politics and Islam in Modern Turkey," pp. 8–9. Zubaida, "Turkish Islam and National Identity," p. 10. Heper, "Islam and Democracy in Turkey," pp. 43–4; White, "Pragmatists or Ideologues?" p. 30; Kohen, "Islamic Party Jumps Out Front"; James M. Dorsey, "Troubled Turkey Getting Seventh Government in Two Years," *Washington Report on Middle East Affairs* (July 1996), p. 58.

weaken as the conditions that have given rise to it – social inequality, exploitation, and political repression – disappear. Islamists' ascendance is based more upon popular discontent with the existing order than with a growing religiosity or a wholesale dissatisfaction with the secular state.[95]

Policy Recommendations

In this context, the United States can be very effective in nudging Turkey's secular elite to address the real causes behind many Turks' protests and grievances. First and foremost, the U.S. government should impress on the Turkish generals the need to solve the country's simmering problems, particularly the Kurdish issue, in accordance with constitutional means. Although the United States made clear its preference for a political solution to the crisis between the military and the Islamist-based government, it still blessed the army's role in the political process. The United States endorsed the military's mandate by publicly praising its indispensability and arranging separate meetings for visiting U.S. officials with some Turkish generals. American officials appear to have a blind faith in the military's capacity to preserve the secular Kemalist state as well as U.S. strategic interests. This fact explains Washington's reluctance to press the army to respect democracy.

Unlike European countries that have stressed the need to strengthen and consolidate a liberal, democratic regime in Ankara, the United States has been willing to tolerate harsh dictatorships in the Muslim world in the interest of stability. U.S. policy circles greeted the three coups d'état – 1960, 1971, and 1980 – with understanding and even relief. In fact, U.S.–Turkish relations were unusually smooth and cordial during the periods of military intervention.[96]

95. Abramowitz, "Dateline Ankara," pp. 177–8; Onis, "Turkey in the Post–Cold War Era," p. 65; Colin Barraclough, "Roll Over Ataturk," *Middle East Insight* 11, no. 2 (January/February 1995), p. 21; Richard Cohen, "If Turkey Went the Way of Iran," *Washington Post*, 29 June 1995; Ahmad, *The Making of Modern Turkey*, p. 223.
96. Steven Greenhouse, "Turk Sees Foray in Iraq Ending in Few Weeks," *New York Times*, 7 April 1995; Kinzer, "Europeans Shut the Door on Turkey's Membership in Union," *New York Times*, 27 March 1997; Paul B. Henze, *Turkish Democracy and the American Alliance* (Santa Monica, CA: Rand Corporation, 1993), p. 2; Barkey, "Turkish Politics after the

With a few exceptions, the United States has mostly sacrificed human-rights concerns in Turkey on the altar of strategic considerations.[97]

American officials and policy experts have not been forceful in their critique of Turkey's dismal human-rights record. Although annual State Department human-rights reports severely criticize abuses in Turkey, various U.S. administrations have somehow attempted to rationalize Ankara's bloody deeds by calling attention to the PKK's terrorist methods. American diplomats say they do not want to publicly criticize Ankara because the best way to prevent that nation from embracing Islamic fundamentalism is to integrate it into Europe sooner rather than later.[98] Even when the State Department criticizes Turkey for its dismal human-rights violations, the various U.S. administrations' policies often do not follow the State Department's findings; they have resisted congressional efforts to condition economic aid on improvement in Ankara's human-rights record on the grounds of national security. In country after country, Washingon has set aside its distaste for human-rights violations in pursuit of good relations.[99]

Elections," p. 5; Ahmad, *The Making of Modern Turkey*, pp. 226, 315; Greenhouse, "U.S. Support for Turks' Anti-Kurd Campaign Dims."

97. Transcript of press conference, U.S. Assistant Secretary of State Richard Holbrooke, Ankara, Turkey, 21 February. 1995; Makovsky, "How to Deal with Erbakan," p. 8; Kohen, "Dollars vs. Diplomacy," and "As Turkey Takes Slice of Iraq, U.S. Nods but Neighbors Fret," *Christian Science Monitor*, 13 September 1996; "Turkey Crosses a Line," *New York Times* editorial, 25 March 1995; Nicole Pope, "Turkey Goes Back into Iraq," p. 4; "Turkish Forces Cross Border into Iraq to Attack Kurdish Guerrillas," *New York Times*, 15 May 1997.

98. *East or West? Turkey Checks Its Compass*, Minority Staff Report for the U.S. Senate Foreign Relations Committee, September 1995, (Washington, DC: U.S. Government Printing Office, 1996), pp. 3, 6; Greenhouse, "Turk Sees Foray in Iraq Ending in Few Weeks," and "U.S. Support for Turks' Anti-Kurd campaign Dims."

99. Thomas W. Lippman, "State Dept. Human Rights Report Chastises Several U.S. Allies." For instance, the State Department conceded that U.S. military equipment was used against the PKK, during which human-rights abuses occurred. However, the Department qualified its statement by noting that there was no evidence that verifies reports of torture or "mystery killings" involving U.S. equipment. See "Human

Washington's ambivalence and vacillation on human rights and democracy have done considerable damage to America's reputation and prestige, as well as to consitutionalism in Turkey; they have also sent the wrong signals to the military brass and alienated mainstream Islamists who played by the rules of the political game. Islamists, not just in Turkey, have scored political points at home by criticizing the United States for its inconsistency and double standards when it comes to the Muslim world.

American diplomacy must show similar concerns with human rights and democratic behavior in Muslim societies as they do elsewhere. Given its consolidated institutions, Turkey is an ideal place for U.S. officials to practice what they preach about democratization. The United States should not only take a more "principled" and consistent stand on human rights but also condition further military aid and sales on Turkish respect for citizens' liberties and rights. American vital interests will be better served in the long term by an unambiguous and consistent stance on human rights and liberalization.

The United States might also contribute to long-term stability in Turkey by signaling its support for rapid, fair, and equitable economic development. A strong connection exists between economic marginalization, alienation, and the steady growth of Islamism across the Muslim world in the last twenty years. Turkey's Islamists have succeeded in exploiting the increasing socioeconomic inequalities and political corruption in a country where 60 percent of the population is under age twenty and four of ten young people are looking for work. The success of Refah at the polls can be credited not only to its ability to manipulate religion but also to its promising economic message.[100]

Rights Abuses by Turkish Military and the Situation in Cyprus," State Department report, *U.S. Department of State Dispatch*, 12 June 1995, p. 502. This assertion flies in the face of evidence provided by independent observers.

100. Mehmet Yasar Geyikdag, *Political Parties in Turkey: The Role of Islam* (New York: Praeger, 1984), p. 119; Heper, "Islam and Democracy in Turkey," p. 36; Barkey, "Turkish Politics after the Elections," pp. 2–3; White, "Pragmatists or Ideologues? p. 26; Ahmad, "Politics and Islam in Modern Turkey," p. 16; Ayata, "Patronage, Party, and State," pp. 52, 54; Zubaida, "Turkish Islam and National Identity," p. 11.

The United States should encourage secular allies to address some of the long-ignored critical issues. These include the plight of the urban poor, the social chaos of large and crowded Turkish cities, corruption, and the militaristic hegemony of the Kemalist state. The political struggle in Turkey cannot be won except by further democratization so that people feel they are in charge of their own destiny. This reality requires opening up both the political and the economic decision-making process. By lending its political weight and foreign aid to such endeavors, U.S. policy makers will contribute to further deepening and consolidation of Turkish democracy and social harmony.

Far from being resolved, Turkey's political crisis continues. Intimidation and exclusion are radicalizing Turkish Islamic politics. Political protests by Islamists have already turned bloody. The potential for escalation of violence is present so long as the military-dominated Kemalist state remains bent on "outlawing Islam" and pushing aside mainstream Islamist politicians such as Erbakan. Dispensing with constitutionalism and democratic procedures will likely intensify the role of the military in Turkish politics further and complicate sociopolitical and economic tensions.

Instead of attempting to ban political Islam, Turkey needs to recognize that Islam constitutes a critical component of its cultural heritage and to draw its values from the East and West, rather than remain heavily dependent on the United States. The latter will help itself and its ally by keeping a measured distance in its relationship; by reminding Turkey's secular elite to seriously tackle socioeconomic and political problems in a serious manner; and by appreciating the need to put a Muslim face on the country's pluralist Western-oriented experience.

10

Conclusion

Despite the myriad pronouncements by American officials, the United States does not have a comprehensive, coherent policy regarding the role of Islam in the political process. American thinking on Islamists has not been translated into concrete policy guidelines. Hence Washington's general and abstract statements should be seen as an ideal type, because no serious attempt has been made to operationalize a policy directive on Islamic resurgence.

Three factors account for the absence of a comprehensive American policy toward Islamic activists. First, neither the Bush nor the Clinton administrations – none of their predecessors made any elaborate statement on Islam – had an overarching, encompassing foreign-policy vision. Both administrations briefly flirted with the idea of creating a new world order in America's image. When faced with the requisite costs, however, presidents Bush and Clinton abandoned their ambitious effort in favor of micro, pragmatic, and selective policies.

Clinton, in particular, seems to be much more concerned with "low," or domestic, politics, and he has essentially delegated foreign-policy formulation to a select team of aides. "High" politics, including the Middle East and the larger Muslim world, is clearly not Clinton's passion. More than any other recent president, Clinton appears to be overly sensitive to internal ethnic politics, conducting foreign-policy on an ad hoc, short-term basis, often geared to satisfy certain domestic constituencies. The result is that American policy has been mostly reactive to crises as they unfold on the world stage. The U.S. approach to Islamic resurgence is a case in point.

A related second point is that former Secretaries of State James

Baker, Warren Christopher, and Madeleine Albright, not being conceptualizers, preferred to tackle concrete and tangible foreign-policy questions. A State Department official cited Christopher's talk, "Open Forum," in which he told the Department personnel that he liked to work on discrete problems – the negotiations for the Panama Canal, the tribunal for Iran, and the Arab-Israeli peace negotiations – not on abstract issues.[1]

The diplomatic style of Baker, Christopher, and Albright explains their decisions to empower medium-level officials like Edward Djerejian, Robert Pelletreau, Martin Indyk, and Mark Paris to grapple with the Islamist phenomenon. This fact illustrates Washington's incremental and piecemeal thinking on Islamism and the continuity that marked the Bush and Clinton administrations' policy approach to the subject. This study shows that Djerejian's Meridian House address has established the large parameters of American policy toward political Islam.

Third, U.S. officials realize that Islamist movements, far from being monolithic, are deeply fragmented, and that their political agendas are driven mainly by particular and unique circumstances in various countries. Here lies the Bush and Clinton administrations' ambivalence about delineating a universal policy toward political Islam. Former Assistant Secretary of State for Near Eastern Affairs Pelletreau criticized those observers who advocate formulating a comprehensive U.S. policy that encompasses the whole Muslim world. Pelletreau stressed that the United States does not have the luxury of articulating a policy across the board toward Islamists, because "we have interests that we deal with every day on a practical, real basis."[2] Other officials agree that the United States treats Islamists on a case-by-case basis, not on any abstract level; policy is determined by analyzing the Islamists' rhetoric and action in each country and assessing their potential threat to American interests.[3]

1. Interview with an official in the State Department's Policy Planning Staff, Washington, DC, 27 March 1995.
2. Robert Pelletreau in "Symposium: Resurgent Islam in the Middle East," p. 16.
3. Interview with an officer in the State Department's Policy Planning Staff, State Department, Washington, DC, 27 March 1995, and interview with an NSC official, Washington, DC, 30 March 1995.

CONCLUSION

Findings of This Study: Rhetoric

Indeed, specificity – analyzing Washington's actual policies toward Islamist movements and states – is critical to understanding American policy toward political Islam. This study, for example, has found major inconsistencies between what U.S. officials say and what they do regarding the role of Islam in the political process. One of the findings of this study is that U.S. pronouncements on political Islam, with the exception of a few deviations, are well anchored within the accommodationist camp. In particular, the discourse of the Bush and Clinton administrations points to a conscious attempt to reach out to moderate Muslims. Both have commended Muslims for "renewed emphasis on traditional values," voicing no alarm at the increasing role of Islam in the political process so long as it remains peaceful.

American foreign policy, stressed Bush and Clinton administration officials, showed willingness to coexist with Islamists who reject violence and extremism and play by the rules of nation–state relations. Although some U.S. officials referred to the importance of values in the relationship between the United States and Islamists, they were basically concerned with Islamists' foreign-policy orientation, not with their internal politics. In this context, the end of the Cold War has not brought about substantive changes in Washington's Middle East policy, which is still preoccupied with stability and with security and economic relationships, rather than with issues of democracy and human rights.

This leads me to another finding of the study: Contemporary security and strategic calculations, not just culture, ideology or history, appear to influence U.S. public and official thinking and discourse on Islamic resurgence. Although some official statements make a reference to culture, they mainly stress current security threats associated with the rise of "extremist" Islam to American vital interests. For as one policy maker noted, neither Clinton nor Bush was intrinsically interested in Islam per se; rather, they feared Islamists' potential to undermine the Arab-Israeli peace process and the stability of the pro-Western regimes, disrupt the West's access to Gulf oil, acquire nonconventional weapons, and undertake terrorist activities. Cultural considerations may unconsciously influence U.S. officials' private thinking on political Islam, but they hardly figure in their public pronouncements.

American policy makers have made it clear that they strongly disagree with confrontationalists' assertion that Islamic activism has replaced Soviet Communism as the new threat to the West. Far from viewing Islamic resurgence as part of an anti-Western Jihad, U.S. officials attribute the rise of Islamic sentiments to worsening socio-economic and political conditions. They have decisively rejected the clash-of-civilizations hypothesis, stressing, instead, the unique role of the United States as a bridge between various spiritual systems. The Bush and Clinton administrations have conducted a well-organized public-relations campaign to allay Muslims' fears about the myth of confrontation that has become popular in some foreign-policy elite circles.

In particular, senior Clinton aides, in addition to the President, Vice President, and first lady, have gone out of their way to praise Islam and stress the religious and civilizational ties between Islam and the Western world. On the whole, Clinton's pronouncements display enlightened sensitivity, realism, and tactfulness. The President has invested some effort in educating and sensitizing himself to Islam. His speech to the Jordanian Parliament in October 1994 was a case in point. According to a senior official who helped draft the speech, Clinton wanted to send an unambiguous message of reassurance to Muslims that America does not subscribe to the clash-of-civilizations hypothesis. Clinton and his senior aides have also taken the time to allay the concerns and fears of the Muslim community in the United States by regularly meeting with its representatives. Again, more than any recent President, Clinton has elevated the art of ethnic politics to new heights. As a result, the Muslim-American community has benefited at least on the symbolic, psychological level by having finally been accorded a little attention and recognition. President Clinton deserves credit for that.

The Clinton administration's statements on political Islam are much more advanced, nuanced, and complex than those of many opinion makers and the general public at large. On the whole, Chapters 1, 2, and 3 show that both the public and the foreign-policy elite perceive political Islam as a menace to the United States and its local allies and call for its containment. In this context, the presidency and its various executive agencies can play a critical role in the education of all American citizens about Islam and Muslims. Unfortunately, the same cannot be said of the legislative branch, some of whose members' views on Islamism parallel those of the public and the foreign-policy elite. In contrast, the discourse on Islamism by present and former U.S. officials – with the exception of a few provocative pronouncements made by several Reagan administration aides – may best be described as culturally sensitive and politically correct.

Findings of This Study: Policies

It is important to stress yet again the fact that U.S. officials' statements, however, do not serve as a guide to understanding American foreign policy toward Islamic activists. Actual American policies toward Islamic movements and states reveal a deep residue of ambivalence, skepticism, and mistrust. A case-by-case survey, such as that done in this study, shows that the United States feels reluctant to engage Islamists in any meaningful dialogue. On a few occasions and in few places, the United States attempted to test the waters by establishing contacts with Islamists in Egypt and Algeria. Washington promptly discontinued those contacts, however, under pressure from its Middle Eastern allies. The United States has not only supported its traditional friends – in their fight against Islamists – but has done little to persuade them to open up the political field to existing, legitimate opposition forces.

Egypt is a case in point. After a brief flirtation with the Egyptian Muslim Brothers in the early 1990s, the U.S. government severed its discreet connection with them by the mid-1990s. President Mubarak's protestations found receptive ears in Washington. The United States did not want to alienate and endanger the Mubarak regime, a critical player in the Arab-Israeli peace process and in regional stability. The United States also harbors deep suspicions about the Brothers' revolutionary agenda at home and abroad. In U.S. eyes, Mubarak is a much safer gamble than Islamists, who are seen to be unknown and unpredictable. The United States appears to be unwilling to take risks on an untested Islamist opposition. The result is that Mubarak feels empowered to emasculate all opposition, Islamist and secular, thus exacerbating Egypt's crisis of political authority and legitimacy.

Egyptians perceive the United States to have – by design or default – sanctioned Mubarak's crackdown on mainstream Muslim Brothers. American officials disavow any endorsement of Mubarak's severe methods; they also stress that they have privately advised him to expand the political space within which the opposition operates. Despite America's having provided Egypt with more than $30 billion in foreign assistance since 1975, U.S. diplomats acknowledge that they have little leverage over Mubarak and, accordingly, little influence to change the course of events there. Wielding influence or not, the United States cannot afford to remain publicly mute in light of the Egyptian regime's dramatic abuse of human rights, restriction of political participation, and constriction of political space.

In the Egyptian case, the United States needs to close, or at least narrow, the gap between its rhetoric and actual behavior. Does the U.S. government consider the mainstream Muslim Brothers as part of the legitimate opposition? And if so, should not the United States impress on the Mubarak regime, both publicly and privately, the need to co-opt the Brothers rather than try to suppress them? Or does the U.S. government view certain manifestations of Islam in power as ultimately inimical to its vital interests? One suspects that the United States considers the Brothers potential troublemakers who might reorient Egypt's regional and foreign policies if they gain power. Hence, Washington's strategy aims to deny Islamists recognition and legitimacy in the hope that the Egyptian state will finally succeed in taming and containing the new Islamic resurgence as it has done in the past.

However, the constriction of legitimate political space drives many Islamists underground and makes the government vulnerable to al-Jama'a's and Jihad's terrorist campaign. Inclusion of the legitimate opposition would expose the falsity of the militants' raison d'être, thus preparing the ground for their isolation and further disintegration. Al-Jama'a's reputation and military organization have been weakened considerably, thanks to its brutal attacks, which have alienated public opinion in Egypt and the larger Muslim world, as well as to the government's crackdown. By helping nudge the Mubarak regime toward mending broken bridges to the legitimate opposition, the United States would serve its own interests and those of its strategic ally.

Unlike its stand toward Egypt, Washington's approach to the Algerian crisis is much more complex and nuanced. Although initially the Bush administration implicitly supported the military's suppression of Islamists, it subsequently adopted a more balanced and sensitive appreciation of the internal struggle for power in Algeria. The U.S. government established discreet contacts with the FIS and pressed the military hard-liners to proceed with the canceled elections and implement real economic and political reforms.

The Clinton administration went further by making its support to the Algerian regime conditional on the latter's commitment to national reconciliation and political pluralism. Important as they are, the administration's policy statements on Algeria have not been accompanied by concrete measures that would convince the Algerian government of Washington's seriousness. In fact, as Chapter 7 shows, the United States has helped the Algerian regime stay afloat by assisting it in rescheduling its debts and providing it with hundreds of millions of dollars in agricultural credits. Furthermore, the United States not only discontinued its contacts with the FIS in 1995, but it also appears to have given up on the FIS altogether by at least tolerating Zeroual's decision to close the door on talks with the FIS.[4]

To be fair to American policy makers, however, one has to stress the limited nature of U.S. influence in Algeria. Unlike its presence in Egypt, the United States has hardly had any bilateral assistance program with Algiers. The military hard-liners are unlikely to be receptive to any pressure emanating from Washington. Nevertheless, U.S. officials have been consistent in calling on the Algerian regime to liberalize and integrate the nonviolent opposition into the political process, including some elements of the FIS. Although the United States does not wish to see Islamists gain power in Algiers, it has expressed its preference – both publicly and privately – for a peaceful settlement that takes into account the concerns and interests of the Algerian regime and the mainstream opposition as well.

A skeptic might say that the United States can afford to be critical and creative in Algeria, because the latter is not seen to be as strategically vital to U.S. interests as Egypt. The fact remains that the Clinton administration did not defer to France in the latter's unlim-

4. Roger Cohen, "Algeria Says Charter Passes, But Critics Charge Vote Fraud."

ited support of the military government in Algiers, and it has also adopted an independent policy of its own. The extent of U.S.–French differences on Algeria manifested themselves in the clash between the late French President François Mitterand and President Clinton when they met in June 1995. Although the Clinton administration has refrained from active engagement in the Algerian conflict, it has attempted with meager means to nudge the Zeroual regime toward a negotiated settlement. In the Algerian case, the United States has shown a willingness to accept nonviolent Islamists' participation in power so long as they accept the rules and norms of civil and international society.

Unlike their reaction to the situations in Egypt and Algeria, U.S. policy makers did not panic when Islamists scored a narrow victory in the 1995 parliamentary elections in Turkey. Initially, the United States feared that the newly elected Islamist Prime Minister, Necmettin Erbakan, would push the traditional secular-leaning country away from its traditional pro-Western orientation and seek new, anti-American alliances with radical Muslim states, particularly Iran. American officials' initial trepidation was put to rest after Erbakan assured visiting U.S. officials that he wanted better and friendlier relations with the United States. Erbakan kept his word. Soon after coming to power, he ceased his anti-Western and anti-Israeli rhetoric; he upheld the military accord with Israel; and he supported the extension of Operation Provide Comfort.

Reassured by Erbakan's respect for its strategic interests, the United States reciprocated by adopting a pragmatic approach toward Refah's ascendence to power. Ignoring the advice of some working-level officials at the State Department, the Clinton administration engaged the newly elected Erbakan before he was confirmed by the Turkish Parliament. Lines of communication were kept open with Erbakan throughout his short tenure in office. Unlike their nervous response to Islamists elsewhere in the Middle East, U.S. officials recognized the inherent limits of Islamists in Turkey. Refah's narrow electoral victory did not allow Islamists to form a government alone. Refah's coalition with the True Path Party served as a check on the former's ambitions. More important in U.S. eyes was the fact that the army seemed determined to prevent Islamists from exercising real power.

On balance, U.S. relations with the Islamist-led government were cordial, though strains persisted between Washington and Ankara. The United States chose not to antagonize or confront the Islamist-based government. Washington's nuanced approach manifested itself in its opposition to a coup d'état by the Turkish military. U.S. officials issued discreet warnings and privately told Turkish generals that the NATO alliance would have great difficulty tolerating a military-led regime. The United States tried hard to balance its stance by walking a fine line between the two warring factions – the military and the Islamist-based government. On the one hand, the United States wanted the generals to keep Erbakan on his toes. On the other, U.S. officials had learned valuable lessons from the Algerian case and feared the effects of a military coup on the long-term political stability of Turkey.

Although U.S. officials did not adopt a hostile stand toward the Islamist-based government, they hardly approved of this new, unpredictable experiment. On the whole, suspicion and apprehension marked U.S. perceptions of Refah's ideology and policies, particularly when Erbakan appeared to challenge American security concerns in the Gulf and the Middle East. For example, the State Department did not utter a word in support of the constitutionally elected government when it was faced with the military's aggressive tactics. No doubt American officials felt pleased when the military succeeded in forcing Erbakan to resign. In U.S. eyes, Islamists were undermined in their attempt to balance Ankara's relations with the Western powers and Muslim states. Turkey remains firmly anchored within the U.S. orbit.

Instead of overreacting to the coming to power of Islamists, American policy makers – to their credit – learned how to coexist with Erbakan by initiating a high-level dialogue with him. Accommodation, not confrontation, typified the U.S. approach. This farsighted U.S. stance has continued after Erbakan was forced out of office. The Unites States is on record as opposing the attempt by the Turkish secular-military establishment to have Refah permanently banned from the political arena on the grounds that it is working to undermine the secular basis of the Turkish state. The State Department has made it clear that banning Refah would have an injurious impact on Turkish democracy and would "end up damaging confidence in Turkey's democratic multi-party system."[5] That assessment stirred one of the Constitutional Court's militant secularists, Gungor Ozden, who accused the United States of trying to interfere and influence the court's decision: "Turkey is not a satellite or servant of the United States."[6]

The case of Turkey shows clearly that the United States may not only learn how to coexist with Islamists in power but also how to preserve its vital interests and strategic relations with its NATO ally. The key is a mutual commitment to serious dialogue, compromise, and recognition of common concerns. In this context, the U.S. stance toward Refah might serve as an effective model to apply to other Islamists who participate in the political process and play by constitutional rules.

The Iranian Complex

Whereas some ambiguity marks U.S. policy approaches toward the Islamist movements in Egypt and Algeria, American rhetoric and actions have been exceptionally – and consistently – hostile toward Iran, the only state ruled directly by revolutionary Islam.[7] Since 1979 Iran has acted as the standard-bearer of Islam, challenging the legitimacy of the existing regional order and of U.S. dominance. Revolutionary Islam as practiced by Iran is seen to be intensely anti-Western and inimical to most American interests. The Islamic revolution and subsequent hostage crisis, coupled with the mullahs' initial campaign to subvert their Arab Gulf neighbors and export revolution, have largely shaped U.S. officials' perceptions of Islamic resurgence.

Indeed, in the minds of many Americans, the politics of Islam is confused with the politics of Iran. Although American policy makers deny drawing any direct linkage between political Islam and Islamic Iran, they seem to have developed the "Iranian complex" – viewing

5. Stephen Kinzer, "Turkish Judge Scolds U.S. for Opposing a Ban on an Islamic Party," *New York Times*, 28 November 1997.
6. Ibid.
7. Sudan is another case whereby revolutionary Islamists, who are represented by the National Islamic Front, indirectly control the government.

other Islamist movements and states through the lens of the bloody revolution in Iran. On balance, this Iranian complex has had a negative affect on American policy toward Islamic activists elsewhere.

Although in the last twenty years U.S.–Iranian relations have witnessed a few short periods of diplomatic thaw, they reached their nadir under the Clinton administration. The latter has declared economic warfare on Iran's cleric-dominated regime and authorized the CIA to mount a covert operation to force it to reform and change its behavior. American officials stress, however, that their disagreement with and opposition to Iran is not related to its being an Islamic state but to its regional and foreign policies. These include Teheran's active opposition to the Arab-Israeli peace process, its support of terrorism, and its drive to obtain nuclear weapons. Again, security and strategic considerations top the list of Washington's complaints about Iran.

Yet the U.S. attempt to downplay the Islamic factor behind the mullahs' behavior has been less than successful. Two reasons account for this failure. First, the Iranian clerics have worked hard at portraying their conflict with the United States as part of a cultural clash between Islam and the secular West. Genuine or not, Iranian leaders insist on defining themselves in Islamic terms, though the weight of evidence indicates that they have strong nationalistic leanings. Second, the outside world, as well as some of the U.S. foreign-policy elite, believes that the United States is motivated by a desire to extract "revenge" for the humiliation it suffered at the hands of the mullahs during the hostage crisis.

Regardless of the importance of the Islamic aspect in U.S. calculations, the Iranian complex has made American policy makers ambivalent and disinclined to accept Islamists' drive to attain power. This complex has also had detrimental effects on Islamists' views of American foreign policy. Islamists often cite U.S. blanket hostility toward Teheran as an example of Washington's intrinsic animosity toward Islam and Muslims. Hence the Islamic revolution in Teheran has been a defining event in the relationship between Islamic resurgence and the United States. American responses to the Iranian revolution and the ensuing events have provided ammunition to those in both camps who believe in the myth of confrontation between the Western and Muslim worlds. The normalization of U.S.–

Iranian relations would probably ease the tensions between the United States and Islamic movements that have been deepening since the 1980s.

What Is to Be Done?

The United States has at different times delivered an impressive set of formal policy statements on political Islam. The tone and substance of this discourse has expressed profound respect for Islam's cultural and religious traditions. American official pronouncements have seemingly put to rest any lingering doubts in people's minds about the likelihood of a clash of civilizations. The challenge still facing the U.S. government is to pursue policies that are consistent and compatible with the lofty ideas expressed by its officials. As a first step, the United States should address the concerns and fears that underlie and account for many Muslims' grievances. These include unfair rules for political participation often leading to exclusion, continuing economic deprivation, and foreign-policy questions, such as the U.S. position toward the Arab-Israeli peace process, Washington's support for corrupt and unpopular Muslim leaders, and American officials' double standard in dealing with the Muslim world.

The longer the pro-Western Middle Eastern regimes keep the gates of political and economic power closed to the new social classes, the more they endanger their own survival. The United States must impress upon the ruling elites of its allies the need to broaden their social base by integrating the new classes into the political mainstream: Exclusive politics is a recipe for disaster, but inclusive politics is the key to survival. All groups that are willing to participate in democratic politics should be actively encouraged to do so.

American officials should engage in an earnest dialogue with nonviolent Islamist movements to determine if they are genuinely committed to constitutional and democratic processes and push them further along in that direction. The United States might support various Middle Eastern governments and their Islamist opposition in order to develop democratic structures and institutions that are appropriate to the needs and culture of the people.

Compounding the explosive political situation is the persistent economic deprivation at the lower end of the social scale evident in many Muslim countries. Growing unemployment and the maldistribution of resources create armies of angry, disillusioned, and resentful youths who become natural recruiting grounds for Islamists. Islamic activism feeds on unemployment, poverty, and alienation. The rank and file of Islamic activists in Egypt and Algeria – as well as Jordan and Sudan, to cite two other obvious examples – have been swelled by those youths of the lower classes who have been most negatively affected by economic scarcity and exclusion. The United States can best support Middle Eastern development by promoting not only privatization and liberalization but also certain economic measures that might alleviate the plight of the impoverished strata: A high priority should be given to the acceleration of structural adjustment in order to create real jobs. Furthermore, the reallocation of military aid and spending to the domestic sector would fuel economic growth.

Although it is debatable whether the United States can truly affect the internal political and economic situation even in Muslim countries with regimes friendly to Washington, the same is not true with regard to foreign affairs. American officials can do much more to improve the image of the United States in the eyes of Muslims, many of whom criticize what they perceive as a double standard in forming U.S. foreign policy, and they question Washington's sincerity in speaking out on issues of human rights, democracy, and the prevention of proliferation of nonconventional weapons for all peoples.

Accordingly, the United States should be more consistent and vocal in its criticism of human rights violations. Washington should make its foreign aid conditional on a respect for basic human, political, and cultural rights. For example, European countries have made it clear to Turkey that their financial, military, and political support is dependent on Ankara's respect for the cultural and human rights of its Kurdish minority. In the case of Turkey, European leaders have been much more rigorous in practicing what they preach than their U.S. counterparts. Little wonder that the Turkish ruling establishment has been diligently trying to compensate for the lack of European support by deepening their ties with Washington.

It is in Washington's long-term interest to maintain a healthy distance from corrupt and unpopular regimes in the Muslim world. Maintaining this healthy distance and remaining engaged in Muslim societies and politics should not be seen as contradictory. In the end, the choices facing the United States in its relations with Muslim societies must not be framed in terms of either having the established regimes abdicate in favor of Islamists or unconditionally supporting the authoritarian governments' crackdown against the Islamist opposition. The challenge is to promote structural reforms and gradually to open up what are today closed political systems. To be sure, the transition into full-fledged parliamentary democracies could take several decades. It would also be misleading to pretend that this process is risk-free. But the alternative is a perpetual instability and the institutionalization of violence – as the cases of Algeria and Egypt have shown.

Similarly, in its attempt to contain dangerously defiant and clearly hostile national leaders in the Muslim world, the United States should avoid inflicting unecessary collective punishment on the population at large. The policy of "dual containment," for example, has done much more damage to the Iranian and Iraqi citizenry than to the regimes in charge in Teheran and Baghdad. Many Muslims find it difficult to square U.S. progressive pronouncements on Islam with the infliction of collective punishment on Muslim peoples and society. In particular, economic sanctions against Iraq have done considerable damage to Iraqi civil society. In this way, U.S. sanctions have radicalized Islamist opposition groups in the rest of the Muslim world, particularly in Saudi Arabia, a critical U.S. client. There exists in the Muslim world a widespread perception of the United States as a ruthless hegemony that is bent on punishing unruly Arabs/Muslims, while co-opting other defiant cultures and countries.

The double-talk on promoting democracy must also end. American prestige and reputation were tarnished when initially the Bush administration supported the military's putsch against the democratic process in Algeria. Democracy implies opportunities as well as risks. To deny Islamists the fruits of electoral victory is to alienate – and radicalize – them further. Algeria, Egypt, and now Turkey are cases in point.

Moreover, many Muslims, while impressed by Clinton's nuanced and sensitive pronouncements on Islam, are baffled by his apparent lack of sensitivity to Arab/Muslim concerns in regard to the Arab-Israeli peace process and the plight of the Palestinians. Muslim commentators often portray Clinton as "the most pro-Israel President in the history of this country." Arabs/Muslims lament the fact that, under Clinton, an almost complete identity of views exists between the United States and Israel over a host of regional issues, including the peace process, security, and terrorism. They feel that Clinton has abandoned Washington's previously advocated policy of even-handedness in favor of a "total commitment" to Tel Aviv. Although tensions exist between the Clinton administration and Israeli Prime Minister Netanyahu, U.S. officials have been reluctant to push the Israeli government hard enough to accept a reasonable compromise. Furthermore, the Clinton administration has endeavored to accommodate Netanyahu at the expense of the broader goal of Arab-Israeli peacemaking and U.S. long-term interests in the region. The Clinton administration's hesitation to confront Netanyahu alienates Arabs/Muslims and provides critics of the United States with plenty of ammunition. As the Arab world's most widely read poet Nizar Qabbani put it:

> Why doesn't America behave justly?
> Why does it use double standards, and speak with two voices?
> Why does America wear two masks in the Middle East?[8]

In April 1996 Muslim public opinion was outraged over Washington's perceived collusion with Israel's bloody military action in Lebanon that resulted in more than one hundred civilian casualties. Expressing the sentiments of many Muslims, Qabbani cried, "Does every American leader who dreams of winning the presidency have to kill us – we the Arabs?"[9] The United States should not only continue its "honest broker" role in the Arab-Israeli peace process but literally push the Arabs and Israelis to a just and comprehensive settlement. What this means in practice is the establishment of a Palestinian state, bringing about the much-hoped-for historical reconciliation between Arabs and Jews.

There are limits to what the United States can do, however. Not only that, but time and again, Islamists have proven to be their own worst enemies. By being equivocal about democractic norms, human rights, peaceful relations with the West, and the use of terror in the

8. In Fawaz A. Gerges, "Clinton and the Middle East: Lost Opportunities?" *Foreign Policy* (Winter 1997).
9. Ibid.

pursuit of domestic political goals, Islamist leaders have provided much ammunition to those in the West, who seek to turn the "Islamic menace" into another bogeyman. Humanist and democratic Islamic voices should assert themselves and be heard. They should also coalesce with their Western counterparts to prevent the hijacking of American foreign policy by those in both camps who are beating the drums of a cultural and civilizational war.

References

Primary Documents

Carter, Jimmy. *Weekly Compilation of Presidential Documents*. U.S. Government Printing Office, vol. 16, no. 4, 28 January 1980.

Christopher, Warren. "Statement by Secretary of State Warren Christopher Regarding U.S. Sanctions Against Iran." State Department briefing. In *Federal News Service*, 1 May 1995.

Clinton, Bill. "A Strategy for Foreign Policy." Speech delivered to the Foreign Policy Association, New York, April 1992. *Vital Speeches* 58, no. 14, May 1992.

Commencement Address at the U.S. Naval Academy for the Class of 1990. Annapolis, MD, 30 May 1990, U.S. Naval Academy Archives, Nimitz Library.

"Remarks by President Bill Clinton to the Jordanian Parliament." The White House: Office of the Press Secretary, Amman, Jordan, 26 October 1994.

"Remarks by President Clinton at a Dinner of the World Jewish Congress." *Federal News Service*, 30 April 1995.

"Statement by the President on the occasion of the Islamic Holy Month Ramadan." The White House: Office of the Press Secretary. Boston, MA, 31 January 1995.

"The President's Remarks at White House Welcoming Ceremony for King Hussein of Jordan and Prime Minister Yitzhak Rabin of Israel, Washington, DC, 25 July 1994." *U.S. Department of State Dispatch* 5, no. 7, August 1994.

Clinton, Bill, and Benazir Bhutto. "Joint Press Conference with President Bill Clinton and Pakistani Prime Minister Benazir Bhutto." *Federal News Service*, 11 April 1995.

Clinton, Bill, and Hosni Mubarak. "U.S.–Egyptian Search for Peace and Stability in the Middle East: President Clinton and President Mubarak's News Conference." *U.S. Department of State Dispatch* 4, no. 15, 12 April 1993.

Clinton, Bill, and King Hassan II. "Remarks by President Clinton and King Hassan of Morocco upon Arrival at the White House." *U.S. Newswire*, 15 March 1995.

"Transcript of Remarks by President Clinton and King Hassan II of Morocco in Press Conference." *U.S. Newswire*, 15 March 1995.

Clinton, Bill, and Tansu Ciller. "The President's News Conference with Prime Minister Tansu Ciller of Turkey, 15 October 1993." *Weekly Compilation of Presidential Documents*. Washington, DC: U.S. Government Printing Office, 18 October 1993.

"The United States and Turkey." Opening statements at a news conference by President Clinton and Prime Minister Ciller, Washington, DC, 15 October 1995. *U.S. Department of State Dispatch*, 1 November 1993.

Djerejian, Edward P. "Review of U.S. Efforts to Achieve Near East Policy Goals." Statement before the Subcommittee on Europe and the Middle East of the House Foreign Affairs Committee, Washington, DC, 24 June 1992. *U.S. Department of State Dispatch*, 29 June 1992.

"United States Policy Toward Islam and the Arc of Crisis." *Baker Institute Study*, no. 1 (1995).

"U.S. Policy Goals in the Near East." Address before the National Association of Arab Americans, Washington, DC, 11 September 1992. *U.S. Department of State Dispatch*, 14 September 1992.

"U.S. Policy on Recent Developments and Other Issues in the Middle East." Statement before the Subcommittee on Europe and the Middle East of the House Foreign Affairs Committee, Washington, DC, 27 July 1993. *U.S. Department of State Dispatch*, 9 August 1993.

"War and Peace: The Problems and Prospects of American Diplomacy in the Middle East." Address before the Los Angeles World Affairs Council, 30 November 1993. *U.S. Department of State Dispatch*, 20 December 1993.

Foreign Relations of the United States, 1955–1957: Arab-Israeli Dispute, January 1–July 26, 1956. Vol. 15. Washington, DC: U.S. Government Printing Office, 1989.

Gore, Al. "Remarks of Vice President Gore As He Meets with Arab and Muslim Ambassadors." *Federal News Service*, 10 June 1994.

Indyk, Martin. "Concluding Remarks: The Implications for U.S. Policy." At "Islam and the U.S.: Challenges for the Nineties," Soref Symposium. Washington, DC: *The Washington Institute for Near East Policy*, 27 April 1992.

Isaacson, Jason F. "On the Threat of Islamic Extremism in Africa." Prepared testimony before the Subcommittee on Africa, House Committee on International Relations. *Federal News Service*, 6 April 1995.

Hicks, Neil. "Human Rights in the Middle East." Testimony before the Subcommittee on Europe and the Middle East of the House Committee on Foreign Affairs, 15 September 1992.

Lake, Anthony. "Building a New Middle East: Challenges for U.S. Policy."

Address by National Security Adviser to the Washington Institute for Near East Policy. Washington, DC, 17 May 1994. *U.S. Department of State Dispatch*, August 1994.

"From Containment to Enlargement: Current Foreign Policy Debates in Perspective." Speech delivered at Johns Hopkins University, School of Advanced International Studie, Washington, DC, September 1993.

"The Need for Engagement." Address given at the Woodrow Wilson School, Princeton University, November 1994. *U.S. Department of State Dispatch*, 5 December 1994.

Lawyers Committee for Human Rights. *Critique: Review of the U.S. Department of State's Country Reports on Human Rights Practices*. Washington, DC: Lawyers Committee for Human Rights, July 1990–6.

Migdalovitch, D. "Turkey's Unfolding Political Crisis." In *Congressional Research Service Report for Congress*. Washington, DC: The Library of Congress, 11 April 1997.

Murphy, Richard. "The Middle East Peace: Facing Realities and Challenges." *U.S. Department of State Bulletin*, September 1988.

National Security Council. *Discussion at the Meeting of the National Security Council (NSC), 25 July 1958 and NSC, U.S. Policy Toward the Near East (NSC 6011), 17 June 1960*. In the U.S. Archives. Center for Lebanese Studies, Oxford.

Parris, Mark R. "Update on the Crisis in Algeria." Statement before the Subcommittee on Africa of the House Foreign Affairs Committee, 22 March 1994. *U.S. Department of State Dispatch*, 4 April 1994.

Pelletreau, Robert H. "Current Issues in the Middle East." Address to the Harvard Law School, Islamic Legal Studies Program, in Cambridge, 11 April 1994.

"Dealing with the Muslim Politics of the Middle East: Algeria, Hamas, Iran." Speech at the Council on Foreign Relations, New York, 8 May 1996. *Muslim Politics Report*, no. 7 (May/June 1996).

"Recent Events in the Middle East." Statement before the Subcommittee on Europe and the Middle East of the House Foreign Affairs Committee, Washington, DC, 14 June 1994. *U.S. Department of State Dispatch*, vol. 5, no. 25, 20 June 1994.

"Statement before the Subcommittee on Europe and the Middle East of the House Foreign Affairs Committee, 4 October 1994." *U.S. Department of State Dispatch*, 10 October 1994.

"U.S. Policy Toward North Africa." Statement before the Subcommittee on Africa of the House Foreign Affairs Committee, 28 September 1994. *U.S. Department of State Dispatch*, 3 October 1994.

Perry, William J. "Address to the Council on Foreign Relations." New York, 18 May 1995.

Quayle, Dan. "Commencement Address at the U.S. Naval Academy for the Class of 1990, Annapolis, Maryland, 30 May 1990." In U.S. Naval Academy Archives, Nimitz Library.

Reagan, Ronald. "Reagan Address on U.S. Air Strike Against Libya," 14 April 1986. In *Historic Documents of 1986*. Washington, DC. Congressional Quarterly, 1987.

Ros-Lehtinen, Ileana. "The Threat of Islamic Extremism in Africa." Prepared testimony of the Honorable Ileana Ros-Lehtinen, Committee on International Relations, U.S. House of Representatives. *Federal News Service*, 6 April 1995.

Russell, Francis J. "U.S. Policies Toward Nasser." Paper delivered by the Secretary of State's Special Assistant on 4 August 1956. In *Foreign Relations of the United States: Suez Crisis, 1956*. Vol. 16. Washington, DC: U.S. Government Printing Office, 1989.

Shultz, George. "The Future of American Foreign Policy: New Realities and New Ways of Thinking." Testimony before the Senate Foreign Relations Committee on 31 January 1985. *U.S. Department of State Bulletin*, May 1985.

"Testimony Before the Joint House–Senate Iran-Contra Investigation Hearings, 23 July 1987." In *Report of the Congressional Committees Investigating the Iran-Contra Affairs, 13 November 1987*. Washington, DC: U.S. Government Printing Office, 1987.

Talbott, Strobe. "U.S.–Turkish Leadership in the Post–Cold War World." Address at Bilkent University, Ankara, Turkey, 11 April 1995. *U.S. Department of State Dispatch*, 24 April 1995.

Tarnoff, Peter. "Containing Iran." *U.S. Department of State Dispatch*, 13 November 1995.

"Sanctions on Iran." *U.S. Department of State Dispatch*, 23 October 1995.

U.S. Department of State. "Enhanced U.S.–Turkish Partnership." Excerpts from press briefing, the White House, 11 February 1992. *U.S. Department of State Dispatch*, 17 February 1992.

"Human Rights Abuses By Turkish Military and the Situation in Cyprus." State Department report. *U.S. Department of State Dispatch*, 12 June 1995.

"Memorandum of Conversation. Subject: U.S.–UAR Relations, 17 September 1965." In *The Lyndon B. Johnson National Security Files, the Middle East: National Security Files, 1963–1969*. Frederick, MD: University Publications of America, 1989.

Patterns of Global Terrorism. Washington, DC: U.S. Government Printing Office, April 1995.

"The U.S., Islam and the Middle East in a Changing World." Address at Meridian House International, Washington, DC, 2 June 1992. *U.S. Department of State Dispatch*, 2 June 1992.

"U.S.–Egyptian Partnership for Economic Growth and Development." Text of joint communiqué issued at the inaugural meeting of the U.S.–Egyptian Sub-Committee on Economic Policy, Trade, Investment, and External Finance, Washington, DC, 2 June 1995. *U.S. Department of State Dispatch* 6, no. 24, 12 June 1995.

U.S. House of Representatives. "Hearing of the House Foreign Affairs

Committee; Developments in the Middle East." *Federal News Service*, 17 March 1992.

'Hearing of the House International Relations Committee; U.S. Assistance to the Palestinians." *Federal News Service*, 6 April 1995.

"Hearing of the U.S. House Committee on Foreign Affairs; U.S. Foreign Policy." *Federal News Service*, 6 February 1992.

"Hearing with Defense Department Personnel; House International Relations Committee; International Economic and Trade Subcommittee–U.S. Sanctions on Iran." *Federal News Service*, 2 May 1995.

"Hearings and Recommendations for U.S. Foreign Assistance to Africa Before the Subcommittee on Africa of the House Committee on Foreign Relations." Printed in *Foreign Assistance Legislation for Fiscal Year 1994*, pt. 7, 12 May 1993.

Hearings Before the Subcommittee on Africa of the Committee on Foreign Affairs, 12 May 1993. Washington, DC: U.S. Government Printing Office, 1994.

"House Foreign Affairs Committee Hearing." *Reuters Transcript Report*, 21 April 1993.

Jordan – The Center of Sunni Islamist Terrorism. 17 April 1991 report to the House Republican Task Force on Terrorism and Conventional Warfare. Washington, DC: July 1998–May 1991.

Report of the Congressional Committees Investigating the Iran-Contra Affair, 13 November 1987. Washington, DC: U.S. Government Printing Office, 1987.

The Future of U.S. Anti-Terrorism Policy. Hearing before the Subcommittee on International Security, International Organizations, and Human Rights of the Committee on Foreign Affairs, 13 July 1993. Washington, DC: U.S. Government Printing Office, 1993.

The Times of the Crusades are Back. 19 March 1990 report to the House Republican Task Force on Terrorism and Unconventional Warfare. Washington, DC: July 1989–May 1991.

U.S. Senate. *East or West? Turkey Checks Its Compass*. Minority staff report for the U.S. Senate Foreign Relations Committee, September 1995. Washington, DC: U.S. Government Printing Office, 1996.

Hearing of the Senate Judiciary Committee, Terrorism and America: A Comprehensive Review of the Threat, Policy, and Law, 21 April 1993. Washington, DC: U.S. Government Printing Office, 1994.

The Battle Looms: Islam and Politics in the Middle East. Study commissioned by the Senate Committee on Foreign Relations. Washington, DC: U.S. Government Printing Office, 1993.

Welch, David. C. "Terrorism in Algeria." *U.S. Department of State Dispatch*, 30 October 1995.

White House. *A National Security Strategy for a New Century*. Washington, DC: U.S. Government Printing Office, May 1997.

National Security Strategy of the United States. Washington, DC: U.S. Government Printing Office, January 1993.

Woolsey, James R. "Testimony Before the Senate Committee on Government Affairs on the Proliferation Threats of the 1990s." Washington, DC, 24 February 1993. Reprinted in *Journal of Palestine Studies* 22 (Summer 1993).

Books

Abramowitz, Morton I. "Forward." In Pierre, Andrew J., and William B. Quant. *The Algerian Crisis: Policy Options for the West.* Washington, DC: Carnegie Endowment for International Peace, 1996.

Abraham, Nabeel. "The Gulf Crisis and Anti-Arab Racism in America." In *Collateral Damage: The 'New World Order' at Home and Abroad.* Ed. Cynthia Peters. Boston, MA: South End Press, 1992.

Abu-Amr, Ziad. *Islamic Fundamentalism in the West Bank and Gaza.* Bloomington: Indiana University Press, 1994.

Acheson, Dean. *Present at the Creation: My Years in the State Department.* New York: New American Library, 1969.

Ahmad, Feroz. *The Making of Modern Turkey.* London: Routledge, 1993.

Ahmed, Ahmed Youssef. *Al-dawr al-Misri fi al-Yaman, 1962–1967* [The Egyptian Role in Yemen, 1962–1967]. Cairo: Al-Hai'a al-Misriya al-amma llkitab, 1981.

Akhtar, Shabbir. *A Faith for All Seasons: Islam and the Challenge of the Modern World.* Chicago: Ivan R. Dee, 1990.

Allison, Robert J. *The Crescent Obscured: The United States and the Muslim World, 1776–1815.* New York: Oxford University Press, 1995.

Amirahmadi, H., ed. *The United States and the Middle East: A Search for New Perspectives.* Albany: State University of New York Press, 1993.

Appleby, R. Scott. "Democratization in the Middle East Does Not Threaten the West." In *Islam: Opposing Viewpoints.* N. ed., n.c. USA: Greenhaven Press, 1995.

Arjomand, Said Amir. *The Turban for the Crown: The Islamic Revolution in Iran.* New York: Oxford University Press, 1988.

Arkoun, Mohammed. *Rethinking Islam.* Trans. and ed. Robert D. Lee. Boulder, CO: Westview Press, 1994.

Art, Robert J. "America's Foreign Policy." In *Foreign Policy in World Politics.* Ed. Roy C. Macridis. Englewood Cliffs, NJ: Prentice-Hall, 1985.

Ayubi, Nazih N. *Political Islam: Religion and Politics in the Arab World.* London: Routledge, 1991.

Baker III, James A., with Thomas M. DeFrank. *The Politics of Diplomacy: Revolution, War and Peace, 1989–1992.* New York: G. P. Putman's Sons, 1995.

Barkey, Henry J., ed. *Reluctant Neighbor: Turkey's Role in the Middle East.* Washington, DC: United Institute of Peace Press, 1996.

Bill, James A. *The Eagle and the Lion.* New Haven, CT: Yale University Press, 1988.

REFERENCES

Bin Sayeed, Khalid. *Western Dominance and Political Islam: Challenge and Response*. Albany: State University of New York Press, 1995.

Bin Yousef, Ahmad, and Ahmad Abul Jobain. *The Politics of Islamic Resurgence: Through Western Eyes*. North Springfield, VA: The United Association for Studies and Research, 1992.

Blank, Stephen J., Stephen C. Pelletiere, and William T. Johnson. *Turkey's Strategic Position at the Crossroads of World Affairs*. N.c.: Strategic Studies Institute, U.S. Army War College, 1993.

Bodansky, Yosseff. *Target America: Terrorism in the U.S. Today*. New York: S.P.I. Books, 1993.

Brown, Seyom. *The Face of Power: United States Foreign Policy from Truman to Clinton*. New York: Columbia University Press, 1994.

Brzezinski, Zbigniew. *Power and Principle: Memoirs of the National Security Advisor, 1977–1981*. New York: Farrar, Straus and Giroux, 1983.

Bulliet, Richard W. "Rhetoric, Discourse, and the Future of Hope." In *Under Siege: Islam and Democracy*. Occasional Papers 1. Ed. Richard W. Bulliet. New York: The Middle East Institute of Columbia University, 1994.

Burgat, François, and William Dowell. *The Islamic Movement in North Africa*. Austin: Center for Middle Eastern Studies at the University of Texas at Austin, 1993.

Caplan, Lionel, ed. *Studies in Religious Fundamentalism*. London: Macmillan, 1987.

Carley, Patricia. *Turkey's Role in the Middle East: A Conference Report*. Washington, DC: United States Institute of Peace, 1995.

Carter, Jimmy. *Keeping Faith: Memoirs of a President*. New York: Bantam Books, 1982.

Castelli, J., and G. Gallup Jr. *The People's Religion: American Faith in the '90s*. New York: Macmillan, 1989.

Chomsky, Noam. *Deterring Democracy*. New York: Hill & Wang, 1992.

Necessary Illusions. Boston, MA: South End Press, 1989.

Toward a New Cold War: Essays on the Current Crisis and How We Got There. New York: Pantheon, 1982.

World Orders: Old and New. New York: Columbia University Press, 1994.

Christopher, Warren, ed. *American Hostages in Iran: The Conduct of a Crisis*. New Haven, CT: Yale University Press, a Council on Foreign Relations Book, 1985.

Chubin, Shahram. *Iran's National Security Policy: Capabilities, Intentions and Impact*. Washington, DC: The Carnegie Endowment for International Peace, 1994.

Clawson, Patrick. "Alternative Foreign Policy Views Among the Iranian Policy Elite." In *Iran: Strategic Intentions and Capabilities*. McNair Paper 29. Ed. Patrick Clawson. Washington, DC: Institute for National Strategic Studies and National Defense University, 1994.

Cole, Juan R. I., and Nikki R. Keddie, eds. *Shi'ism and Social Protest*. New Haven, CT: Yale University Press, 1986.

Copeland, Miles. *The Game of Nations: The Amorality of Power Politics*. London: Weidenfeld & Nicolson, 1969.

Cottam, Richard W. "U.S. and Soviet Responses to Islamic Political Militancy." In *Neither East nor West: Iran, the Soviet Union and the United States*. Ed. Nikki R. Keddie and Mark J. Gasiorowski. New Haven, CT: Yale University Press, 1990.

Daniel, Norman. *Islam and the West: The Making of an Image*. Edinburgh: Edinburgh University Press, 1960.

The Arabs and Medieval Europe. London: Longman, 1975.

De Marenches, Count, and David A. Adelman. *The Fourth World War: Diplomacy and Espionage in the Age of Terrorism*. New York: William Morris & Co., 1992.

Djait, Hichem. *Europe and Islam: Cultures and Modernity*. Berkeley and Los Angeles: University of California Press, 1985.

Dolbeare, Kenneth M., and Patricia Dolbeare. *American Ideologies*. Chicago: Markham, 1971.

Donohue, John J., and John L. Esposito, eds. *Islam in Transition: Muslim Perspectives*. New York: Oxford University Press, 1982.

Dorman, William. "Media, Public Discourse, and U.S. Policy Toward the Middle East." In *The United States and the Middle East: A Search for New Perspectives*. Ed. H. Amirahmadi. Albany: State University of New York Press, 1993.

Enayat, Hamid. *Modern Islamic Political Thought*. Austin: University of Texas Press, 1982.

Esposito, John L. *Political Islam: The Challenges of Change*. Annandale, VA: United Association for Studies and Research, 1995.

The Islamic Threat: Myth or Reality? New York: Oxford University Press, 1992.

Esposito, John L., ed. *Voices of Resurgent Islam*. New York: Oxford University Press, 1983.

Esposito, John L., and James P. Piscatori. "The Global Impact of the Iranian Revolution: A Policy Perspective." In *The Iranian Revolution: Its Global Impact*. Ed. John L. Esposito. Miami: Florida International University Press, 1990.

Fuller, Graham E. *Algeria: The Next Fundamentalist State?* Santa Monica, CA: Rand Corporation, 1996.

"Alternative Turkish Roles in the Future Middle East." In *Reluctant Neighbor: Turkey's Role in the Middle East*. Ed. Henry J. Barkey. Washington, DC: United Institute of World Peace Press, 1996.

Fuller, Graham E., and Ian O. Lesser. *A Sense of Siege: The Geopolitics of Islam and the West*. Boulder, CO: Westview Press, 1995.

Central Asia: The New Geopolitics. Santa Monica, CA: Rand Corporation, 1992.

Islamic Fundamentalism in the Northern Tier Countries: An Integrative View. Santa Monica, CA: Rand Corporation, 1991.

Gaddis, John Lewis. *The United States and the End of the Cold War: Implica-*

tions, Reconsiderations, Provocations. New York: Oxford University Press, 1992.

Geertz, Cliford. *The Interpretation of Cultures*. New York: Basic Books, 1973.

Gerges, Fawaz A. *The Superpowers and the Middle East: Regional and International Politics, 1955–1967*. Boulder, CO: Westview Press, 1994.

Geyikdag, Mehmet Yasar. *Political Parties in Turkey: The Role of Islam*. New York: Praeger, 1984.

Ghannoushi, Rashid. "Islamic Civilization Need Not Clash with Western Civilization." In *Islam: Opposing Viewpoints*. N. ed., n.c. USA: Greenhaven Press, 1995.

Ghareeb, Edmund, ed. *Split Vision: The Portrayal of Arabs in the American Media*. Washington, DC: American-Arab Affairs Council, 1983.

Goldberg, Jacob. "The Shi'i Minority in Saudi Arabia." In *Shi'ism and Social Protest*. Ed. Juan R. I. Cole and Nikkie R. Keddie. New Haven, CT: Yale University Press, 1986.

Grimmett, Richard F. *Conventional Arms Transfers to the Third World*. Washington, DC: Congressional Research Service, 1993.

Guvenc, Bozkurt. *Culture and Education in Turkey* [in Turkish]. Ankara: Gundogan, 1995.

Hadar, Leon T. "Political Islam is Not a Threat to the West." In *Islam: Opposing Viewpoints*. No ed., n.c. USA: Greenhaven Press, 1995.

Quagmire: America in the Middle East. Washington, DC: Cato Institute, 1992.

"The Media and Islam." In *Under Seige: Islam and Democracy*. Occasional Papers 1. Ed. Richard W. Bulliet. New York: The Middle East Institute of Columbia University, 1994.

Haddad, Yvonne Yazbeck. "Islamist Perceptions of the U.S. Policy in the Middle East." In *The Middle East and the United States: A Historical Reassessment*. Ed. David W. Lesch. Boulder, CO: Westview Press, 1996.

"The 'New Enemy'? Islam and Islamists after the Cold War." In *Altered States: A Reader in the New World Order*. Ed. Michel Moushabeck and Phyllis Bennice. New York: Olive Branch Press, 1993.

Halliday, Fred. *Islam and the Myth of Confrontation: Religion and Politics in the Middle East*. London: I. B. Tauris, 1995.

Hamroush, Ahmed. *Qissa taura 23 Yulio: Karif Abdel-Nasser* [The Story of 23 July Revolution: The Autumn of Abdel-Nasser]. Vol. 5. Cairo: Maktaba al-madbuli, 1984.

Hartz, Louis. *The Liberal Tradition in America*. New York: Harcourt Brace & World, 1955.

Hastedt, Glenn P., ed. *American Foreign Policy: Past, Present, Future*. Englewood Cliffs, NJ: Prentice-Hall, 1997.

Haviland, William A. *Cultural Anthropology*. Fort Worth, TX: Holt, Reinhart & Winston, 1990.

Hentsch, Thierry. *Imagining the Middle East*. Trans. Fred A. Reed. Montreal: Black Rose Books, 1992.

Henze, Paul B. *Turkey: Toward the Twenty-First Century*. Santa Monica, CA: Rand Corporation, 1994.

   Turkish Democracy and the American Alliance. Santa Monica, CA: Rand Corporation, 1993.

Hippler, Jochen. "The Islamist Threat and Western Foreign Policy." In *The Netx Threat: Western Perceptions of Islam*. Ed. Jochen Hippler and Andrea Lueg. Boulder, CO: Pluto Press, 1995.

Hippler, Jochen, and Andrea Lueg, eds. *The Next Threat: Western Perceptions of Islam*. Boulder, CO: Pluto Press, 1995.

Hoffmann, Stanley. *Dead Ends: American Foreign Policy in the New Cold War*. Cambridge: Ballinger, 1983.

Hourani, Albert. *Islam in European Thought*. New York: Cambridge University Press, 1991.

Hunt, Michael H. *Ideology and U.S. Foreign Policy*. New Haven, CT: Yale University Press, 1987.

Hunter, Shireen T. *Iran and the World*. Bloomington: Indiana University Press, 1990.

   Turkey at the Crossroads: Islamic Past or European Future. Brussels: Centre for European Policy Studies, 1995.

Husain, Asaf. *Western Conflict with Islam: Survey of the Anti-Islamic Tradition*. Leicester: Volcano Books, 1990.

Hybel, Alex Roberto. *Power over Rationality: The Bush Administration and the Gulf Crisis*. Albany: State University of New York Press, 1993.

Indyk, Martin. "The Clinton Administration's Approach to the Middle East." Address by special assistant to the President to the Soref Symposium, 18–19 May 1993. In *Challenges to U.S. Interests in the Middle East: Obstacles and Opportunities*. Ed. Y. Mirsky, Matt Ahrens, and J. Sultan. Washington, DC: The Washington Institute for Near East Policy, May 1993.

Islam and the U.S.: Challenges for the Nineties. Soref Symposium. Washington, DC: The Washington Institute for Near East Policy, 27 April 1992.

Islam: Opposing Viewpoints. N. ed., n.c. USA: Greenhaven Press, 1995.

Johnson, William T. "Turkey and Europe: Expectations and Complications." In *Turkey's Strategic Position at the Crossroads of World Affairs*. Ed. Stephen J. Blank, Stephen C. Pelletiere, and William T. Johnson. N.c.: Strategic Studies Institute, U.S. Army War College, 1993.

Jordan, Hamilton. *Crisis: The Last Year of the Carter Presidency*. New York: Bantam Books, 1982.

Jouejati, Muhraf. "Water Politics as High Politics: The Case of Turkey and Syria." In *Reluctant Neighbor: Turkey's Role in the Middle East*. Ed. Henry J. Barkey. Washington, DC: United Institute of Peace Press, 1996.

Juergensmeyer, Mark. *The New Cold War? Religious Nationalism Confronts the Secular State*. Berkeley and Los Angeles: University of California Press, 1993.

Kabbani, Rana. *Europe's Myths of the Orient*. London: Macmillan, 1986.

   Letter to Christendom. London: Virago Press, 1989.

Keddie, Nikki R., and Mark J. Gasiorowski, eds. *Neither East nor West: Iran, the Soviet Union and the United States.* New Haven, CT: Yale University Press, 1990.

Kegley, Charles W., Jr., and Eugene R. Wittkoff. *American Foreign Policy: Pattern and Process.* London: Macmillan Education, 1987.

Kelsay, John. *Islam and War: A Study in Comparative Ethics.* Louisville, KY: Westminster/John Knox Press, 1993.

Kemp, Geoffrey. *Forever Enemies: American Policy and the Islamic Republic of Iran.* Washington, DC: The Carnegie Endowment for International Peace, 1994.

Kepel, Gilles. *The Revenge of God: The Resurgence of Islam, Christianity and Judaism in the Modern World.* Trans. Alan Braley. University Park: Pennsylvania State University Press, 1994.

Kissinger, Henry. *White House Years.* Boston: Little, Brown & Company, 1979.

Klare, Michael T., and Daniel C. Thomas, eds. *World Security: Challenges for a New Century.* 2d ed. New York: St. Martin's Press, 1994.

Kung, Hans, and Jurgen Moltmann, eds. *Islam: A Challenge for Christianity.* London: SCM Press, 1994.

Lenczowski, George. *American Presidents and the Middle East.* Durham, NC: Duke University Press, 1990.

Lesch, David W., ed. *The Middle East and the United States: A Historical and Political Reassessment.* Boulder CO: Westview Press, 1996.

Lewis, Bernard. *Islam and the West.* New York: Oxford University Press, 1993.

The Emergence of Modern Turkey. New York: Oxford University Press, 1961.

The Political Language of Islam. Chicago: University of Chicago Press, 1988.

Lueg, Andrew. "The Perception of Islam in Western Debate." In *The Next Threat: Western Perceptions of Islam.* Ed. Jochen Hippler and Andrea Lueg. Boulder, CO: Pluto Press, 1995.

Macrides, Roy C., ed. *Foreign Policy in World Politics.* Englewood Cliffs, NJ: Prentice-Hall, 1985.

Makovsky, Alan. "Israeli-Turkish Relations: A Turkish 'Periphery Strategy'?" In *Reluctant Neighbor: Turkey's Role in the Middle East.* Ed. Henry J. Barkey. Washington, DC: United Institute of Peace Press, 1996.

Marr, Phebe, and William Lewis, eds. *Riding the Tiger: The Middle East Challenge after the Cold War.* Boulder, CO: Westview Press, 1993.

Marty, Martin E., and R. Scott Appleby, eds. *Fundamentalism Observed.* Chicago: University of Chicago Press, 1991.

Mayall, Simon V. *Turkey: Thwarted Ambition.* Paper 56. Washington, DC: National Defense University, January 1997.

Mazrui, Ali A. *Cultural Forces in World Politics.* London: James Currey, 1990.

McDowall, David. *A Modern History of the Kurds.* London: I. B. Tauris, 1996.

Mirsky, Y., Matt Ahrens, and J. Sultan, eds. *Challenges to U.S. Interests in the*

Middle East: Obstacles and Opportunities. Washington, DC: The Washington Institute for Near East Policy, May 1993.

Mohaddessin, Mohammed. *Islamic Fundamentalism: The New Global Threat.* Washington, DC: Seven Locks Press, 1993.

Mountcastle, Colonel W. "Forward." In *Turkey's Strategic Position at the Crossroads of World Affairs.* Ed. Stephen J. Blank, Stephen C. Pelletiere, and William T. Johnson. N.c.: Strategic Studies Institute, U.S. Army War College, 1993.

Moushabeck, Michel, and Phyllis Bennice, eds. *Altered States: A Reader in the New World Order.* New York: Olive Branch Press, 1993.

Muslih, Muhammad. "Syria and Turkey: Uneasy Relations." In *Reluctant Neighbor: Turkey's Role in the Middle East.* Ed. Henry J. Barkey. Washington, DC: United Institute of Peace Press, 1996.

Mustapha, Hala. *The State and the Islamic Opposition Movements: Between Truce and Confrontation During the Sadat and Mubarak Administrations.* Cairo: Markaz Al-Mahrousa Lilnasahr, 1995.

Ozubudun, Ergun. "Islam and Politics in Modern Turkey." In *The Islamic Impulse.* Ed. Barbara Freyer Stowasser. Washington, DC: Center for Contemporary Arab Studies, Georgetown University, 1996.

Payne, Richard J. *The Clash with Distant Cultures: Values, Interests, and Force in American Foreign Policy.* New York: State University of New York Press, 1995.

Pelletiere, Stephen C. "Turkey and the United States in the Middle East: The Kurdish Connection." In *Turkey's Strategic Position at the Crossroads of World Affairs.* Ed. Stephen J. Blank, Stephen C. Pelletiere, and William T. Johnson. N.c.: Strategic Studies Institute, U.S. Army War College, 1993.

Perkins, "The American Approach to Foreign Policy." Cambridge: Harvard University Press, 1962.

Peters, Cynthia, ed. *Collateral Damage: The 'New World Order' at Home and Abroad."* Boston: South End Press, 1992.

Pierre, Andrew J., and William B. Quandt. *The Algerian Crisis: Policy Options for the West.* Washington, DC: Carnegie Endowment for International Peace, 1996.

Pipes, Daniel. "Political Islam Is a Threat to the West." In *Islam: Opposing Viewpoints.* N. ed., n.c. USA: Greenhaven Press, 1995.

Piscatori, James P. *Islam in a World of Nation–States.* New York: Cambridge University Press, 1986.

Piscatori, James P., ed. *Islamic Fundamentalists and the Gulf War.* Chicago: American Academy of Arts and Sciences, 1991.

Pollack, David, and Elaine El Assal, eds. *In the Eye of the Beholder: Muslim and Non-Muslim Views of Islam, Islamic Politics, and Each Other.* Washington, DC: Office of Research and Media Reaction, United States Information Agency, August 1995.

Pryce-Jones, David. *At War with Modernity: Islam's Challenge to the West.* London: Institute for European Defense and Strategic Studies, 1992.

Quandt, William B. *Camp David: Peacemaking and Politics*. Washington, DC: The Brookings Institution, 1986.

    Decade of Decisions: American Policy Toward the Arab-Israeli Conflict, 1967–1976. Berkley and Los Angeles: University of California Press, 1977.

    Peace Process: American Diplomacy and the Arab-Israeli Conflict Since 1967. Berkeley and Los Angeles: University of California Press, 1993.

Ramazani, Rouhollah K., ed. *Iran's Revolution*. Washington, DC: Middle East Institute, 1990.

Reagan, Ronald. *An American Life: The Autobiography*. New York: Pocket Books, 1990.

Rodinson, Maxime. *Europe and the Mystique of Islam*. Roger Veinus, trans. London: I. B. Tauris, 1987.

Rubin, Barry. *Paved with Good Intentions: The American Experience and Iran*. New York: Oxford University Press, 1980.

Rugman, Jonathan. *Ataturk's Children: Turkey and the Kurds*. London: Cassell, 1996.

Said, Edward. *Covering Islam: How the Media and the Experts Determine How We See the Rest of the World*. New York: Pantheon Books, 1981.

    Orientalism. New York: Vintage Books, 1978.

Satloff, Robert. "An American Strategy to Respond to Political Islam." Soref Symposium. In *Challenge to U.S. Interests in the Middle East: Obstacles and Opportunities*. Ed. Y. Mirsky, Matt Ahrens, and J. Sultan. Washington, DC: Washington Institute for Near East Policy, May 1993.

Saunders, Harold. "Diplomacy and Pressure, November 1979–May 1980" and "The Crisis Begins." In *American Hostages in Iran: The Conduct of a Crisis*. Ed. Warren Christopher. New Haven, CT: Yale University Press, a Council on Foreign Relations Book, 1985.

Schleiermacher, Friedrich. *Der Christliche Glaube in Samtliche Werke*. 2d ed., vol. 3, pt. 1. Berlin: 1842. *The Christian Faith*. English trans. Edinburgh, 1928.

Sha'ban, Fuad. *Islam and Arabs in Early American Thought: The Roots of Orientalism in America*. Durham, NC: The Acorn Press, 1991.

Shawcross, William. *The Shah's Last Ride*. London: Pan Books, 1989.

Sick, Gary. *All Fall Down: America's Fateful Encounter with Iran*. London: I. B. Tauris, 1985.

    "Islam and the Norms of Democracy." In *Under Seige: Islam and Democracy*. Occasional Papers 1. Ed. Richard W. Bulliet. New York: The Middle East Institute of Columbia University, 1994.

    "Military Options and Constraints." In *American Hostages in Iran: The Conduct of a Crisis*. Ed. Warren Christopher. New Haven, CT: Yale University Press, a Council on Foreign Relations Book, 1985.

Sigal, Leon V. *Reporters and Officials: The Organization and Politics of News-making*. Lexington, MA: D. C. Heath, 1973.

Sisk, Timothy D. *Islam and Democracy: Religion, Politics, and Power in the Middle East*. Washington, DC: United States Institute for Peace, 1992.

Smith, Tony. *America's Mission: The United States and the Worldwide Struggle for Democracy in the 20th Century*. Princeton, NJ: Princeton University Press, 1994.

Southern, R. W. *Western Views of Islam in the Middle Ages*. Cambridge: Harvard University Press, 1980.

Spanier, John, and Steven W. Hook. *American Foreign Policy Since World War II*. Washington, DC: *Congressional Quarterly*, 13th ed., 1995.

Steel, Ronald. *Temptations of a Superpower*. Cambridge: Harvard University Press, 1995.

Stowasser, Barbara Freyer, ed. *The Islamic Impulse*. Washington, DC: Center for Contemporary Arab Studies, Georgetown University, 1987.

Suleiman, Michael W. *The Arabs in the Mind of America*. Brattleboro, VT: Anana Books, 1988.

"The Effects of American Perceptions of Arabs on Middle East Issues." In *Split Vision: The Portrayal of Arabs in the American Media*. Ed. Edmund Ghareeb. Washington, DC: American-Arab Affairs Council, 1983.

Suleiman, Michael W., ed. *U.S. Policy on Palestine: From Wilson to Clinton*. Normal, IL: Association of Arab-American University Graduates, 1995.

Tapper, Richard, ed. *Islam in Modern Turkey*. London: I. B. Tauris, 1991.

Tapper, Richard, and Nancy Tapper. " 'Thank God We're Secular!' Aspects of Fundamentalism in a Turkish Town." In *Studies in Religious Fundamentalism*. Ed. Lionel Caplan. London: Macmillan, 1987.

Turan, Ilter. "Religion and Political Culture in Turkey." In *Islam in Modern Turkey*. Ed. Richard Tapper. London: I.B. Taurus, 1991.

Vance, Cyrus. *Hard Choices: Critical Years in American Foreign Policy*. New York: Simon & Schuster, 1983.

Wales, Charles, Prince of. *Islam and the West*. New York: Oxford Centre for Islamic Studies, 1993.

Weinberger, Caspar. *Fighting for Peace: Seven Critical Years in the Pentagon*. New York: Warner Books, 1990.

Woodward, Bob. *Veil: The Secret Wars of the CIA, 1981–1987*. New York: Simon & Schuster, 1987.

Wolfowitz, Paul. "Challenges to U.S. Interests in the Middle East." In *Challenges to U.S. Interests in the Middle East: Obstacles and Opportunities*. Ed. Y. Mirsky, Matt Ahrens, and J. Sultan. Washington, DC: The Washington Institute for Near East Policy, May 1993.

Wright, Robin. *Sacred Rage: The Wrath of Militant Islam*. New York: Simon & Schuster, 1985.

Journals

Abdallah, Ahmed. "Egypt's Islamists and the State." *Middle East Report* (July/August 1993).

Abramowitz, Morton I. "Dateline Ankara: Turkey After Ozal." *Foreign Policy*, no. 91 (Summer 1993).

REFERENCES

Ahmad, Feroz. "Politics and Islam in Modern Turkey." *Middle Eastern Studies* 27, no. 1 (January 1991).

Ajami, Fouad. "The Sorrows of Egypt." *Foreign Affairs* 74, no. 5 (September/October 1995).

Ali, M. M. "Refah Foreign Affairs Expert: Turkey's Outreach to Muslim States 'Realistic.' " *Washington Report on Middle Eastern Affairs* (April/May 1997).

Al-Marayati, Salam. "The Rising Tide of Hostile Stereotyping of Islam." *Washington Report on Middle Eastern Affairs* (June 1994).

Al-Sayyid, Mustapha K. "A Civil Society in Egypt." *Middle East Journal* 47, no. 2 (Spring 1993).

Amuzegar, Jahangir. "The Truth and Illusion of Islamic Fundamentalism." *SAIS Review* 13 (Summer/Fall 1993).

Ayata, Spencer. "Patronage, Party, and State: The Politicalization of Islam in Turkey." *Middle East Journal* 50, no. 1 (January 1995).

Banu, U.A.B., and Razia Akhter Banu. "Fundamentalist Islam: A Threat to the West?" *Islamic Studies* 32 (Spring 1993).

Barraclough, Colin. "Roll Over Ataturk." *Middle East Insight* 11, no. 2 (January/February 1995).

Bill, James A. "The United States and Iran: Mutual Mythologies." *Middle East Policy* 2, no. 3 (1993).

Bird, Gene. "Administration Official Assures Middle East the 'Crusades Are Over.' " *Washington Report on Middle Eastern Affairs* 11, no. 2 (July 1992).

Brown, James. "Islamic Fundamentalism and Turkey." *Journal of Politics and Military Sociology* 16 (Fall 1998).

Brzezinski, Zbigniew, Brent Scowcroft, and Richard Murphy. "Differentiated Containment." *Foreign Affairs* 76, no. 3 (May/June 1997).

Cassandra. "The Impending Crisis in Egypt." *Middle East Journal* 49, no. 1 (Winter 1995).

Chase, Robert S., Emily B. Hill, and Paul Kennedy. "Pivotal States and U.S. Strategy." *Foreign Affairs* 75, no. 1 (January/February 1995).

Christopher, Warren. "America's Leadership, America's Opportunity." *Foreign Policy*, no. 98 (Spring 1995).

Chubin, Shahram. "Does Iran Want Nuclear Weapons." *Survival* 37, no. 1 (Spring 1995).

Clarke, Duncan L., and Daniel O'Connor. "U.S. Base-Rights Payments after the Cold War." *Orbis* 37, no. 3 (Summer 1993).

Clawson, Patrick. "Liberty's the Thing, not Democracy: Ripostes." *Middle East Quarterly* 1, no. 3 (September 1994).

Connelly, Mathew. "Déjà Vu All Over Again: Algeria, France and U.S." *National Interest*, no. 42 (Winter 1995–6).

Coulombis, Theodore, and Thanos Veremis. "In Search of New Barbarians: Samuel P. Huntington and the Clash of Civilizations." *Mediterranean Quarterly* 5 (Winter 1994).

Dallal, Shaw J. "Islam and the U.S. National Interest." *The Link* 26 (February/March 1993).

Djerejian, Edward P. "One Man, One Vote, One Time." *New Perspectives Quarterly* 10, no. 3 (Summer 1993).

Dorsey, James M. "Erbakan Striking Balance Between Islamic Neighbors and Secular Army." *Washington Report on Middle Eastern Affairs* (October 1996).

"Troubled Turkey Getting Seventh Government in Two Years." *Washington Report on Middle Eastern Affairs* (July 1996).

"Turkish Military 'Advice' Reins in Islamist Erbakan Government." *Washington Report on Middle Eastern Affairs* (June/July 1997).

"With Friends Like Qaddafi, Islamist Erbakan Doesn't Need Enemies." *Washington Report on Middle Eastern Affairs* (November/December 1996).

Drake, Laura. "Still Fighting the Last Cold War." *Middle East Insight* 10 (September/October 1994).

Esposito, John L. "Political Islam: Beyond the Green Menace." *Current History* 93 (January 1994).

"Fehim Adak: Erbakan Seeks Cooperation with America." Interview in *Middle East Quarterly* (March 1997).

"Focus – Islam and Turkey: The Regional Impact." *Bulletin of Regional Cooperation in the Middle East* 6, no. 2 (Summer 1997).

Fuller, Graham E. "The Appeal of Iran." *National Interest* (Fall 1994).

"The Next Ideology." *Foreign Policy*, no. 98 (Spring 1995).

Gerges, Fawaz A. "Clinton and the Middle East: Lost Opportunities?" *Foreign Policy* (Winter 1997).

"Egyptian-Israeli Relations Turn Sour." *Foreign Affairs* 74, no. 3 (May/June 1995).

"The Kennedy Administration and the Egyptian-Saudi Conflict in Yemen: Co-opting Arab Nationalism." *Middle East Journal* 49, no. 2 (Spring 1995).

Gole, Nilufer. "Secularism and Islamism in Turkey: The Making of Elites and Counter-Elites." *Middle East Journal* 51, no. 1 (Winter 1997).

Haass, Richard. "Paradigm Lost." *Foreign Affairs* (January/February 1995).

Hadar, Leon T. "What Green Peril?" *Foreign Affairs* 72 (Spring 1993).

Hashemi, William D. "Nixon's Children: Bill Clinton and the Permanent Arms Bazaar." *World Policy Journal* 12 (Summer 1995).

Heper, Metin. "Islam and Democracy in Turkey: Toward a Reconciliation." *Middle East Journal* 51, no. 1 (Winter 1997).

Herman, Edward S. "The Media's Role in U.S. Foreign Policy." *Journal of International Affairs* 47, no. 1 (Summer 1993).

Howe, Marvine. "Tensions Between Islamists and Secularists Grow in Turkey." *Washington Report on Middle Eastern Affairs* (May/June 1996).

"House Imposes New Limits on U.S. Military Aid Programs." *Arms Control Today* (July/August 1994).

Hunter, Jane. "Making Islam the Enemy." *Israeli Foreign Affairs* 8 (May/June 1994).

Huntington, Samuel. "America's Changing Strategic Interests." *Survival* 33 (January/February 1991).

"If Not Civilizations, What?: Paradigms of the Post–Cold War World." *Foreign Affairs* 72 (November/December 1993).

"Religion and the Third Wave." *National Interest* (Summer 1991).

"The Clash of Civilizations?" *Foreign Affairs* (Summer 1993).

"The Islamic-Confucian Connection." Interview by Nathan Gardels. *New Perspectives Quarterly* 10 (Summer 1993).

"Will More Countries Become Democratic?" *Political Science Quarterly* 99, no. 2 (Summer 1984).

Indyk, Martin. "Beyond the Balance of Power: America's Choice in the Middle East." *National Interest*, no. 26 (Winter 1991–2).

"Interview With James A. Baker III." *Middle East Quarterly* 1, no. 3 (September 1994).

Karabell, Zachary. "The Wrong Threat: The United States and Islamic Fundamentalism." *World Policy Journal* 12 (Summer 1995).

Kechichian, Joseph, and Jeanne Nazimek. "Challenges to the Military in Egypt." *Middle East Policy* 5, no. 3 (September 1997).

Kuniholm, Bruce. "Turkey and the West." *Foreign Affairs* (Spring 1991).

Kurkcii, Ertugrul. "The Crisis of the Turkish State." *Middle East Report* (April/June 1996).

Lake, Anthony. "Confronting Backlash States." *Foreign Affairs* 73, no. 2 (March/April 1994).

Layne, Christopher, and Benjamin Schwarz. "American Hegemony Without an Enemy." *Foreign Policy* 92 (Fall 1993).

Lewis, William A. "Algeria at 35: The Politics of Violence." *Washington Quarterly* (Summer 1996).

Lowrie, Arthur L. "The Campaign Against Islam and American Foreign Policy." *Middle East Policy* 4, no. 1–2 (September 1995).

Makovsky, Alan. "Erbakan on the Ropes." *Policywatch*, no. 239. Published by the Washington Institute for Near East Policy, 12 March 1997.

"How to Deal with Erbakan." *Middle East Quarterly* 4, no. 1 (March 1997).

Makram, Ebeid. "Democratization in Egypt: The 'Algeria Complex.' " *Middle East Policy* 3, no. 3 (1994).

Margulies, Ronnie, and Ergin Yildizoglu. "The Political Uses of Islam in Turkey." *Middle East Report* (July/August 1988).

Marr, Phebe. "Islamic Revival: Security Issues." *Mediterranean Quarterly* 3 (Fall 1992).

McArthur, Shirl. "Turkey Defies Iran Sanctions." *Washington Report on Middle Eastern Affairs* (October 1996).

Middle East Policy Council. "The Middle East: What Is Our Long-Term Vision?" Discussion with Bruce Riedel, William Quandt, Richard Falk, and Thomas R. Mattair in *Middle East Policy* 3, no. 3 (1994).

Miller, Judith. "Faces of Fundamentalism." *Foreign Affairs* 73, no. 6 (November/December 1994).

"The Challenge of Radical Islam." *Foreign Affairs* (Spring 1993).

Muravchik, Joshua. "Blaming America First." *Middle East Quarterly* 1, no. 3 (September 1994).

Noorbaksh, Mehdi. "The Middle East, Islam and the United States: The Special Case of Iran." *Middle East Policy* 2, no. 3 (1993).

Nurhan, Aydin. "Turkey and Middle Eastern Stability." *Vital Speeches of the Day* 63, no. 5 (15 December 1996).

Onis, Ziya. "Turkey in the Post–Cold War Era: In Search of Identity." *Middle East Journal* 49, no. 1 (Winter 1995).

Paris, Jonathan S. "When to Worry in the Middle East," *Orbis* (Fall 1993).

Pierre, Andrew J., and William B. Quandt. "Algeria's War on Itself." *Foreign Policy*, no. 99 (Summer 1995).

Pipes, Daniel. "Fundamentalist Muslims: Between America and Russia." *Foreign Affairs* 64 (Summer 1986).

"Interview with Jesse Helms." *Middle East Quarterly* (March 1995).

"Interview with Martin Indyk on 13 November 1993 – Perspectives from the White House." *Middle East Quarterly* 1, no. 1 (March 1994).

Roberson, Barbara Allen. "Islam and Europe: An Enigma or a Myth?" *Middle East Journal* 48 (Spring 1994).

Robins, Philip. "Between Sentiment and Self-Interest: Turkey's Policy Toward Azerbaijan and the Central Asian States." *Middle East Journal* 47, no. 4 (Autumn 1993).

Rodman, Peter W. "Policy Brief: Co-opt or Confront Fundamentalist Islam?" *Middle East Quarterly* (December 1994).

Rouleau, Eric. "The Challange to Turkey." *Foreign Affairs* 72, no. 5 (November/December 1993).

"Turkey Beyond Ataturk." *Foreign Policy*, no. 91 (Summer 1993).

Sadowski, Yahya. "The New Orientalism and the Democracy Debate." *Middle East Report* 23 (July/August 1983).

Said, Abdul Aziz. "Islamic Fundamentalism and the West." *Mediterranean Quarterly* 3 (Fall 1992).

Salame, Ghassan. "Islam and the West." *Foreign Policy*, no. 90 (Spring 1993).

Salt, Jeremy. "Nationalism and the Rise of Muslim Sentiment in Turkey." *Middle East Studies* 31, no. 1 (January 1995).

Sayari, Sabri. "Turkey: The Changing European Security Environment and the Gulf Crisis." *Middle East Journal* 46, no. 1 (Winter 1992).

"Turkey's Islamist Challenge." *Middle East Quarterly* 3, no. 3 (September 1996).

Shahak, Israel. "With Iraq Neutralized, Israelis Seek Catalyst for War with Iran." *Washington Report on Middle Eastern Affairs* (April/May 1993).

Shirley, Edward G. "The Iran Policy Trap." *Foreign Policy*, no. 96 (Fall 1994).

Sick, Gary. "A Sensible Policy Toward Iran: Consistency in American Policy

Should Be a Top Priority." *Middle East Insight* (July/August 1995).

. "The United States and Iran: Truths and Consequences." *Contention* 5, no. 2 (Winter 1996).

Slade, Shelley. "The Image of the Arab in America: Analysis of a Poll on American Attitudes." *Middle East Journal* 35, no. 2 (Spring 1981).

Stav, Arye. "The Muslim Threat to the Western World." *Midstream* 39 (January 1993).

Sullivan, Denis J. "State and Civil Society in Conflict in Egypt." *Journal of Middle East Affairs* 3, no. 1–2 (Winter/Spring 1997).

"Symposium: Resurgent Islam in the Middle East." Transcript in *Middle East Policy* 3, no. 2 (1994).

Thompson, John. "Exaggeration of American Vulnerability." *Diplomatic History* 16 (Winter 1992).

"Turkey: The Emerging Market Bridging East and West." *Foreign Affairs* 75, no. 3 (May/June 1996).

Twing, Shawn L. "Mideast Policy Makers Conference Examines Peace Process, Gulf Security." *Washington Report on Middle Eastern Affairs* (October/November 1995).

Unal, Hasan. "Bosnia II: A Turkish Critique." *World Journal Today* 1, no. 7 (July 1995).

Van Bruinessen, Martin. "Turkey's Death Squads." *Middle East Report* (April/June 1996).

Voll, John O., and John L. Esposito. "Islam's Democratic Essence." *Middle East Quarterly* 1, no. 3 (September 1994).

White, Jenny B. "Pragmatists or Ideologues? Turkey's Welfare Party in Power." *Current History* (January 1997).

Wright, Robin. "Islam, Democracy, and the West." *Foreign Affairs* (Summer 1992).

Zubaida, Sami. "Turkish Islam and National Identity." *Middle East Report* (April/June 1996).

Newspapers & Magazines

Adams, James. "Mubarak at Grave Risk of Being Overthrown by March of Islam." *Sunday Times*, London, 20 February 1994.

Al-Din, Randa Taqi. "France's Algeria Policy Is in Crisis." *Al-Hayat*, 1 February 1997.

Alemdar, Zeynep. "Turk Military on Anti-Islam Offense." *Associated Press*, 10 June 1997.

"Turkey to Combat Islam Influence." *Associated Press*, 11 June 1997.

"Algeria Calls on France Not to Interfere in Its Affairs." *Al-Hayat*, 2 January 1997.

"Algerian Elections Were Not Problem-Free." *New York Times, 18 June 1997.*

"Algeria's Sham Elections." Editorial. *New York Times*, 7 June 1997.

Al-Husseini, Jihan, and Ishraf al-Fiqi. "Mubarak: The Terrorists in Britain; No Dialogue with Them Because It Strengthens Them." *Al-Hayat*, 24 November 1997.

Al-Majid, Wahid Abd. "A Fundamentalist Threat?" *Al-Hayat*, 28 July 1997.

"America and Islam: A Wobbly Hand of Friendship." *Economist*, 26 August 1995.

"America Arms Turkey's Repression." Editorial. *New York Times*, 17 October 1995.

"America Reviews Its Policy in Algeria: No Fundamental Shift Is Expected." *Al-Hayat*, 19 October 1997.

"Amnesty International Requests 'International Investigation' of Massacres in Algeria." *Al-Hayat*, 19 November 1997.

"An Arab-International Consensus on Condemning the Luxor Attack." *Al-Hayat*, 19 November 1997.

"An Interview With Ronald Reagan." *Time*, 17 November 1980.

"Anwar Haddam Is on Food Strike: Grant Me Political Asylum or Hand Me in to Algeria." *Al-Hayat*, 16 May 1997.

"ARCO to Produce Oil with Algerians." *New York Times*, 16 February 1996.

Avineri, Shlomo. "The Return to Islam." *Lies of Our Times*, March/April 1993.

Baram, Haim. "The Demon of Islam." *Middle East International*, 2 December 1994.

Baram, Zeyno. "Too Little Stability in Turkey." *Christian Science Monitor*, 18 February 1997.

Barzin, Saeed. "Iran Rides High." *Middle East International*, 16 August 1996.

"Ben Bellah: Nobody Knows Who Kills in Algeria." *Al-Hayat*, 19 November 1997.

Bermudes, Robert W. "Jihad: Violence or Spiritual Struggle?" *Middle East International*, 18 February 1994.

Bin Jida, Ghassan. "Khomeini Stresses the Need to Preserve Fundamentalism and Warns Against the 'Threat of Cultural Invasion.'" *Al-Hayat*, 11 December 1996.

Blustein, Paul. "House Passes Measure Against Foreign Firms Investing in Iranian, Libyan Oil." *Washington Post*, 24 July 1996.

Bohlen, Celestine. "European Parliament Admits Turkey to Its New Customs Union." *New York Times*, 14 December 1995.

"Turkish Army in New Battle." *New York Times*, 30 March 1996.

Borderwich, Fergus M. "A Holy War Heads Our Way: A Rising Tide of Islamic Radicalism Is Sweeping over the Middle East and Threatening Western Security Interests." *Readers Digest*, January 1995.

Borowiec, Andrew. "French–U.S. Clash over Algeria Policy Escalates." *Washington Times*, 5 August 1994.

Brooke, James. "Attacks on U.S. Muslims Surge Even as Their Faith Takes Hold." *New York Times*, 28 August 1995.

Cohen, Richard. "If Turkey Went the Way of Iran." *Washington Post*, 29 June 1995.

Cohen, Roger. "A Chance to Try to End an Agony." *New York Times*, 2
February 1997.
"Algeria Says Charter Passes, But Critics Charge Vote Fraud." *New York
Times*, 30 November 1996.
"Algerian Links Rebels to 'Foreign Interests.'" *New York Times*, 25 January 1997.
"Algerians Seem Poised to Embrace Authority." *New York Times*, 29
November 1996.
"Algeria's Main Rebel Faction Takes Risks and Calls Truce." *New York
Times*, 25 September 1997.
"Divisions Deepen Among Algeria's Military Rulers." *New York Times*, 11
September 1997.
"In Algeria, Oil and Islam Make a Volatile Mixture." *New York Times*, 28
December 1996.
"Islamic Front in Algeria Calls for Truce and Peace Talks." *New York
Times*, 28 September 1997.
"Military Tightens Grip in Algeria Elections." *New York Times*, 7 June
1997.
"West's Fear in Bosnia: 1) Chaos 2) Islam." *New York Times*, 13 March
1994.
"With Leading Party Banned, Algeria Elects a New Parliament." *New
York Times*, 6 June 1997.
Coll, Steve. "The U.S. Case Against Iranian Nukes." *Washington Post*, 15–
21 May 1995, National Weekly edition.
"Condemnation of Luxor Massacre Continues and Consensus Regarding Its
Harm to Islam." *Al-Hayat*, 20 November 1997.
Couturier, Kelly. "Ignoring U.S., Turkey and Iran Sign Trade Accords."
Washington Post, 22 December 1996.
"New Turkish Leader's Islamic Vision Clouded by Political Reality."
Washington Post, 25 July 1996.
"Turkey, Israel Launch a Military Partnership." *Washington Post*, 16 April
1996.
"Turkish Parties Vow Coalition to Keep Islamists out of Power." *Washington Post*, 26 December 1995.
"Turk's Libya Trip Causes Political Crisis at Home." *Washington Post*, 8
October 1996.
Cowell, Alan. "Berlin Court Says Top Iran Leaders Ordered Killings." *New
York Times*, 11 April 1997.
"Mixed Response from Europe on Ruling Linking Iran to Killings." *New
York Times*, 30 April 1997.
"U.S. Fails to Enlist European Allies in Iranian Trade Embargo." *New
York Times*, 3 May 1995.
Crossman, Daniel. "U.S. and Iran Cooperating on Ways to End Afghan
War." *New York Times*, 15 December 1997.
Crossette, Barbara. "Democracies Love Peace, Don't They?" *New York
Times*, Sunday, 1 June 1997.

"U.S. Aide Calls Muslim Militants Big Concern in World." *New York Times*, 1 January 1992.

Darnton, John. "Discontent Seethes in Once-Stable Turkey." *New York Times*, 2 March 1995.

"Delicate Relations with Turkey." Editorial. *New York Times*, 8 March 1997.

Dergham, Rhagida. "Amman Reserves Request to Call for Dialogue in Algeria." *Al-Hayat*, 12 September 1997.

Dickey, Christopher. "Islam Is Not the Issue." *Newsweek*, 30 May 1994.

Driefus, Claudia. "Who's the Enemy Now?" *New York Times*, Sunday, 21 May 1995 Magazine section.

"Egypt Is Upset by Britain's Noncooperation in Combatting Terrorism." *Al-Hayat*, 30 November 1997.

Emerson, Steven. "The Great Satan Wins One." *Wall Street Journal*, 25 June 1993.

Evans, Rowland, and Robert Novak. "Ripe for Retaliation." *Washington Post*, 1 August 1996.

"Fadllalh Accuses Israel and America in the Luxor Operation." *Al-Hayat*, 21 November 1997.

Farhan, Haq. "Algeria–U.S.: Washington Reaches Out to Muslim Moderates." *Inter Press Service*, 6 March 1995.

Feldman, Trude B. "Christopher: Mideast Gains Will Hold." *Washington Times*, 18 January 1995.

Frazer, Suzan. "Turkey Islamic Leader Cedes Power." *Associated Press*, 13 June 1997.

Friedman, Robert I. "One Man's Jihad." *Nation*, 15 May 1995.

Friedman, Thomas L. "Baker's Trip to Nations Unready for Independence." *New York Times*, 16 February 1992.

"Republics Promise to Protect Rights." *New York Times*, 13 February 1992.

"Too Much of a Good Thing." *New York Times*, 18 June 1995.

"Fundamentalist Fear." *Economist*, 6–12 August 1994.

Gelb, Leslie. "U.S. Sees Opportunities and Risks in Mideast after War in Lebanon." *New York Times*, 31 October 1982.

Glastris, Steve. "A Fundamental Turn by the Bosporus." *U.S. News and World Report*, 26 February 1996.

Glazer, Nathan. "Debate on Aliens Flares Beyond the Melting Pot." *New York Times*, 23 April 1995.

Goshko, John M. "U.S. Modifies Statement on Algerian Move." *Washington Post*, 15 January 1992.

Greenhouse, Steven. "U.S. Gives Russia Secret Data on Iran to Fight Atom Deal." *New York Times*, 3–4 April 1995.

"U.S. Support for Turks' Anti-Kurd Campaign Dims." *New York Times*, March 29 1995.

Haberman, Clyde. "Israel Focuses on the Threat Beyond the Arabs – in Iran." *New York Times*, Sunday, 8 November 1992.

Hasan, Daoud. "Iranian President To Mubarak: Foreign Powers Conspire Against Egypt." *Al-Hayat*, 20 November 1997.

Hasan, Sana. "My Lost Egypt." *New York Times*, Sunday, 22 October 1995, Magazine section.

Hedges, Chris. "Iran May Be Able to Build an Atomic Bomb in Five Years, U.S. and Israeli Officials Fear." *New York Times*, 5 January 1995.

Hoagland, Jim. "Political Con Game in Turkey." *Washington Post*, 11 July 1996.

Hoffman, David. "Israel Seeking to Convince U.S. That West is Threatened by Iran." *Washington Post*, 13 March 1993.

Holmes, Steven A. "U.S. Says Terrorist Attacks Dropped Sharply in 1992." *New York Times*, 1 May 1993.

Hope, Hugh. "The New Middle: Turks Add Their Voices to Contest of Generals and Fundamentalists." *Wall Street Journal*, 14 March 1997.

Howaidi, Fahmi. "Political Thinking!" *Al-Ahram*, 2 March 1993.

Hussain, Mushahid. "America's Quest for an Islam Policy." *Middle East International*, 3 March 1995.

Ibrahim, Youssef. M. "Algeria Gains a Vote of Confidence with Foreign Oil Contracts," *New York Times*, 12 December 1995.

Ignatius, David. "Islam in the West's Sights: The Wrong Crusade?" *Washington Post*, 8 March 1992.

"Iran Eases Stand on Peace Process." *Jordan Times*, 4 July 1995.

Islam, Shada. "Cautious EU Response." *Middle East International*, 5 July 1996.

"Turkey and NATO." *Middle East International*, 21 February 1997.

"It's Racist, But Hey, It's Disney." *New York Times*. 14 July 1993.

Jehl, Douglas. "Egypt Is Playing Down Sheik's Jail Term in U.S.," *New York Times*, 20 January 1996.

"In the Face of Criticism, Egypt Sentences 54 Muslim Leaders," *New York Times*, 24 November 1995.

"In Uneasy Time, Saudi Prince Provides a Hope of Stability." *New York Times*, 19 January 1996.

"Iran-Backed Terrorists are Growing More Aggressive, U.S. Warns." *New York Times*, 18 March 1993.

"Iranian President Calls for Opening Dialogue with the U.S." *New York Times*, 15 December 1997.

"Islamic Militants' War on Egypt: Going International," *New York Times*, 20 November 1995.

"Killings Erode Cairo's Claim to 'Control' Militants." *New York Times*, 15 March 1997.

"Shake-up in Cairo Follows Tourists' Killings." *New York Times*, 20 November 1997.

"Jospin Criticizes the Violence of the Government and the Islamists in Algeria." *Al-Hayat*, 1 October 1997.

Kamal, Hassam. "Egyptian Official Blames America for the 'Arab Afghani' Phenomenon." *Al-Hayat*, 26 May 1997.

Kamal, Hassam, and Mohammed Saleh. "Al-Alfi: No Dialogue with al-Jama'a al-Islamiyya in Egypt." *Al-Hayat*, 7 September 1997.

Kaplan, Robert. "Tales From the Bazaar." *Atlantic Monthly*, August 1992.

Kashana, Rashid. "Algerian Massacres and the Reconciliation Project." *Al-Hayat*, 25 September 1997.

Kennedy, Paul, and Matthew Connelly. "Must It Be the Rest Against the West?" *Atlantic Monthly*, December 1994.

"Kharazi: Relations with America Do Not Conflict with Revolution's Principles." *Al-Hayat*, 16 September 1997.

Khatami, Mohammed. "The Dialogue of Civilizations and Its Difficulties." *Al-Hayat*, 11 July 1997.

"Khatami Promises to Adhere to His Program: We Will Avoid Discord with the World." *Al-Hayat*, 5 August 1997.

Kifner, John. "Alms and Arms: Tactics in a Holy War." *New York Times*, 15 March 1995.

King, John. "A 'Clash of Civilizations': Pentagon Rhetoric on the 'Islamic Threat.' " *Middle East International*, 3 March 1995.

Kinzer, Stephen. "Brussels Meeting Dims Turkey's Bid to Join European Union." *New York Times*, 11 March 1997.

"Europeans Shut the Door on Turkey's Membership in Union." *New York Times*, 27 March 1997.

"In Defense of Secularism, Turkish Army Warns Rulers." *New York Times*, 2 March 1997.

"Islam and Liberty: Struggles in Two Lands." *New York Times*, 22 June 1997.

"Meeting U.S. Envoy, Turkish Premier Takes Pro-Arab Stance." *New York Times*, 3 July 1996.

"Once the Hope of Secular Turks, Ex-Leader Is Now Widely Reviled." *New York Times*, 6 April 1997.

"Pro-Islamic Premier Steps Down in Turkey Under Army Pressure." *New York Times*, 19 June 1997.

"The Islamist Who Runs Turkey, Delicately." *New York Times*, Sunday, 23 February 1997, Magazine section.

"Turkey Sending Envoy to U.S. to Clear up 'Misunderstanding.' " *New York Times*, 27 December 1996.

"Turkey's Islamic Leaders Vow to Keep Secularism." *New York Times*, 14 March 1997.

"Turkish Ex-Premier's Comeback Hits a Snag." *New York Times*, 2 July 1997.

"Turkish Generals Raise Pressure on Premier." *New York Times*, 13 June 1997.

"Turkish Judge Scolds U.S. for Opposing a Ban on an Islamic Party." *New York Times*, 28 November 1997.

"Turk's Chief Surprisingly Silent on Iraq." *New York Times*, 14 September 1996.

"Turks March in Campaign to Preserve Secularism." *New York Times*, 16 February 1997.

Kohen, Sami. "Dollars vs. Diplomacy: Turks Differ with U.S." *Christian Science Monitor*, 25 May 1995.

"In a First Test, Pro-Islamic Turkey Stays the Course on Western Ties." *Christian Science Monitor*, 26 July 1996.

"Islamic Party Jumps Out Front." *Christian Science Monitor*, 29 November 1995.

"Islamic Party Win Worsens Turkey's East vs. West Woes." *Christian Science Monitor*, 27 December 1995.

"Pro-Islamic Premier Stays in Power, but the Future of Turkey Still Murky." *Christian Science Monitor*, 10 October 1997.

"Regional Conflicts on U.S.–Turkey Agenda." *Christian Science Monitor*, 18 October 1993.

"Secular Turks Hope to Check Nation's First Islamic Leader." *Christian Science Monitor*, 1 July 1996.

"To U.S., Turk Leader's Tour Goes to All the Wrong Places." *Christian Science Monitor*, 3 October 1996.

"Turkey's Military Tries Political Moves to Squelch Premier's Islamic Ambition." *Christian Science Monitor*, 3 July 1997.

"Who Runs Turkey?" *Christian Science Monitor*, 9 May 1997.

"With Islam's Crescent Rising over Turkey, the Army Howls." *Christian Science Monitor*, 2 June 1997.

Kramer, Martin. "Islam vs. Democracy." *Commentary*, January 1993.

"The Jihad Against the Jews." *Commentary*, October 1994.

Krauthammer, Charles. "Iran: Orchestrator of Disorder." *Washington Post*, 1 January 1993.

Lake, Anthony. "The Middle East Moment: At the Heart of Our Policy, Extremism Is the Enemy." *Washington Post*, 24 July 1994.

Lane, Charles. "Rock the Casbah." *New Republic*, 27 February 1995.

Larsen, Alan P. "Building U.S.–Turkey Economic Cooperation." Address before the U.S.–Turkey Business Council, 20 February 1997, printed in *Turkish Times*, 1 March 1997.

Lauter, David. "Clinton Seeks to Build Bridge to Muslim World." *Los Angeles Times*, 27 October 1994.

Law, John. "Martin Indyk Lays Out the Clinton Approach." *Middle East International*, 11 June 1993.

Lewis, Anthony. "This is America." *New York Times*, 1 May 1995.

Lewis, Bernard. "Islam and Liberal Democracy." *Atlantic Monthly*, February 1993.

"The Roots of Muslim Rage." *Atlantic Monthly*, September 1990.

Lippman, Thomas W. "No More Mr. Nice Guy: On the Subject of Iran, Warren Christopher Is the Hardest of the Hard-Liners." *Washington Post*, 15–21 May 1995, National Weekly edition.

"State Dept. Human Rights Report Chastises Several U.S. Allies." *Washington Post*, 31 January 1997.

"U.S. Prepared to Airlift Dissidents." *Washington Post*, 12 September 1996.

"Living with Islam." *Economist*, 17 April 1992.

"Living with Islam." *Economist*, 18–24 March 1994.

"Makeup of Iran's Cabinet Defies the Hard-Liners." *New York Times*, 13 August 1997.

Marquand, Robert. "Religious Right Elbows Way onto World's Political Stage." *Christian Science Monitor*, 13 June 1996.

McDowall, David. "The Destruction of Turkey's South East." *Middle East International*, 6 December 1996.

"Military Meddling in Turkey." Editorial. *New York Times*, 14 June 1997.

Millward, William. "The Rising Tide of Islamic Fundamentalism I." *Commentary* (Ottawa), April 1993.

"The Rising Tide of Islamic Fundamentalism II." *Commentary* (Ottawa), April 1993.

Mitchell, Alison. "Clinton Sees Hope in the Election of Moderate as President of Iran." *New York Times*, 30 May 1997.

Mohammed, Hazem. "Changes in the Egyptian Security Apparatus Highlights the Role of 'Political Security.'" *Al-Hayat*, 21 November 1997.

"Muslims Don't Fare Well in Poll," *Pantagraph*, 13 May 1993.

Mustapha, Hala. "The Brothers and the Egyptian State: New Confrontation." *Al Wasat*, 7 August 1995.

Myers, Steven Lee. "White House Says Iran Won't Violate Sanctions Act." *New York Times*, 28 July 1997.

Nasser, Salim. "Zeroual Attempts to Clean the Reputation of the Military Institution." *Al-Hayat*, 18 October 1997.

Neff, Donald. "Agony in Washington." *Middle East International*, 10 October 1997.

"Clinton Places U.S. Policy at Israel's Bidding." *Middle East International*, 31 March 1995.

"U.S. and Iran: Congressional Cowboys." *Middle East International*, 17 November 1995.

"U.S. and Iran: Policy under Fire." *Middle East International*, 2 May 1997.

Negus, Steve. "Copts Massacred." *Middle East International*, 7 March 1997.

"Tourists Slain in Cairo." *Middle East International*, 26 September 1997.

Olson, Robert. "An Israeli-Kurdish Conflict?" *Middle East International*, 5 July 1996.

"Democratization and the Kurdish Question." *Middle East International*, 7 March 1997.

"Israel and Turkey – Consolidating Relations." *Middle East International*, 4 April 1997.

"PKK the Target." *Middle East International*, 21 February 1997.

"The Turkey-Israel Agreement and the Kurdish Question." *Middle East International*, 24 May 1996.

Onaran, Yalman. "Muslim Leaders Pledge Cooperation." *Associated Press*, 15 June 1997.

"Turkey's Military Boycotts Islam." *Associated Press*, 7 June 1997.

"Outlawing Islam." Editorial. *New York Times*, 19 June 1997.

Pelletreau, Robert. "Symposium: Resurgent Islam." Op-ed article. *New York Times*, 2 October 1995.

Perlmutter, Amos. "Wishful Thinking about Islamic Fundamentalism." *Washington Post*, 19 January 1992.

Peterson, Scott. "Mideast Balance of Power Shifts as an 'Axis' Is Born." *Christian Science Monitor*, 29 August 1996.

"Turkey's Army Keeps the Faith at Bay." *Christian Science Monitor*, 9 April 1996.

"Turkey Ties Trade Knot with Iran, Sparks Alarm." *Christian Science Monitor*, 24 December 1996.

Phillips, James. "The Rising Threat of Revolutionary Islam in Algeria." *The Heritage Foundation: Backgrounder*, 9 November 1995.

Pianin, Eric. "Clinton Approves Sanctions for Investors in Iran, Libya." *Washington Post*, 6 August 1996.

Pipes, Daniel. "Same Difference: The Islamic Threat – Part I." *National Review*, 7 November 1994.

"The Muslims Are Coming! The Muslims Are Coming!" *National Review*, 19 November 1990.

Pomfret, John. "Turkey's Identity Crisis." *Washington Post*, 17 April 1995.

Pope, Hugh. "A Troubled System." *Middle East International*, 8 November 1996.

"Attempt on Demirel's Life." *Middle East International*, 24 May 1996.

"Erbakan at the Helm." *Middle East International*, 5 July 1996.

"Erbakan's Strange Travels." *Middle East International*, 25 October 1996.

"The Erbakan Whirlwind Sweeps Through Turkey." *Middle East International*, 19 July 1996.

"Turkey's Generals Behind the Israel Axis." *Middle East International*, 16 May 1996.

Pope, Nicole. "Long Live Provide Comfort." *Middle East International*, 10 January 1997.

"The Crisis Drags On." *Middle East International*, 13 June 1997.

"The End of Provide Comfort?" *Middle East International*, 6 December 1996.

"Turbulent Times." *Middle East International*, 7 March 1997.

"Turkey: Erbakan Versus the Generals." *Middle East International*, 2 May 1997.

"Turkey Goes Back into Iraq." *Middle East International*, 30 May 1997.

"Punishing Iran." *Economist*, 6 May 1996.

Purdum, Todd S. "Clinton Fears Partisan Fight on Anti-Terrorism Proposal." *New York Times*, 29 April 1995.

"Clinton Pays Homage to an Extraordinary Generation." *New York Times*, 9 May 1995.

"Clinton to Order a Trade Embargo Against Teheran." *New York Times*, 1 May 1995.

"Rafsanjani: We Support the Palestinian Struggle but We Reject Any Terrorist Act." *Al-Hayat*, 12 March 1996.

"Rebel Group Forswears Tourist Attacks in Egypt." *New York Times*, 9 December 1997.

"Reform to Confront Terrorism." *Al-Hayat*, 23 November 1997.

Rodman, Peter W. "Mullah Moola." In "The Islamic Threat," pt. 2. *National Review*, 7 November 1994.

Rosenfeld, Stephen S. "Through the Minefield of Political Islam." *Washington Post*, 31 March 1995.

Rosenthal, A. M. "How to Trade with Iran." *New York Times*, 24 March 1995.

"Things America Can Do to Curtail Terrorism, Domestic and Foreign." *New York Times* column. Rpt. in *International Herald Tribune*, 26 April 1995.

"Rules of Engagement." *Economist*, 2 October 1993.

Safire, William. "Sending in Marines." *New York Times*, 14 February 1980.

Said, Edward W. "The Phony Islamic Threat." *New York Times*, Sunday, 21 November 1993, Magazine section.

Saleh, Heba. " 'Rigged' Elections." *Middle East International*, 7 November 1997.

"The FIS Calls a Cease-Fire." *Middle East International*, 10 October 1997.

Saleh, Mohammed. "Egypt: 'al-Jama'a al-Islamiyya' Decides to Stop Operations Against Tourism." *Al-Hayat*, 8 December 1997.

"Egypt: Confrontation Between the Government and Human Rights Organizations." *Al Hayat*, 10 August 1995.

"Egypt: Failure of Attempts to Convince Leaders of 'al-Jama'a' and 'Jihad' Overseas to Support the Cease-Fire." *Al-Hayat*, 4 August 1997.

"Egypt: Imprisoned Leaders of 'al-Jama'a' Considered the Luxor Operation a Violation of the Safety Vows." *Al-Hayat*, 23 November 1997.

"Egypt: Leaders of 'al-Jama'a' and 'Jihad' Join the Cease-Fire." *Al-Hayat*, 13 July 1997.

"Egypt: Leaders of the 'al-Jama'a al-Islamiyya' Decide to Cease Hostilities." *Al-Hayat*, 6 July 1997.

"Egypt: The Moment of Reckoning for the Islamic Brothers." *Al-Wasat*, 7 August 1995.

"Egypt: Two Leaders of Jihad Join the Declaration of Cease-Fire." *Al-Hayat*, 10 July 1997.

"Investigations Inside the 'al-Jama'a al-Islamiyya' Look at Irregularities in the Luxor Operation." *Al-Hayat*, 29 November 1997.

"Members in 'al-Jama'a' and 'Jihad' Join Cease-Fire." *Al-Hayat*, 25 July 1997.

"Mubarak: 'The Brothers' Practice Terrorist Activities." *Al-Hayat*, 27 September 1995.

" 'The Case of Big Assassination' in Egypt: The Accused Support the Cease-Fire." *Al-Hayat*, 25 September 1997.

Saleh, Mohammed, and Hussam Kamal. "Leaders of 'al-Jama'a' and 'Jihad' Overseas Reject the Cease-Fire." *Al-Hayat*, 12 July 1997.

Saleh, Mohammed, Hussam Kamal, and Hazem Mohammed. "Egypt: The Army Participates for the First Time in the Protection of Tourist Areas." *Al-Hayat*, 23 November 1997.

Schmitt, Eric. "Republicans Warn Russia That Its Deal with Iran Threatens Aid." *New York Times*, 8 May 1995.

Schwed, Barry. "Albright Backs Secular Turkey." *Associated Press*, 13 June 1997.

Sciolino, Elaine. "Calling Iran an 'Outlaw State,' Christopher Backs U.S. Trade Ban." *New York Times*, 2 May 1995.

"Christopher Proposes Tighter Curbs on Trade with Iran." *New York Times*, 31 March 1995.

"Christopher Signals a Tougher U.S. Line Toward Iran." *New York Times*, 31 March 1993.

"C.I.A. Asks Congress for $19 Million to Undermine Iraq's Rulers and Rein in Iran." *New York Times*, 12 April 1995.

"Egypt Warned U.S. of Terror, Mubarak Says." *New York Times*, 5 April 1993.

"In World of Flux, a Constant: U.S. and Iran Still Foes." *New York Times*, Sunday, 29 December 1996.

"Iranian Leader Says U.S. Move on Oil Deal Wrecked Chance to Improve Ties," *New York Times*, 16 May 1995.

"The Point Man: Berger Manages a Welter of Crises in the Post–Cold War White House." *New York Times*, 18 May 1998.

"The Red Menace Is Gone. But Here's Islam." *New York Times*, Sunday, 21 January 1996, Week in Review section.

"U.S. Asserts Iranians Plotted to Disrupt Rally in Germany." *New York Times*, 25 June 1995.

"U.S. Pressure Put on Iran and Iraq." *New York Times*, 5 April 1995.

Singer, David E. "Two-Edged Sword: Anti-Terrorism Law Risks American Relations with Allies." *New York Times*, 30 September 1997.

"Sixty-Six Percent of Egyptians Do Not Pay Attention to Politics." *Al-Hayat*, 19 April 1997.

Swanson, David. "Secular Turkey Teeters over Plan to Close Islamic Schools." *Christian Science Monitor*, 12 June 1997.

"The Clinton Administration Condemned the Outrageous Massacres in Algeria." *Al-Hayat*, 4 September 1997.

"Turkey Crosses a Line." Editorial. *New York Times*, 25 March 1995.

"Turkey Is a European Country." Interview with Minister of State Abdullah Gul. *Turkish Times*, 1 March 1997.

"Turkey, Star of Islam." *Economist*, 14 December 1991.

"Turkey's Meddlesome Generals." Editorial. *New York Times*, 25 March 1997.

"Turkish Prosecutor Seeks to Outlaw Islamic Party." *New York Times*, 22 May 1997.

"U.S. Criticizes Turkish Leader for Libya Trip and Trade Deal." *New York Times*, 8 October 1996.

"U.S. Views Threat by Iraq as Strategy to Split Critics." *New York Times*, 25 September 1990.

"U.S. Voices Support for Algeria Bid to End Civil Strife." *Reuters*, 12 April 1996.

"Washington and the Kurds." Editorial. *New York Times*, 4 April 1995.

"Washington Supports the Algerian Government in Its Military Effort." *Al-Hayat*, 11 September 1997.

Weaver, Mary Ann. "The Battle for Cairo." *New Yorker*, 30 January 1995.

Weiner, Tim. "U.S. Plan to Change Iran Leaders Is an Open Secret Before It Begins." *New York Times*, 26 January 1996.

Weymouth, Lally. "Saddam's New Friend." *Washington Post*, 30 July 1996.

"Turkey: An Anti-Western Tilt?" *Washington Post*, 23 January 1996.

"What Turkey Needs." *Washington Post* editorial. Rpt. in *International Herald Tribune*, 21–2 June 1997.

"Where Islam Recruits." *Economist*, 12 November 1994.

Wright, Robin. "Islamist's Theory of Relativity." *Los Angeles Times*, 27 January 1995.

Zuckerman, Mortimer. "Beware the Religious Stalinists." *U.S. News and World Report*, 22 March 1993.

Misc. Reports, Papers, Documentaries, & Surveys

American-Arab Anti-Discrimination Committee. *1990 ADC Annual Report on Political and Hate Violence*. Washington, DC: American-Arab Anti-Discrimination Committee, February 1991.

Barkey, Henry J. "Turkish Politics after the Elections." Unpublished paper delivered to the Commission on Security and Cooperation in Europe, 25 January 1996.

Council on American-Islamic Relations (CAIR). "A Rush to Judgments." Special report on anti-Muslim bias and harassment following the Oklahoma City bombing, June 1995.

Davis, Edward B. "Changing National Security Policy in the Clinton Administration." Unpublished paper delivered at the annual meeting of the International Studies Association, Chicago, IL, January 1995.

Entelis, John P. "Islam and Democracy: A Dilemma for U.S. Policy – A Panel Discussion." At "Islam and the U.S.: Challenges for the Nineties," Soref Symposium, The Washington Institute for Near East Policy, Washington, DC, 27 April 1992.

"Islamic Activism in North Africa: The View from Within – Algeria and Tunisia." Unpublished paper given at the Institute for National Strategic Studies, National Defense University, Department of Defense, Washington, DC, 29 March 1996.

Jihad in America. Produced for PBS by journalist Steven Emerson and aired on 21 November 1994. SAE Productions, 1994.

Khomeini's Message to Gorbachev. BBC Summary of World Broadcast, ME/0354/A/4–6, 10 January 1989.

Makovsky, Alan. "Assessing the Intentions of Turkey's Refah Party." In *Muslim Politics Report*, pub. by the Council on Foreign Relations, New York, November/December 1996.

Middle East Watch. *Behind Closed Doors: Torture and Detention in Egypt*. New York: Human Rights Watch, 1992.

Egypt: Hostage-Taking and Intimidation by Security Forces. New York: Human Rights Watch, January 1995.

Egypt: Trials of Civilians in Military Courts Violate International Law. New York: Human Rights Watch, July 1993.

Mufti, Malik. "Daring and Caution in Turkish Foreign Policy." Unpublished paper presented at the Middle East Studies Association, Providence, RI, November 1996.

Naveh, Chanan. "Foreign Policy of Regional Powers in the 1990s: The Cases of Israel and Turkey." Unpublished paper delivered at the 35th annual convention of the International Studies Association, Washington, DC: 29–31 April/May 1994.

Survey sponsored by the American Muslim Council and conducted by the John Zogby Group International. Number of respondents: 905. Survey dates: 16–23 March 1993.

Survey sponsored by the National Conference on Inter-Group Relations, the Ford Foundation, and the Joyce Foundation. Conducted by L. H. Research. Number of respondents: 2755. Survey dates: 6–8 August 1993.

Index

Turkey (*cont.*)
  Libya, 212, 213, 214
  military, 192, 193, 198, 201, 203, 204, 206, 208–209,215, 216, 217–219, 223, 225, 226, 235
  NATO, 130, 194, 197, 199, 210, 213, 216, 219, 235, 236
  Soviet Union, 194, 197–198, 210
  terrorism, 203, 209
  U.S. foreign aid, 199
Turkish nationalism, 221

United Kingdom, *see* Britain
United Nations (UN), 45, 166, 202, 212
  Iraq sanctions, 198
USS Vincennes, 72

Vance, Cyrus, 43, 65, 67
Velayati, Ali Akbar, 119
Vietnam war, 126

Washington Institute for Near East Policy, 22, 28, 90–91, 98, 112

weapons of mass destruction, 14, 25–26, 30, 90, 229, 239 *see also* nuclear proliferation *and* chemical weapons
Weinberger, Casper, 69, 73
Welch, David, 149–150
West Bank, *see* Palestinian territories
Wirth, Timothy, 96–97
Wolfowitz, Paul, 187
World Bank, 211
World Jewish Congress, 57
World Trade Center bombing, 45, 46, 47, 52, 56, 106, 176
World War I, 38
World War II, 39, 68, 128, 194, 197
Wright, Robin, 29–30, 33–34

Yilmaz, Mesut, 192, 219

Zeroual, Liamine, 144, 147, 149, 156, 157–158, 159, 160, 161, 164, 166–167, 168, 233, 234
Zuckerman, Mortimer, 24